New Frontiers in Enterprise Risk Management

David L. Olson • Desheng Wu
Editors

New Frontiers in Enterprise Risk Management

Springer

Editors
Prof. David L. Olson
University of Nebraska
Department of Management
Lincoln, NE 68588-0491
USA
dolson3@unl.edu

Prof. Desheng Wu
University of Toronto
RiskLab
Toronto, ON M5S 3G3
Canada
DWu@Rotman.Utoronto.ca

ISBN 978-3-540-78641-2 e-ISBN 978-3-540-78642-9

DOI: 10.1007/978-3-540-78642-9

Library of Congress Control Number: 2008922455

Cover Design: WMX Design GmbH, Heidelberg, Germany

Printed on acid-free paper

5 4 3 2 1

springer.com

Preface

Risk management has become a critical part of doing business in the twenty-first century. This book is a collection of material about enterprise risk management, and the role of risk in decision making. Part I introduces the topic of enterprise risk management. Part II presents enterprise risk management from perspectives of finance, accounting, insurance, supply chain operations, and project management. Technology tools are addressed in Part III, including financial models of risk as well as accounting aspects, using data envelopment analysis, neural network tools for credit risk evaluation, and real option analysis applied to information technology outsourcing. In Part IV, three chapters present enterprise risk management experience in China, including banking, chemical plant operations, and information technology.

Lincoln, USA
Toronto, Canada
February 2008

David L. Olson
Desheng Wu

Contents

Part I
Preliminary

Chapter 1
Introduction

D.L. Olson and D. Wu

Enterprise risk management (ERM) developed in the mid-1990s in industry, with a managerial focus. There are over 80 risk management frameworks reported worldwide, to include that of the Committee of Sponsoring Organizations of the Treadway Commission (COSO) 2004. COSO is a leading accounting standards organization in the U.S. ERM is a systematic, integrated approach to managing all risks facing an organization.[1] It focuses on board supervision, aiming to identify, evaluate, and manage all major corporate risks in an integrated framework.[2] It was undoubtedly encouraged by traumatic recent events such as 9/11/2001 and business scandals to include Enron and WorldCom.[3]

Part I: Preliminary

Part I of the book is introductory, to include this chapter. It also includes an overview of human decision making and how it deals with risk. This chapter is written by David R. Koenig, Executive Director of the Professional Risk Managers' International Association (PRMIA).

We published a book focusing on different perspectives of enterprise risk management.[4] That book discussed key perspectives of ERM, to include financial, accounting, supply chain, information technology, and disaster planning aspects. There are many others. Part II of this book gives other views of the impact of ERM in financial and accounting, insurance, supply chain, and project management fields. Part III presents papers addressing technical tools available to support ERM. Most of these papers address financial aspects, as is appropriate because finance and insurance are key to ERM. There also is a chapter addressing the impact of the Sarbanes–Oxley Act on ERM in the U.S. Part II ends with a chapter addressing analytic tools for information technology outsourcing analysis. Part IV of the book includes three chapters related to ERM in China. These include applications in banking, operations, and information technology.

D.L. Olson, D. Wu (eds.) *New Frontiers in Enterprise Risk Management*,

Part II: ERM Perspectives

Chapter 3 addresses core perspective of financial risk management, and perspectives of accounting through COSO framework. In the financial perspective, the relationship between ERM and financial operations, various risks including market risk, credit risk, and operational risks are all discussed. A description of the COSO ERM cube is provided, to include the series of activities involved from the accounting perspective.

Chapter 4 presents a model of ERM in the insurance sector. The initiatives of four major European insurers for their ERM program were studied inductively. Key issues are identified and explored under four dimensions (i.e., evolution, design, challenges and performance of Enterprise Risk Management). It is revealed that the benefits of Enterprise Risk Management are mostly intangible. This provides a foundation of integrating risks in a holistic framework beyond disciplinary silos, which initiates further research directions.

Chapter 5 reviews the benefits of supply chains in marketing products to customers, with focus on manageable risks. Supply chain management issues with respect to risk are analyzed. Risk reduction in supply chain is the focal point of the chapter, and multicriteria analysis is used as a means to quantify evaluation of alternative risk reduction proposals.

Chapter 6 addresses risk in project management. A state-of-the art of Risk Management Process (RMP) relies on two main phases, (a): Risk Assessment and (b): Risk Response. Most studies have risk assessment but we can find a limited study on the subject of risk response. The main objective of the research upon which this chapter is based is to emphasize the need for a shift of our perspectives to a more "Equilibrant" RMP, both for risk assessment and risk response. A two-polar generic RMP framework for projects is proposed. It is argued that a two-polar perspective proposed in this research study can be used for risk management projects in most effective and productive manner in real world's problems.

Part III: ERM Technologies

Part III presents technical tools applicable for a variety of risk management needs. Chapter 7 presents an historical account of the evolution of mathematics and risk management over the last twenty years, with focus on current credit market developments. The tool presented is collateralized fund obligations as a new credit derivative, applied to dealing with the risk of snow in Montreal.

Chapter 8 addresses to the role of stable laws in risk management. After a review on calibration methods for stable laws, Autoregressive Moving Average processes (ARMA) and Generalized Autoregressive Conditionally Heteroscedastic processes (GARCH) driven by stable noises are studied. Value at Risk computation under several models is discussed.

Chapter 9 presents research relative to stable forecasting models in financial analysis. Hybrid calibration techniques in pricing and risk management are given. A credit risky markets of defaultable bonds with an arbitrary number of factors is considered, more precisely a term structure model using Gaussian random yields.

In such a model the forward rates are driven by infinitely many factors which leads to hedges akin to practice, more stable calibrations and allows for more general shapes of the yield curve. Hybrid calibration has two main advantages: on one side it combines the advantages of estimation and classical calibration. On the other side it can be used in a market which suffers from scarcity of (liquid) credit derivatives data as the combination with historical estimation provides high stability. Risk measures are derived using the results from the calibration procedure.

Chapter 10 employs alternate techniques to examine whether passage of the Sarbanes–Oxley act (SOX) has had positive effects on the efficiency of public accounting firms. These alternate techniques extend from use of the non-parametric, "frontier" oriented method of Data Envelopment Analysis (DEA), and include more traditional regression based approaches using central tendency estimates. Using data from 58 of the 100 largest accounting firms in the U.S. we find that efficiency increased at high levels of statistical significance and discover that this result is consistent for all of the different methods – frontier and central tendencies used in this article. We also find that this result is not affected by inclusion or exclusion of the Big 4 firms. All results are found to be robust as well as consistent.

Credit risk evaluation and credit default prediction attract a natural interest from both practitioners and regulators in the financial industry. Chapter 11 reviews various quantitative methods in credit risk management. Case study to identify credit risks is demonstrated using two neural network approaches, Backpropagation Neural Networks (BPNN) and Probabilistic Neural Network (PNN). The results of the empirical application of both methods confirm their validity. BPNN yeilds a convincing 54.55% bankruptcy and 100% non-bankruptcy out-of-sample prediction accuracy. PNN produces a 54.55% bankruptcy and 96.52% non-bankruptcy out-of-sample prediction accuracy. The promising results potentially provide tremendous benefit to the financial sector in the areas of credit approval, loan securitization and loan portfolio management.

Information technology (IT) outsourcing is one of the major issues facing organizations in today's rapidly changing business environment. Due to its very nature of uncertainty, it is critical for companies to manage and mitigate the high risks associated with IT outsourcing practices including the task of vendor selection. Chapter 12 explores the two-stage vendor selection approach in IT outsourcing using real options analysis. In the first stage, the client engages a vendor for a pilot project and observes the outcome. Using this observation, the client decides either to continue the project to the second stage based upon pre-specified terms or to terminate the project. A case example of outsourcing the development of supply chain management information systems for a logistics firm is also presented in the paper. Our findings suggest that real options analysis is a viable project valuation technique for IT outsourcing.

Part IV: Applications of ERM in China

Assessment of operational risk (oprisks) in banking is multiple attribute decision analysis (MADA) problems. MADA problems having both quantitative and qualitative attributes under uncertainty can be modeled and analyzed using the evidential reasoning (ER) approach. Because of the assessment under uncertainty it is valuable to use the uncertainty reasoning theory to quantify the information gathered from experts, according to the key role of the experts' knowledge to the oprisk measurement. Several types of uncertainty such as ignorance and fuzziness can be consistently modeled in the ER framework. Chapter 13 uses DS evidential theory to establish the frame of discernment, collected the information from experts, and adopted two kinds of weight coefficients, weights in same group experts and weights between different groups, to modify the Dempster's combining formula to find the final assessment of oprisk. The validity of this method is confirmed through demonstration on three commercial banks in China.

As a Large-scale State-owned Corporation in China, Cailing Chemical Corporation encounters several risks that impede its business activities. Chapter 14 identifies these risks and their factors. In additional, the paper examines the relationship among risks and puts forward a risk network diagram. Then, the paper investigates risk distribution from three profiles such as business process, spatial layout and organization structure, which is the basis of total risk management. Finally, the study proposes some suggestions for risk management in Cailing Chemical Corporation.

Enterprise risk management (ERM) has become an important topic in today's more complex, interrelated global business environment, replete with threats from natural, political, economic, and technical sources. Chapter 15 presents development and current status information technology (IT) outsourcing risks. We review the IT risks in the ERM framework and consider risks of evaluating IT proposals. Outsourcing is attractive to many types of organizations, since it has evolved into a way for IT to gain cost savings to organizations. China is beginning to offer compelling advantages over India since India's original cost benefits are reaching wage and capacity limits. The status and trend of outsourcing risks in China is presented.

Thanks to Authors

This book collects works from many authors throughout the world. We would like to thank them for their valuable contributions, and hope that this collection provides value to the growing research community in ERM.

End Notes

1. Dickinson, G. (2001). Enterprise risk management: Its origins and conceptual foundation, *The Geneva Papers on Risk and Insurance* 26:3, 360–366.
2. Gates, S. and Nanes, A. (2006). Incorporating strategic risk into enterprise risk management: A survey of current corporate practice, *Journal of Applied Corporate Finance* 18:4, 81–90.
3. Walker, L., Shenkir, W.G. and Barton, T.L. (2003). ERM in practice 60:4, 51–55; Baranoff, E.G. (2004). Risk management: A focus on a more holistic approach three years after September 11, *Journal of Insurance Regulation* 22:4, 71–81.
4. Olson, D.L. and Wu, D. (2008). Enterprise Risk Management. World Scientific.

Chapter 2
The Human Reaction to Risk and Opportunity

D.R. Koenig

Introduction

Enterprise risk management is about increasing the value of an enterprise or system. The value of a system today is the discounted present value of some perceived set of possible future states of value of that system. By creating ductile systems that respond well to risk events we can positively change the distribution of and perception about expected future states of value of the system. We can also increase the expected life over which the system is being valued.

Quantitative methods, cultural awareness, processes and control are all important to an enterprise risk management framework that is ductile. However, a subtle but important contributor to the impact of a risk event, which defines future states of value, is often ignored in present-day enterprise risk management programs. This may lead to under-appreciation of the value of addressing risks and even false comfort levels in our programs. Intriguing psychological research has been published that shows that the impact of a "risk event" can be either attenuated or exacerbated by the human reaction to that risk event. The human reaction can be affected by present-day risk perceptions and framing, for example, or how risk is processed psychologically. Further, the weighting of possible future states of value, can be impacted by factors such as loss avoidance, small probabilistic changes in state and framing.

We are warned, by research in this area, that an over-reliance on quantitative measures can provide a false sense of security, lead to greater amplification of risk events and even generate unexpected risk events when incentives are improperly aligned with risk management objectives. Yet, we naturally seek this security as part of our psychological makeup, perhaps to our own detriment.

In total, our awareness of the psychological contributions to how risk events can change the value of our systems is important in any enterprise risk management program and to increasing the value of our enterprise.

D.L. Olson, D. Wu (eds.) *New Frontiers in Enterprise Risk Management*,

Risk and Risk Events

Risk can be defined as the unknown change in the future value of a system. Kloman defined risk as "a measure of the probable likelihood, consequences and timing of an event."[1] Slovik and Weber identified four common conceptions of risk:[2]

- Risk as hazard
  - Examples: "Which risks should we rank?" or "Which risks keep you awake at night?"
- Risk as probability
  - Examples: "What is the risk of getting AIDS from an infected needle?" or "What is the chance that Citigroup defaults in the next 12 months?"
- Risk as consequence
  - Examples: "What is the risk of lettering your parking meter expire?" (answer: "Getting a ticket.") or "What is the risk of not addressing a compliance letter?" (answer: "Regulatory penalties.")
- Risk as potential adversity or threat
  - Examples: "How great is the risk of riding a motorcycle?" or "What is your exposure to rising jet fuel prices?"

While these last four conceptions all tend to have a negative tonality to them, the classical definition of "risk" refers to both positive and negative outcomes, which the first two definitions of risk capture.

A *risk event*, therefore, can be described as the actualization of a risk that alters the value of a system or enterprise, either increasing or decreasing its present value by some amount.

Ductile Systems

Recent use of the term risk has been focused on negative outcomes, or loss. In particular, attention has been highly concentrated on extreme losses and their ability to disrupt a system or even to cause its collapse. This may be every bit a function of preference described as loss avoidance by Kahneman and Tversky where the negative utility from loss greatly exceeds the positive utility from an equal gain.[3]

By definition, a ductile system is one that "breaks well" or never allows a risk event to cause the entire system to collapse.[4] A company cares about things that can break its "system" like the drying-up of liquidity sources or a dramatic negative change in perception of its products by customers, for example, as such events could dramatically reduce or eliminate the value of the enterprise. Figure 2.1 below depicts the path a risk event takes to its full potential. In other words, absent any intervention, the full change in value of the system that would be realized from the risk event is 100% of the potential impact of the risk event.

In this figure, the horizontal axis represents steps in time, noting that all risk events take some amount of time to reach their full potential impact. The vertical axis is the percent of the full impact that has been realized. All risk events eventually reach 100% of their potential impact if there is no intervention.

Hundreds of thousands of risk events are likely to be realized in any system and some very small percentage would, if left unchecked, break the system. In a corporate setting, these system-breaking events would be those that resulted in losses that exceed the company's capital.

Through interventions, which include enterprise risk management programs, dissemination of knowledge and risk-awareness can help make systems more ductile and thus more valuable. If the players in a system are risk-aware, problems are less likely

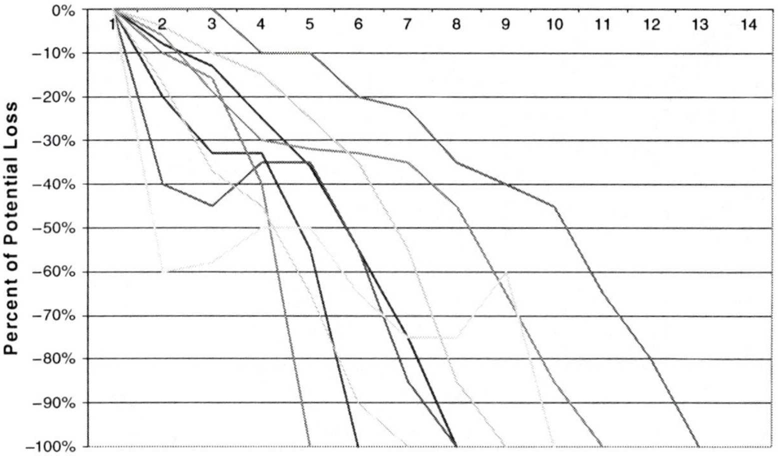

Fig. 2.1 The path of a risk event

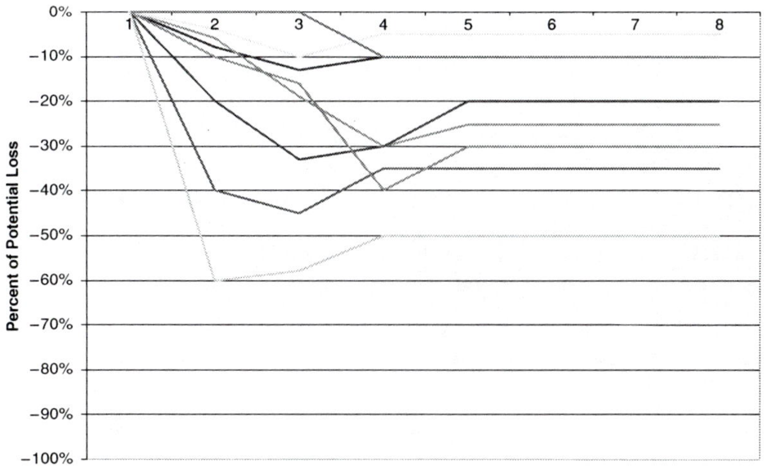

Fig. 2.2 The path of a risk event in a ductile system

to reach their full potential for damage. This is so simply because some element of the system, by virtue of the risk-awareness, takes an action to stop the problem before it realizes its full impact. Figure 2.2 depicts the path of a risk event in a ductile system.

In a ductile system, no risk event reaches its full potential impact.

The Value of the System

The general notion behind creating a ductile system is that if you can positively alter the perception of possible future states of value of the system through enterprise risk management, you can greatly increase the system's present value. This comes about through a reduced need for capital (reduced potential loss from a given risk event) and its associated expense, a greater ability to take business risks (perceived and real increases in growth) and more benefit from investor perception of the firm.

In classic theories of finance, risk has been used as a theoretical construct assumed to influence choice.[5] Underlying risk-return models in finance (e.g., Markowitz 1954) is the psychological assumption that greed and fear guide behavior, and that it is the final balance and trade-off between the fear of adverse consequences (risk) and the hope for gain (return) that determines our choices, like investing or supply of liquidity.[6] How many units of risk is a person willing to tolerate for one unit of return? The acceptable ratio of risk to return is the definition of risk attitude in these models.[7]

In our ductile system, we can easily recognize how a trimming of the possible negative risk events and a shift right-ward towards higher expected gains from greater business growth can positively impact value in the Markowitz world (Fig. 2.3).

But, the variance (i.e., the square of the standard deviation of outcomes around the mean) used in such models is a symmetric measure, meaning the variation above the mean has equal impact to variation below the mean. Psychological research indicates that humans care much more about much more about downside variability (i.e., outcomes that are worse than the average) than upside variability.[8]

The asymmetric human perception and attitudes towards risk mean that there is more that we must understand in terms of the human impact on risk events and valuation of a system than a standard Markowitz risk-return framework would suggest, or our enterprise risk management system might not be as effective as it could be. In other words, the enterprise risk management program will not be as valuable and some cost/benefit calculations will incorrectly reach the conclusion that no action is economically justified.

How does understanding the way in which risk events can be amplified matter? How do transparency and confidence lead to an attenuation of risk events? How do people psychologically process risk events and why does that matter? These are just a few of the questions that must be asked about our enterprises and the risks they face.

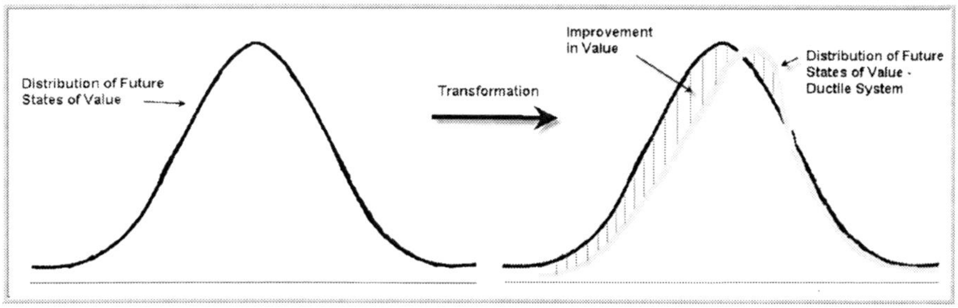

Fig. 2.3 Ductile systems shift the distributions of changes of value

Social Amplification of Risk

In the late 1980s, a framework for understanding how the human response to risk events could contribute to the final "value" of the impact of a risk event was conceived under the Social Amplification of Risk Framework or SARF.[9]

The theoretical starting point of the SARF is the belief that unless humans communicate to each other, the impact of a risk event will be localized or irrelevant. In other words, its potential negative impact will be less than if the risk event is amplified through human communication. Even though this framework was developed in a setting focused on natural or physical risks, this foundation is essential to understanding the transmission mechanism that can lead to things like credit crunches, liquidity crises or dramatic devaluation of a system, firm or assets.

A key component of the human communication process about risk is portrayed through various risk signals (images, signs and symbols), which in turn interact with a wide range of psychological, social, institutional and cultural processes in ways that either intensify or attenuate perceptions of risk and its manageability through *amplification* stations.[10] Events may be interpreted as clues regarding the magnitude of the risk and the adequacy of the risk management process.[11]

Amplification stations can include social networks, expert communities, institutions, the mass media and government agencies, etc. These individual stations of amplification are affected by risk heuristics, qualitative aspects of risk, prior attitudes, blame and trust.

In the second stage of the framework, some risk events will produce ripple effects that may spread beyond the initial impact of the risk event and may even impact unrelated entities. Consider consumer reaction to the Tylenol poisonings. Tylenol tampering resulted in more than 125,000 stories in the print media alone and inflicted losses of more than $1 billion upon the Johnson & Johnson company, including a damaged image of the product.[12] Further, consumer demand and regulation following this led to the ubiquity of tamper-proof packages (and associated costs) at completely unrelated firms.

Similarly, the reaction to the events of 9/11 has led to an enormous cost on all who travel, businesses wishing to hire foreign talent the United States or businesses involved in import/export, for example. Other impacts from risk amplification can include potentially system-breaking events like capital flight as in the Asian currency crisis of 1997–1998.

This process has been equated to the ripples from dropping a stone into a pond.[13] As the ripples spread outward, there is a first group directly impacted by the risk event, then it touches the next higher institutional level (a business line, company or agency) and in extreme cases reaches other parts of the industry or even extra-industry entities.

In 1998, the Asian currency and Russian debt crises had ripple effects that led to the demise of the hedge-fund Long Term Capital Management (LTCM). This demise, in turn, was perceived as having the potential to lead to a catastrophic disruption of the entire global capital markets system and resulted in substantial financial losses (and gains) for firms that believed they had no exposure to either Asia or Russia and certainly not to hedge funds. This amplification came through human stations.

In 1992, the same researchers who conceived of SARF evaluated their theory by reviewing a large database of 128 risk events, primarily physical risks, in the United States. In their study, they found strong evidence that the social amplification of a risk event is as important in determining the full set of risk consequences as is the direct physical impact of the risk event. Applying this result to internal risk assessments suggests that it would be easy to greatly underestimate the impact of a risk event if only first order effects are considered and not the secondary and tertiary impacts from social amplification or communication and reaction to the risk event.

Again, considering the Tylenol tampering case, an internal risk assessment of a scenario that included such an event might result in the risk being limited to be legal liability from the poisonings and perhaps some negative customer impact. However, it would be unlikely that any ex-ante analysis would have concluded the long-term impact on product packaging and associated costs that were a result of the amplification of the story. Or, if the scenario had involved such an event at a competing firm, the impact might have even been assumed to be positive for the "unaffected" firm.

The Perception of Risk, Dread and Knowledge

So, what are the factors that can increase the likelihood of social amplification or attenuation? How are hazards or risks perceived? It turns out, not surprisingly, that what people do not understand and what they perceive as having potentially wide-ranging effects are the things they are most likely respond to with some kind of action, e.g., a change in the valuation of a system.

Weber reviewed three approaches to risk perception: axiomatic, socio-cultural and psychometric.[14] Axiomatic measurements focus on the way in which people subjectively transform objective risk information (e.g., the common credit risk measure Loss Given Default and the equally common Probability of Default) into how the realization of the event will impact them personally (career prospects, for example).

The study of socio-cultural paradigms focuses on the effect of group- and culture-level variables on risk perception. Some cultures select some risks that require attention, while others pay little or no attention to these risks at all. Cultural differences in trust in institutions (corporation, government, market) drive a different perception of risk.[15]

But, most important, is the *psychometric paradigm* which has identified people's emotional reactions to risky situations that affect the judgments of the riskiness of events that go beyond their objective consequences. This paradigm is characterized by risk dimensions called *Dread* (perceived lack of control, feelings of dread and perceived catastrophic potential) and *risk of the Unknown* (the extent to which the risk is judged to be unobservable, unknown, new or delayed in producing harmful impacts).

Recall that SARF holds that risk events can contain "signal value." Signal value might warn of the likelihood of secondary or tertiary effects. The likelihood of a risk event having high signal value is a function of perceptions of that risk in terms of the source of the risk and its potential impact. Slovic developed a dread/knowledge chart represented below, that measures the factors that contribute to feelings of dread and knowledge.[16]

In Fig. 2.4, "Dread risk," captures aspects of the described risks that speed up our heart rate and make us anxious as we contemplate them: perceived lack of control over exposure to the risk, with consequences that are catastrophic, and may have global ramifications or affect future generations.[17] "Unknown risk," refers to the degree to which exposure to a risk and its consequences are predictable and observable: how much is known about the risk and is the exposure easily detected.

Research has shown that the public's risk perceptions and attitudes are closely related to the position of a risk within the factor space. Most important is the factor Dread risk. The higher a risk's score on this factor, the higher its perceived risk, the more people want to see its current risks reduced, and the more they want to see strict regulation employed to achieve the desired reduction in risk.[18]

In the unknown risk factor space, familiarity with a risk (e.g., acquired by daily exposure) lowers perceptions of its riskiness.[19] In this factor, people are also willing to accept far greater voluntary risks (risks from smoking or skiing for example) than involuntary risks (risks from electric power generation for example). We are loath to let others do on to us what we haply do to ourselves.[20]

From this depiction, we can recognize that both dread and our lack of familiarity with something will likely amplify the human response to a risk event. In other words, risks that are in the upper right hand corner of the dread/knowledge chart are the ones most likely to lead to an amplification effect.

Slovic and Weber use terrorism as an example, noting that the concept of accidents as signal helps explain our strong response to terrorism.[21] Because the risks associated with terrorism are seen as poorly understood and catastrophic, accidents anywhere in the world may be seen as omens of disaster everywhere, thus producing responses that carry immense psychological, socioeconomic, and political impacts.

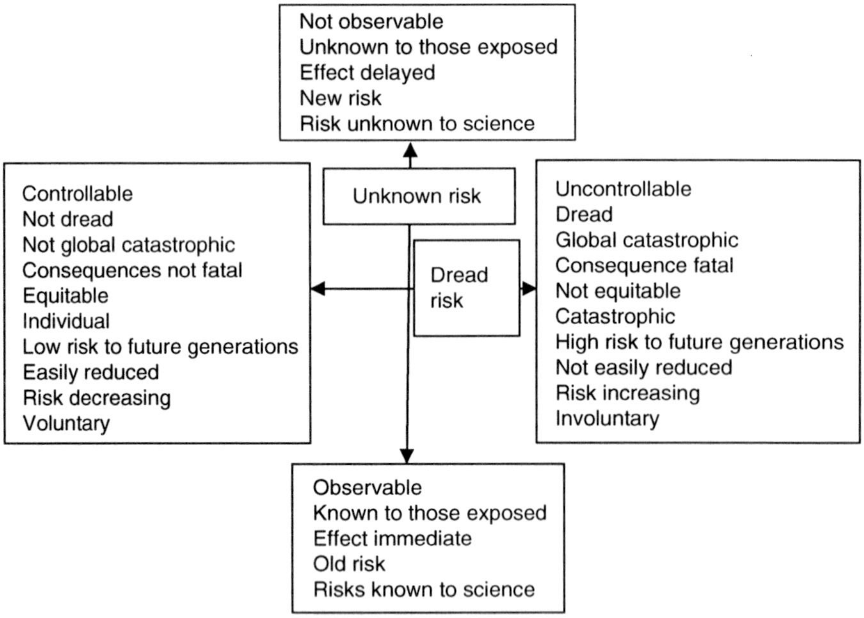

Fig. 2.4 The dread/knowledge spectrum

We might also include the 2007 subprime mortgage crisis as an example of a risk event being amplified to affect general liquidity being provided to financial service companies. The Unknown in this case is the extent to which companies are exposed to subprime default risk and the Dread is that these defaults might affect home prices, thus affecting consumer spending and thus affecting the general well-being of banks and other companies.

One implication of the signal concept is that effort and expense beyond that indicated by a first-order cost-benefit analysis might be warranted to reduce the possibility of high signal events and that transparency may be undervalued, underappreciated or improperly feared.

The examination of risks that face a system should include a qualitative, and even quantitative assessment of where those risks fall on the dread/knowledge spectrum to assess the risk to underestimating their impact through traditional risk assessment techniques.

The Processing of Risk: Emotion Versus Reason

We have looked at the way in which people perceive risk in terms of dread and their knowledge of a risk. But, what about how people process information about a risk event once it has occurred? How are people likely to react to risk event? Research indicates that people process information about risk events in two substantially different manners.[22]

The first system of information processing is more reactive, developed as an evolutionary response system, but also based on knowledge and experience. This experience or association-based processing enabled humans to survive during a long period of evolution and remains the most natural and most common way to respond to a threat.[23]

This is an *affective* paradigm, relying on images and associations, linked by experience to emotions, good or bad. It transforms uncertainty and threats into emotional or affective responses (e.g., fear, dread, anxiety) and represents risk as a feeling, which tells us whether it is safe to walk down a dark street or drink strange smelling water.[24]

The second paradigm for processing is more analytic and rule-based. Examples include formal logic, probability calculus and utility maximization as modes of process. As a result, it is slower and requires awareness and conscious control.[25] Its algorithms need to be taught explicitly and its appropriateness of use for a given situation needs to be obvious, i.e., it does not get triggered automatically.[26]

While these two processes work simultaneously, situationally, one can dominate the other. Weber uses the example of how a mind responds to the question "Is a whale a fish?"[27] The first process immediately says that the whale sure looks like a great big fish, while the second process says that it cannot be a fish because it is warm-blooded. When these two processes are in conflict, evidence strongly suggests that the affective, or emotion-based system will prevail.

This matters significantly in financial risk management, especially in market reactions to bad news. Consider an investor, with an open financial exposure to a company, who sees a 20% decline in that company's stock overnight. The affective response may be to immediately assume there is trouble and to cut-off further investment in or credit-extension to that company. Up to that point, though, the analytic process had indicated to the investor that the exposure was prudent. Further exposure might even have been possible. The fear that the drop in stock prices has been correlated with deterioration of the company, though, may immediately override the analytic process, even if it was still correct and the change in stock price presented a new and better opportunity.

A visceral reaction like fear or anxiety serves as early warning to indicate that some risk management action is in order and motivate us to execute that action.[28] Stepping into the realm of emotion, certain market behaviors like foreign-exchange overshooting, liquidity crises and the tendency of asset prices to move down more quickly and violently than they move up can easily be associated with the dominance of the affective process.

Quantification as a Coping Mechanism

Risk and uncertainty make us uneasy. We naturally prefer to move further down on the unknown risk factor chart, making ourselves more comfortable with things that we may not understand initially. Quantifications are one manner by which we try to turn subjective risk assessments into objective measures. We attempt to convert uncertainty, which is not measurable, into risk, which is believed to be measurable.

Consider a firm reviewing an unsecured $20 MM line of credit to ABC Corporation. If the market price of a 1-year credit default swap on ABC trades at such a price as to imply a 0.5% probability of default, that firm could use this metric to decide what to do with the "risk as probability" by either buying or selling credit protection, selling any credit exposure that it has to ABC, taking on more ABC exposure or not accepting any more ABC exposure.

The firm providing liquidity to ABC, absent complete transparency, does not know the actual probability that ABC will default in the next 12 months. But, it does have a metric that makes it think that it does and it is thus more comfortable and likely to extend the credit.

Slovik and Weber note that much social science analysis rejects the concept of measuring uncertainty, arguing that "objective characterization of the distribution of possible outcomes is incomplete at best and misleading at worst."[29] Risk, they say, is "a concept that human beings have invented to help them understand and cope with the dangers and uncertainties of life."

The assignment of numbers to that which is not measurable creates its own risk, much in the way that an earthquake can disrupt ones faith in the stability of the ground on which we stand. This is particularly true if one has never experienced an earthquake and is in an area where earthquakes are not supposed to happen, as Prospect theory has found dramatic effect on human perceptions when a risk changes its state from the impossible to possible.

Define the terms "public" and "expert" in a general sense that conveys information asymmetry. The term expert is used to refer to someone or a group with, or perceived to have, more information, and public is used to refer to a group with less or no information about a realized or potential risk. In the ABC Company example above, we consider the market for credit default swaps to be our proxy "expert." Should our expert prove to be wrong, we may alter our response to the realization of risk, figuring it to be farther up the unknown risk spectrum than first believed and perhaps even of increasing risk and greater dread. This could trigger a greater emotional reaction and social amplification.

What is the impact when an expert is wrong? Reduced trust in institutions or experts results in stronger negative affective responses to potential risks and thus greater chance for amplification.[30] In the subprime crisis, early in 2008, we see less trust in credit risk models (proxy experts) and in guarantors of credit, suggesting further risk events resulting in credit losses will spur larger negative reactions, absent any change in transparency. Risk signals and blame attributable to incompetent risk management seems particularly important to public concerns.[31]

Incentives and Operational Risk

In addition to understanding how human perceptions and the processing of negative risk events can alter our value perception with respect to the true value of an enterprise risk management system or the value of an enterprise, there are also important psychological aspects to how humans within our systems will respond to incentives to perform better. In particular, work by Darley notes that rigid or overly quantified incentive or criterial control systems can create new risks of their own which are unknown or unexpected to those involved in the system.[32]

Darley's Law says that "The more any quantitative performance measure is used to determine a group or an individual's rewards and punishments, the more subject it will be to corruption pressures and the more apt it will be to distort and corrupt the action patterns and thoughts of the group or individual it is intended to monitor."

Darley's Law is a good warning to organizations that employ overly objective incentive or valuation systems. Humans are quite adept at manipulating rules to personal benefit. Success in recognizing this and in aligning incentives with behavioral objectives means that incentives must be carefully crafted so that the mix of measurable and qualitative inputs to the award match the behavior desired from the individual being incented. We must, as a first root, understand how humans respond to incentives and controls before we are able to build structures to match desired behaviors with compensation.

In 2001 the Risk Management Group (RMG) of the Basel Committee on Banking Supervision defined operational risk in a causal-based fashion: "the risk of loss resulting from inadequate or failed internal processes, people and systems…"

Darley describes compensation and incentive programs as being "criterial control systems."[33] We set criteria for people's performances, measure, and reward or punish according to a process or system. The general intent of criterial control systems is to develop calculations or, in the business vernacular, "metrics" of how individual contributions have helped the organization to reach corporate goals. By inference, the corporate goals are metrics like share price, earnings and market share, expecting that the company will be rewarded by "the market" for making goals and punished for not doing so. Such systems are designed to pay off those who make their numbers and punish those who do not.

Incentive systems, simple or complicated, are typically based on objective measures upon which all parties agree, ex ante. Employers formulate a choice and employees respond to the potential outcomes perceived and the risks with which they associate them.

The appeal for the employer of such systems is in the perception that they provide more predictable budgeting, they may make employees behave more like owners and they help to retain attractive human capital.

Such systems, though, may inadvertently attract a concentration of a certain type of human capital. Employees who are averse to subjective systems under which they perceive less control are more likely to be drawn to highly objective or criterial control systems. The cause of their preference may be related to a level of trust in organizations, or something deeper in the personality of the employee. Whatever the source, the more rigidity there is in a criterial control formula; the more tightly defined will be the personality attracted to it and the greater the potential impact of concentrated misalignment.

Prospect Theory research has yielded numerous examples of how the framing of a choice can greatly alter how that choice is perceived by humans. If the behavior that an organization is seeking to stimulate through criteria-based incentives provides the employee with a choice in an "incorrect" manner, the organization might be creating risk of which it is not aware, or, in fact, exacerbating risk that it thought the incentive system was reducing. Further, this risk might be highly concentrated in places where its realization it is also likely to have high impact, like trading desks, sales teams or business line management.

Darley also suggests that a highly objective system is not necessarily a morally neutral system.[34] Objective systems may create certain pressures on the actors within the system that may be not at all what the performance measurers intended. This goes beyond the framing issue of Prospect Theory and into even more complex behavioral notions.

Three general sorts of occasions arise when the criterial control system is not morally neutral:[35]

1. *A person, in hopes of advancement or in fear of falling behind, "cheats" on the performance measurement system by exploiting its weaknesses to "make his or her numbers." Others who see this, and see this action succeeding, are then under pressure to cheat also. There is a diffusion of a corrupt innovation that corrupts the individuals within the system.*

This group behavior can become pervasive. Consider two employees at the same level in an organization, both seeking advancement within the organization. If one succeeds in cheating, the second may perceive his/her chances for promotion slipping away. That person is thus pressured to engage in the same or "better" cheating. The increased cheating is more likely to stimulate cheating behavior by other advancement-hungry peers.

2. *Or a person, with the best will in the world, does what optimizes his or her performance measurements, without realizing that this is not what the system really intended. A performance measurement system is a powerful communication that the authorities have thought these issues through, and want what they reward. The individuals in the system are to some extent relieved of their responsibilities to think through the system goals, and to independently determine their contributions to those goals.*

In this instance, the rules of the game have been defined and the employee simply plays the game to their highest benefit.

3. *Or a person who has the best interests of the system in mind, may "game" the performance measurement system in various ways, to allow the continuation of the actions that best fulfill his or her reading of the system goals. However, this "takes underground" those activities, and diminishes the possibilities of dialogue about system goals or modifications in system measurements.*

There is ample evidence of Darley's Law being realized in financial loss case studies like Enron, Joseph Jett and Kidder Peabody, National Australia Bank and Barings. See Koenig, for a more detailed examination of these cases in this context.[36]

Another approach to understanding the human response to the framing of incentives or expectations is highlighted by Angelova as risk-sensitive foraging theory.[37] The argument made is that real-life has baselines, such as death, or total capital, below which one must not fall. These baselines can affect how one chooses risk or processes risky options.

Suppose that a sales person needs to realize $2 MM in sales in order to keep their job. Two sales approaches that both have a $2 MM expected value are available, but one has greater variability, while the other guarantees $2 MM in sales. The rational sales person should choose the approach with no variability as that ensures their survival. However, if the requirement to maintain employment is shifted to $2.1 MM, the sales person must choose the riskier approach or realize the loss of their job with certainty. They will, therefore, move from risk-averse behavior to risk-loving with only a modest change in the paradigm that they face.

Poorly framed incentive structures have broken systems. These structures are often not given enough attention, if any at all, by traditional enterprise risk management programs. Yet, they fall into the category of low-probability, high-impact events and have the potential to dramatically affect the value of the firm in a negative sense when their crafting was an attempt to shift the value upward.

Conclusion

Within most organizations the debate about whether an enterprise risk management function adds value is less contentious than even five years ago. However, there are still ample situations in which risk management is either not being used, is not well understood or is undervalued because of a lack of appreciation for the importance of how humans respond to risk and opportunity and how risk management programs can be structured to mitigate the risks of such reactions.

In effect, through enterprise risk management, we are attempting to reframe the perceptions, of investors, customers and liquidity providers, of the system to which risk management is being applied. We are seeking to increase its value by understanding what risks are perceived to be most important by those most important to our enterprise.

Psychological research being applied in past decades to finance and economics suggests that many of our traditionally held assumptions about valuation and utility are not as complete or effective as had been previously assumed. In particular, traditional models of valuation have not placed enough emphasis on the perceived impact on value assigned by humans to loss, extreme loss and rare events. When this increased valuation or *loss avoidance* is taken into account, enterprise risk management systems, designed to create ductile systems (corporations, firms or other), receive greater importance and the cost-benefit decisions about preemptive risk management initiatives become less subject to error via a negative decision.

Understanding that risk events need not lead to an amplification of their impacts, which risk events might spur emotional reactions, how transparency can reduce this effect via a movement down the unknown risk spectrum and understanding how people evaluate prospects can dramatically and positively alter the value of our systems.

The literature on human responses to risk and opportunity, while relatively new, is quite vast. Only a very small segment of that research has been discussed in this chapter. Readers are recommended to study the works of Kahneman and Tversky, Weber, Slovic and Darley in particular. For those interested in a highly concentrated review of some of the psychological influences on finance theory, see Shiller.[38]

One final note which serves as a warning is that some of the research has found evidence of something called *single-action bias*. This expression was coined by Weber for the following phenomenon observed in a wide range of contexts.[39] Decision-makers are very likely take one action to reduce the risk that they encounter but are much less likely to take additional steps that would provide incremental protection or risk reduction. The single action taken is not necessarily the most effective one. Regardless of which single action is taken first, decision-makers have a tendency to stop from taking further action presumably because the first action suffices in reducing the feeling of fear or threat. In the absence of fear or dread response to a risk, purely affect driven risk management decisions will likely result in insufficient responsiveness to the risk.[40]

As the understanding of human behavior advances so too will the practice of enterprise risk management, adding greater value to the systems in which it is practiced.

End Notes

1. Kloman, F. (2007). What Is Risk Management?, Unpublished, Seawrack, Lyme, CT 06371.
2. Slovic, P., and Weber, E. (2002). Perception of Risk Posed by Extreme Events, prepared for discussion at "Risk Management Strategies in an Uncertain World", April 12–13.
3. Kahnemann, D., and Tversky, A. (1979). Prospect theory: An analysis of decision under risk, *Econometrica*, 47:2, 263–291.
4. Koenig, D.R. (2004). Understanding risk management as added value, *Derivatives and Risk Management Handbook*, Euromoney Yearbooks
5. Weber, E. (2003). Origins and Functions of Perceptions of Risk, presentation at NCI Workshop on Conceptualizing and Measuring Risk Perceptions, Feb. 14–4.
6. Markowitz. (1954).
7. Weber (2003), op cit.
8. Ibid.
9. Pidgeon, N., Kasperson, R.E., and Slovic, P. (2003). *The Social Amplification of Risk*, 13–46, Cambridge University Press, Cambridge, UK.
10. Kasperson, J.X., Kasperson, R.E., Pidgeon, N. and Slovic, P. (2003). The social amplification of risk: assessing fifteen years of research and theory, in Pidgeon, N., Kasperson, R.E., and Slovic, P. (Eds.), *The Social Amplification of Risk*, Cambridge Press, Cambridge, UK.
11. Slovik and Weber. (2002). op cit.
12. bid.
13. Kasperson et al. (2003). op cit.
14. Weber, E. (2001). *Risk: Empirical studies on decision and choice, in International Encyclopedia of the Social and Behavioral Sciences*, Elsevier Science, Ltd.
15. Ibid.
16. Slovik and Weber. (2002). op cit.

17. Weber, E. (2004). Who's afraid of poor old age? Risk perception in risk management decisions, in Olivia S. and Utkus, Stephen P. (Eds.), *Pension and Design Structure by Mitchell*, Oxford University Press.
18. Slovik and Weber. (2002). op cit.
19. Weber. (2004). op cit.
20. Angelova, R. (c. 2000). *Risk-Sensitive Decision-Making Examined Within an Evolutionary Framework*, Blagoevgrad, Bulgaria.
21. Slovik and Weber. (2002). op cit.
22. Ibid.
23. Ibid.
24. Ibid.
25. Weber. (2004). op cit.
26. Weber, E. (2006). Experience-based and description-based perceptions of long-term risk: Why global warming does not scare us (yet), *Climate Change* 77: 103–120.
27. Weber. (2004). op cit.
28. Weber. (2006). op cit.
29. Slovik & Weber (2002) op cit.
30. Weber. (2001). op cit.
31. Kasperson et al. (2003). op cit.
32. Darley, J.M. (2001). The dynamics of authority in organizations and the unintended action consequences, in Darley, J.M., Messick, D.M., and Tyler, T.R. (Eds.), *Social Influences on Ethical Behavior in Organizations*, pp. 37–52 , Mahwah, NJ: L.A. Erlbaum Assoc.
33. Darley, J.M. (1994). Gaming, Gundecking, Body Counts, and the Loss of Three British Cruisers at the Battle of Jutland: The Complex Moral Consequences of Performance Measurement Systems in Military Settings, Unpublished Speech to Air Force Academy, April 6, 1994.
34. Ibid.
35. Ibid.
36. Koenig. (2004). op cit.
37. Angelova. (2000). op cit.
38. Shiller, R.J. (1999). Human behavior and the efficiency of the financial system, in Taylor, J.B. and Woodford, M. (Eds.), *Handbook of Macroeconomics*, Chap. 20, Vol. 1C.
39. Weber, E. (1997). Perception and expectation of climate change: Precondition for economic and technological adaptation, in Bazerman, M., Messick, D, Tenbrunsel, A., and Wade Benzoni, K. (Eds.), *Psychological Perspectives to Environmental and Ethical Issues in Management* (pp. 314–341). San Francisco, CA: Jossey-Bass.
40. Weber (2004), op cit.

Part II
ERM Perspectives

Chapter 3
Enterprise Risk Management: Financial and Accounting Perspectives

D. Wu and D.L. Olson

ERM and Finance Operations: Key Financial Risks

Recent financial disasters in financial and non-financial firms and in governmental agencies have led to increased emphasis on various forms of risk management such as market risk management, credit risk management, and operational risk management. Financial institutions like banks are further motivated by the need to meet various regulatory requirements for risk measurement and capital. There is an increasing tendency toward an integrated or holistic view of risks. A framework for thinking about the collective risk of a group of financial instruments and an individual security's contribution to that collective risk would be useful. A Tillinghast-Towers Perrin survey has reported that nearly half of the insurance industry used an integrated risk management process (with another 40% planning to do so), and 40% had a chief risk officer.[1]

Enterprise Risk Management (ERM) is an integrated approach to achieving the enterprise's strategic, programmatic, and financial objectives with acceptable risk. The philosophy of ERM generalizes these concepts beyond financial risks to include all kinds of risks. For example, a portfolio of equity investments has been generalized to the entire collection of risks facing an organization. A number of principles have often been found useful in practice:

1. Portfolio risk can never be the simple sum of various individual risk elements.
2. One has to understand various individual risk elements and their interactions in order to understand portfolio risk.
3. The key risk, i.e., the most important risk, contributes most to the portfolio risk or the risk facing the entire organization. Therefore, decision makers should be most concerned about key risk decisions.
4. Using quantitative approaches to measure risk is very important. For example, a key financial market risk can broadly be defined as volatility relative to the capital markets. One measure of this risk is the cost of capital, which can be measured through models such as the Weighted Average Cost of Capital (WACC) and Capital Asset Pricing Model (CAPM).[2]

D.L. Olson, D. Wu (eds.) *New Frontiers in Enterprise Risk Management*,

ERM and Financial Operations

Traditional finance operations have focused on cost and efficiency in operations and processes.[3] A firm is assumed to seek efficiency either through information technologies such as enterprise systems, or through newer operations management techniques such as shared cost/services and outsourcing. While this has been sufficient to preserve competitive advantage when these methods were novel and not widely used, use by competitors makes heavy investment in information technology highly risky. Companies, financial or not, have achieved high performance by utilizing information technology to capture and process data. The challenge today is to process the inherent uncertainties of business, in this case, through finance operations data, in order to develop a coherent strategy. Efficiency is a means to achieve strategic objectives. Where there is strategy, there is an attempt to overcome uncertainty and incomplete knowledge, to act in the face of risk.

To make clear where ERM takes over from finance operations, we must examine best and first principles. While finance operations in an enterprise vary across different industries and products and services provided, effective finance operations rely on four competencies: (1) Transaction processing: creating satisfied efficiency in core finance functions, e.g., accounts payable and general ledger which are increasingly delivered through shared services or outsourcing strategies. (2) Financial and regulatory reporting: capturing regulatory and tax reporting requirements from a transactional and systems perspective. (3) Management reporting: providing various data and information for management decision making. And (4) Internal controls: providing support to effective risk management within the enterprise through the disciplined oversight of financial, accounting and audit systems.

These four competencies are similar to the COSO ERM framework,[4] where three objective categories are identified: operational objectives, financial reporting objectives, and compliance objectives. The COSO framework defines ERM as an ongoing process for identifying and managing potential events and operations that could affect the entity's ability to manage business risks such that they remain within its risk appetite.[5]

Finance operational activities are usually managed through various quantitative models that can be used by ERM. Value-at-Risk models have been popular, partially in response to Basel II banking guidelines.[6] Other analytic approaches include simulation of internal risk rating systems using past data and decision analysis models.[7] Swedish banks have been found to use credit rating categories, and that each bank reflected its own risk policy.[8] One bank was found to have a higher level of defaults, but without adversely affecting profitability due to constraining high risk loans to low amounts. Systemic risk from overall economic systems as well as risk from networks of banks with linked loan portfolios are important.[9] Overall economic system risk was found to be much more likely, while linked loan portfolios involved high impact but very low probability of default.[10]

Key Financial Risks

Typically, the major sources of value loss in financial institutions are identified as:

Market risk is exposure to the uncertain market value of a portfolio, where the underlying economic factors are such as interest rates, exchange rates, and equity and commodity prices.

Credit risk is the risks that counterparty may be unable to perform on an obligation.

Operational risk is the risk of loss resulting from inadequate or failed internal processes, people and systems, or from external events. The committee indicates that this definition excludes systemic risk, legal risk and reputational risk.[11]

During the early part of the 1990s, much of the focus was on techniques for measuring and managing market risk. As the decade progressed, this shifted to techniques of measuring and managing credit risk. By the end of the decade, firms and regulators were increasingly focusing on Operational risk.

A trader holds a portfolio of commodity forwards. She knows what its market value is today, but she is uncertain as to its market value a week from today. She faces market risk. The trader employs the derivatives "greeks" to describe and to characterize the various exposures to fluctuations in financial prices inherent in a particular position or portfolio of instruments. Such a portfolio of instruments may include cash instruments, derivatives instruments, borrowing and lending. In this article, we will introduce two additional techniques for measuring and reporting risk: Value-at-Risk assessment and scenario analysis.

Market risk is concerned both internally and externally. Internally, managers and traders in financial service industry need a measure that allows active, efficient management of the firm's risk position. Externally, regulators want to be sure a financial company's potential for catastrophic net worth loss is accurately measured and that the company's economic capital is sufficient to survive such a loss. Although both managers and regulators want up-to-date measures of risk, they do estimate exposure to risks based on different time horizons. Bank managers and traders measures market risks on a daily basis, which is very costly and time consuming. Thus, bank managers compromise between measurement precision on the one hand and the cost and timeliness of reporting on the other.

Regulators are concerned with the maximum loss a bank is likely to experience over a given horizon so that they can set the bank's required capital (i.e., its economic net worth) to be greater than the estimated maximum loss and be almost sure that the bank will not fail over that horizon. As a result, they are concerned with the overall riskiness of a bank and have less concern with the risk of individual portfolio components.[12] The time horizon used in computation is relatively long. For example, Under Basel II capital for market risk is based on the 10-day 99% VaR and for credit risk and operational risk is based on a 1-year 99.9% VaR.

Market Risk Measurement

There are two principle approaches to risk measurement: value-at-risk analysis and scenario analysis.

VaR: Value at Risk

Value at Risk, or VaR, represents a measure of the risk inherent in a portfolio of financial instruments or contracts, such as a trading portfolio. It can be characterized as a maximum expected loss, given some time horizon and within a given confidence interval. Its utility is in providing a measure of risk that illustrates the risk inherent in a portfolio with multiple risk factors, such as portfolios held by large banks, which are diversified across many risk factors and product types. The VaR and other analytics are primarily run in a series of overnight, automated batch processes. The flow of information and processing is roughly as outlined in the diagram below.

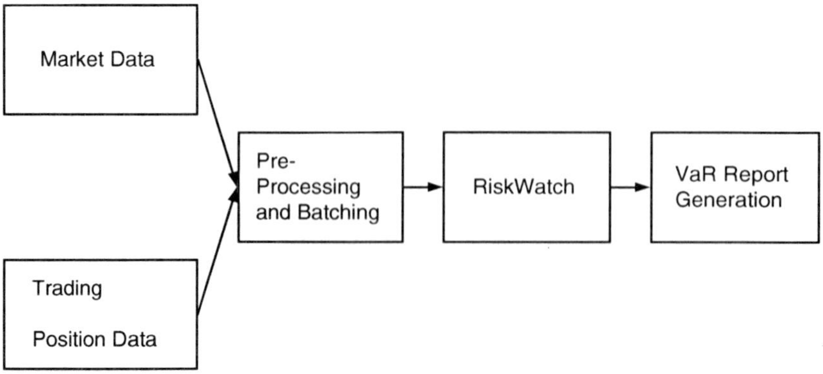

VaR is a measure of risk that is globally accepted by regulatory bodies responsible for supervision of banking activities. These regulatory bodies, in broad terms, enforce regulatory practices as outlined by the Basel Committee on Banking Supervision of the Bank for International Settlements (BIS). The regulator that has responsibility for financial institutions in Canada is the Office of the Superintendent of Financial Institutions (OSFI), and OSFI typically follows practices and criteria as proposed by the Basel Committee.

A key agreement of the Basel Committee is the Basel Capital Accord (generally referred to as "Basel" or the "Basel Accord"), which has been updated several times since 1988. From the point of view of Market Risk Operations, the most significant Amendment to the Basel Accord occurred in January 1996.

In the 1996 (updated, 1998) Amendment to the Basel Accord, banks are encouraged to use internal models to measure Value at Risk, and the numbers produced by these internal models support capital charges to ensure the capital adequacy, or liquidity, of the bank. Some elements of the minimum standard established by Basel are:

- VaR should be computed daily, using a 99th percentile, one-tailed confidence interval
- A minimum price shock equivalent to ten trading days be used. This is called the "holding period" and simulates a 10-day period of liquidating assets in a period of market crisis
- The model should incorporate a historical observation period of at least one year
- The capital charge is set at a minimum of three times the average of the daily value-at-risk of the preceding 60 business days.

In practice, these minimum standards mean that the VaR that is produced by the Market Risk Operations area is multiplied first by the square root of 10 (to simulate 10 days holding) and then multiplied by a minimum capital multiplier of 3 to establish capital held against regulatory requirements.

In summary, VaR provides the worst expected loss at the 99% confidence level. That is, a 99% confidence interval produces a measure of loss that will be exceeded only 1% of the time. But this does mean there will likely be a larger loss than the VaR calculation two or three times in a year. This is compensated for by the inclusion of the multiplicative factors, above, and the implementation of Stress Testing, which falls outside the scope of the activities of Market Risk Operations. Various approaches can be used to compute VaR, of which three are widely used: Historical Simulation, Variance-covariance approach, and Monte Carlo simulation

Scenario Analysis

Scenario analysis typically refers to varying a wider range of parameters at the same time. Scenario analyses often examine the impact of catastrophic events on the firm's financial position, for example, simultaneous movements in a number of risk categories affecting all of a firm's business operations, such as business volumes, investment values and interest rate movements. Scenarios can also be generally considered under three broad headings. Changes to the business plan, changes in business cycles and those relating to extreme events. The scenarios can be derived in a variety of ways including stochastic models or a repetition of an historical event. Scenarios can be developed with varying degrees of precision and depth. One specific scenario analysis is Stress testing, which typically refers to shifting the values of individual parameters that affect the financial position of a firm, and then determining the effect on the firm's business. A stress test isolates the impact on a portfolio's value of one or more predefined moves in a particular market risk factor or a small number of closely linked market risk factors. This approach has the advantage of not requiring a distributional assumption for the risk calculation. Scenario analyses are based on the analysis of the impact of unlikely, but not impossible, events. These events can be financial, operational, legal or relate to any other risk that might have an economic impact on the firm.

Because there is generally more focus on the specific question, stress and scenario tests can generally be constructed and get to the point of producing reliable results much more quickly than in the case for stochastic models. The actual scenarios used will be comprehensible to management of the business, and the subjectivity in the assessment of relative likelihood will clear for all to see.[13]

Measuring Credit Risk

Credit risks are defined as the risk of loss due to a debtor's non-payment of a loan or other line of credit (either the principal or interest (coupon) or both). Examples of Credit Risk Factors in the insurance industry are:

- Adequacy of reinsurance program for the risks selected
- Reinsurance failure of the company's reinsurance program and the impact on claim recoveries
- Credit deterioration of the company's reinsurers, intermediaries or other counterparties
- Credit concentration to a single counterparty or group
- Credit concentration to reinsurers of particular rating grades
- Reinsurance rates increasing
- Bad Debts greater than expected

A financial service firm has used a number of methods, e.g., credit scoring, ratings, credit committees, to assess the creditworthiness of counter-parties (Refer to Chap. 10 for details of these methods). This would make it difficult for the firm to integrate this source of risk with the market risks. Many financial companies are aware of the need for parallel treatment of all measurable risks and are doing something about it.[14]

If financial companies can "score" loans, they can determine how loan values change as scores change. Then, a probability distribution of value changes can be modeled relating to these changes produce over time due to credit risk. Finally, the time series of credit risk changes could be related to the market risk, which enable market risk and credit risk to be integrated into a single estimate of value change over a given horizon.

Measuring Operational Risk

"Operational risk is the risk of loss resulting from inadequate or failed internal processes, people, and systems, or from external events." The definition includes people risks, technology and processing risks, physical risks, legal risks, etc, but excludes reputation risk and strategic risk. The Operational Risk Management framework should include identification, measurement, monitoring, reporting, control and mitigation frameworks for Operational Risk. Basel II proposed three alternatives to measure operational risks: (1) Basic Indicator, which requires Financial Institutions to reserve 15% of annual gross income; (2) Standardized Approach, which is based on annual revenue of each of the broad business lines of the Financial Institution; and (3) Advanced Measurement Approach (AMA), which is based on the internally developed risk measurement framework of the bank adhering to the standards prescribed.

The following lists the official Basel II defined business lines:

- Corporate finance
- Trading and sales
- Retail banking
- Commercial banking
- Payment and settlement
- Agency services
- Asset management
- Retail brokerage

The following lists the official Basel II defined event types with some examples for each category:

- Internal Fraud – misappropriation of assets, tax evasion, intentional mismarking of positions, bribery: Loss due to acts of a type intended to defraud, misappropriate property or circumvent regulations, the law or company policy, excluding diversity/discrimination events, which involves at least one internal party.
- External Fraud – theft of information, hacking damage, third-party theft and forgery: Losses due to acts of a type intended to defraud, misappropriate property or circumvent the law, by a third party.
- Employment Practices and Workplace Safety – discrimination, workers compensation, employee health and safety: Losses arising from acts inconsistent with employment, health or safety laws or agreements, from payment of personal injury claims, or from diversity/discrimination events.
- Clients, Products, and Business Practice – market manipulation, antitrust, improper trade, product defects, fiduciary breaches, account churning; Losses arising from an unintentional or negligent failure to meet a professional obligation to specific clients (including fiduciary and suitability requirements), or from the nature or design of a product.
- Damage to Physical Assets – natural disasters, terrorism, vandalism: Losses arising from loss or damage to physical assets from natural disaster or other events.
- Business Disruption and Systems Failures – utility disruptions, software failures, hardware failures: Losses arising from disruption of business or system failures.
- Execution, Delivery, and Process Management – data entry errors, accounting errors, failed mandatory reporting, negligent loss of client assets: Losses from failed transaction processing or process management, from relations with trade counterparties and vendors

Financial Institutions need to estimate their exposure to each type of risk for each business line combination. Ideally this will lead to $7 \times 8 = 56$ VaR measures that can be combined into an overall VaR measure. Other techniques to measure operational risks includes: Scenario Analysis, Identifying Causal Relationships, key risk indicator (KRI), Scorecard approaches, etc.

The Accounting Perspective: The COSO ERM Cube

Accounting is responsible for providing stockholders with measures of organizational performance. This includes assurance of accurate financial reporting, which has proven to be fundamental in organizational risk management. Motivated by corporate governance malfeasance exemplified by Enron Corporation, Sarbanes–Oxley placed responsibilities for disclosure and procedures seeking to guarantee honest accounting.

The accounting approach to risk management is centered to a large degree on the standards promulgated by the Committee on Sponsoring Organizations of the Treadway Commission (COSO), generated by the Treadway Commission beginning in 1992. The Sarbanes–Oxley Act of 2002 had a synergistic impact with COSO. While many companies have not used it, COSO offers a framework for organizations to manage risk.[15] Use of COSO was found to be used to a large extent by only 11% of the organizations surveyed, and only 15% of the respondents believed that their internal auditors used the COSO 1992 framework in full. This finding was supported by a 2005 study conducted by the IIA Research Foundation which found under 12% of responding organizations to have complete implementation of ERM, while 14% were not going to adopt it.[16] Chief Executive Officers and Chief Financial Officers are required to certify effective internal controls. These controls can be assessed against COSO.[17] This benefits stakeholders. Risk management is now understood to be a strategic activity, and risk standards can ensure uniform risk assessment across the organization. Resources are more likely to be devoted to the most important risk, and better responsiveness to change is obtained.

The COSO ERM Cube

In 2004, COSO published an *Enterprise Risk Management-Integrated Framework*.[18] The COSO ERM cube considers dimension of objective categories, activities, and organizational levels Table (3.1).

Categories

The *strategic level* involves overarching activities such as organizational governance, strategic objectives, business models, consideration of external forces, and other factors. The *operations level* is concerned with business processes, value chains, financial flows, and related issues. *Reporting* includes information systems as well as means to communicate organizational performance on multiple dimensions, to include finance, reputation, and intellectual property. *Compliance* considers organizational reporting on legal, contractual, and other regulatory requirements (including environmental).

Table 3.1 COSO ERM cube

Categories	Activities	Levels
Strategic	Internal environment	Entity level
Operations	Objective setting	Division
Reporting	Event identification	Business unit
Compliance	Risk assessment	Subsidiary
	Risk response	
	Control activities	
	Information and communication	
	Monitoring	

Activities

The COSO process consists of a series of actions.[19]

1. *Internal Environment:* The process starts with identification of the organizational units, with *entity level* representing the overall organization. This includes actions to develop a risk management philosophy, create a risk management culture, and design a risk management organizational structure.
2. *Objective Setting:* Each participating *division, business unit*, and *subsidiary* would then identify business objectives and strategic alternatives, reflecting vision for enterprise success. These objectives would be categorized as strategic, operations, reporting, and compliance. These objectives need to be integrated with enterprise objectives at the entity level. Objectives should be clear and strategic, and should reflect the entity-wide risk appetite.
3. *Event Identification:* Management needs to identify events that could influence organizational performance, either positively or negatively. Risk events are identified, along with event interdependencies. (Some events are isolated, while others are correlated.) Measurement issues associated with methodologies or risk assessment techniques need to be considered. O'Donnell (2004) provided a systems view to create a map of the organization's value chain and a taxonomy of categories to identify events that might threaten business performance.
4. *Risk Assessment:* Each of the risks identified in Step 3 are assessed in terms of probability of occurrence, as well as the impact each risk will have on the organization. Thus both impact and likelihood are considered. Their product provides a metric for ranking risks. Assessment techniques can include point estimates, ranges, or best/worst-case scenarios.
5. *Risk Response:* Strategies available to manage risks are developed. These can include risk acceptance, risk avoidance, risk sharing, or risk reduction. Options have been summarized into the four Ts

    a. *Treating a Risk:* taking direct action to reduce impact or likelihood
    b. *Terminate a Risk:* discontinue activity exposing the organization to the risk
    c. *Transfer a Risk:* insurance or contracts
    d. *Take (or tolerate) a Risk:* for areas of organizational expertise, they may decide to accept risk with the idea that they are expert at dealing with it

Another view considers risk avoidance, reduction, acceptance, transfer, or seeking risks fitting the organization's risk appetite.[20] This is compatible with the four Ts. Avoidance is akin to terminating, acceptance to treating, reduction and transfer to transfer above, and seeking risks to toleration. Risks are necessary to lead to situations likely to offer profit, but risks should be taken only after informed business analysis.

The effects of risk response on other risks should be considered.

6. *Control Activities:* Controls needed to mitigate identified risks are selected. Implicit in this step is assessment of the costs of each risk response available, and consideration of activities to reduce risks.
7. *Information and Communication:* Control and other risk response activities are put in place to ensure appropriate action is taken within the organization. Organizations need to ensure that information systems can measure and report risk accurately. ERM effectiveness and cost should be communicated to stakeholders.

Monitoring: As part of an ongoing process, the effectiveness of plan implementation is monitored, feeding back to the control step if problems are encountered. Monitoring includes risk evaluations comparing actual event occurrences with prior estimates of probability, frequency, and cost.

Event Identification: As an example of how step 3 above can be implemented, Table 3.2 provides a categorization of risks for financial institutions.

Risk Appetite

Risks are necessary to do business. Every organization can be viewed as a specialist at dealing with at least one type of risk. Insurance companies specialize in assessing the market value of risks, and offer policies that transfer special types of risks to themselves from their clients at a fee. Banks specialize in the risk of loan repayment, and survive when they are effective at managing these risks. Construction companies specialize in the risks of making buildings or other facilities. However, risks come at organizations from every direction. Those risks that are outside of an organization's specialty are outside that organization's risk appetite. Management needs to assess risks associated with the opportunities it is presented, and accept those that fit their risk appetite (or organizational expertise), and offload other risks in some way (see Step 6 above).

Example of Risk Quantification

Matyjewicz and D'Arcangelo gave simple examples of how risk assessment could be applied. First, a matrix of risk level (high or low) and control strength (weak or strong) could be generated for each identified risk. Risk impact could be further categorized as critical, significant, moderate, low, or insignificant, while risk probability could have categories of highly probable, probable, likely, unlikely, or remote.

Table 3.2 Financial institution enterprise risk management model

	Top level	Internal		Specific risks
External				Regulatory/legal
				Investor relations
				Competitors
				Financial markets
				Catastrophic loss
				Sovereign/political issues
	Strategic			Corporate governance
				Leadership
				Alignment
				Planning
				Communication
	Legal			Compliance
				Litigation
				Contractual/obligations
				Fiduciary
	Reputation			Fraud
				Ethics
				Privacy
		Credit		Domestic
				Foreign
		Market		Valuation
				Foreign exchange
		Interest rate risk		Repricing
				Yield curve
				Basis
				Options
			Operational	Accounting
				Performance measurement
				Product development, pricing
				Business interruption
				Technology
				Budgeting and planning
				Human resources
				Policy/procedure compliance
				Customer loyalty/retention
				Financial reporting
				Third-party relationships

The likely actions of internal auditing were identified. Those risks involving high risk and strong controls would call for checking that inherent risks were in fact mitigated by risk response strategies and controls. Risks involving high risk and weak controls would call for checking for adequacy of management's action plan to improve controls. Those risks assessed as low call for internal auditing to review accuracy of managerial impact evaluation and risk event likelihood.

Implementation Issues

Past risk management efforts have been characterized by bottom-up implementation.[21] Effective implementation calls for top-down management, as do most organizational efforts. Without top support, lack of funding will starve most efforts. Related to that, top support is needed to coordinate efforts so that silo mentalities do not take over. COSO requires a holistic approach. If COSO is adopted within daily processes, it can effectively strengthen corporate governance. Another important issue is the application of sufficient resources to effectively implement ERM.
One view of ERM, parallel to that of the CMI system used in software engineering, is as follows.[22]

1. Level 1: *Compliance* – review of policy and procedure with a checklist orientation, providing low value to the organization in terms of ERM.
2. Level 2: *Control* – implementation of control frameworks, still using a checklist orientation, also providing low value to organizations.
3. Level 3: *Process* – taking a process view across departments, focusing on effectiveness as well as efficiency, to include process mapping.
4. Level 4: *Risk Management* – use of shared risk language, with the ability to prioritize efforts based on process mapping.
5. Level 5: *Enterprise Risk Management* – the Nirvana of holistic risk reviews tied to entity strategy based on common risk language, viewing risk management as a process, providing high value to organizational risk management.

Conclusions

Risks in a financial firm can be quantified and managed using various models. Models also provide support to organizations seeking to control enterprise risk. ERM provides tools to integrate enterprise-wide operations and finance functions and better inform strategic decisions. The promise of ERM lies in allowing managers to better understand and use their firms' fundamental relation to uncertainty in a scientific framework: from each risk, strategy may create opportunity. We have discussed various risk modeling and reviewed some common risk measures in financial service company from the core financial and accounting perspective.

Gupta and Thomson identified problems in implementing COSO.[23] Small companies (fewer than 1,000 employees) reported a less favorable impression of COSO. Complaints in general included vagueness and nonspecificity for auditing. COSO was viewed as high-level, and thus open to interpretation at the operational level. This seems to reflect a view by most organizations reflective of Level 1 and Level 2 in Bowling and Rieger's framework. Other complaints about COSO have been published.[24] One is that the 1992 framework is not completely appropriate for 2006. The subsequent COSO ERM is more current, but some view it as vague, simplistic, and provides little implementation guidance.

A number of specific approaches for various steps have been published. Later studies have indicated about one half of the surveyed organizations to have either adopted or were in the process of implementing ERM, indicating some increase.[25] Carnaghan reviewed procedures for business process modeling.[25] If such approaches are utilized, more effective ERM can be obtained through COSO.

End Notes

1. Walker, L., Shenkir, W.G., and Barton, T.L. (2003). ERM in practice 60:4, 51–55.
2. Baranoff, E.G. (2004). Risk management: A focus on a more holistic approach three years after September 11, *Journal of Insurance Regulation*, 22:4, 71–81.
3. Sharpe and William, F. (1964). Capital asset prices: A theory of market equilibrium under conditions of risk, *Journal of Finance*, 19:3, 425–442.
4. Donnellan, M., and Sutcliff, M. (2006). *CFO Insights: Delivering High Performance*. Wiley, New York.
5. Levinsohn, A. (2004). How to manage risk – Enterprise-wide, *Strategic Finance*, 86(5), 55–56.
6. Committee of Sponsoring Organizations of the Treadway Commission (COSO) (2004). *Enterprise risk management – integrated framework*. Jersey City, NJ: American Institute of Certified Public Accountants.
7. Alexander, G.J., and Baptista, A.M. (2004). A comparison of VaR and CVaR constraints on portfolio selection with the mean-variance model. *Management Science* 50(9), 1261–1273; Chavez-Demoulin, V., Embrechts, P., and Nešlehová, J. (2006). Quantitative models for operational risk: Extremes, dependence and aggregation. *Journal of Banking and Finance* 30, 2635–2658.
8. Florez-Lopez, R. (2007). Modelling of insurers' rating determinants. An application of machine learning techniques and statistical models. *European Journal of Operational Research*, 183, 1488–1512.
9. Jacobson, T., Lindé, J., and Roszbach, K. (2006). Internal ratings systems, implied credit risk and the consistency of banks' risk classification policies. *Journal of Banking and Finance* 30, 1899–1926.
10. Elsinger, H., Lehar, A., and Summer, M. (2006). Risk assessment for banking systems. *Management Science* 52(9), 1301–1314.
11. Crouhy M., Galai D., and Mark, R. (2000). A comparative analysis of current credit risk models. *Journal of Banking and Finance* 24, 59–117; Crouhy M., Galai D., and Mark, R. (1998). Model Risk. *Journal of Financial Engineering* 7(3/4), 267–288, reprinted in Model Risk: Concepts, Calibration and Pricing, (ed. R. Gibson), *Risk Book*, 2000, 17–31; Crook, J. N., Edelman, D.B., and Thomas, L.C. (2007). Recent developments in consumer credit risk assessment. *European Journal of Operational Research*, 183, 1447–146.
12. Basel Committee on Banking Supervision (June 2004). International Convergence of Capital Measurement and Capital Standards, Bank for International Settlements.
13. Pritsker, M. (1996). Evaluating value at risk methodologies: accuracy versus computational time, unpublished working paper, Board of Governors of the Federal Reserve System.
14. Hull, J.C. (2006). Risk Management and Financial Institutions.
15. Morgan, J.P. (1997). CreditMetrics™-technical document.
16. Gupta, P.P., Thomson, J.C. (2006). Use of COSO 1992 in management reporting on internal control. *Strategic Finance* 88:3, 27–33.
17. Gramling, A.A., and Myers, P.M. (2006). Internal auditing's role in ERM. *Internal Auditor* 63:2, 52–58.
18. Matyjewicz, G., and D'Arcangelo, J.R. (2004). Beyond Sarbanes–Oxley. *Internal Auditor* 61:5, 67–72.

19. Matyjewicz and D'Arcangelo (2004), op. cit.; Ballou, B., and Heitger, D.L. (2005). A building-block approach for implementing COSO's enterprise risk management-integrated framework. *Management Accounting Quarterly* 6:2, 1–10.
20. Drew, M. (2007). Information risk management and compliance – Expect the unexpected. *BT Technology Journal* 25:1, 19–29.
21. Extracted and modified from Bowling, D.M., and Rieger, L.A. (2005). Making sense of COSO's new framework for enterprise risk management, Bank Accounting and Finance 18:2, 29–34.
22. Bowling and Rieger (2005). op cit.
23. Gupta and Thomson (2004). op. cit.
24. Quinn, L.R. (2006). COSO at a crossroad, Strategic Finance 88:1, 42–49.
25. Carnaghan, C. (2006). Business process modeling approaches in the context of process level audit risk assessment: An analysis and comparison. *International Journal of Accounting Information Systems* 7:2, 170–204.

Chapter 4
An Empirical Study on Enterprise Risk Management in Insurance

M. Acharyya

Enterprise Risk Management in Insurance

Enterprise Risk Management (hereinafter referred as "ERM") interests a wide range of professions (e.g., actuaries, corporate financial managers, underwriters, accountants, and internal auditors), however, current ERM solutions often do not cover all risks because they are motivated by the core professional ethics and principles of these professions who design and administer them. In a typical insurance company all such professions work as a group to achieve the overriding corporate objectives. Risk can be defined as factors which prevent an organization in achieving its objectives and risks affect organizations holistically. The management of risk in isolation often misses its big picture. It is argued here that a holistic management of risk is logical and is the ultimate destination of all general management activities. Moreover, risk management should not be a separate function of the business process; rather, managing downside risk and taking the opportunities from upside risk should be the key management goals. Consequently, ERM is believed as an approach to risk management, which provides a common understanding across the multidisciplinary groups of people of the organization. ERM should be proactive and its focus should be on the organizations future. Organizations often struggle to see and understand the full risk spectrum to which they are exposed and as a result they may fail to identify the most vulnerable areas of the business. The effective management of risk is truly an interdisciplinary exercise grounded on a holistic framework.

Whatever name this new type of risk management is given (the literature refers to it by diverse names, such as Enterprise Risk Management, Strategic Risk Management, and Holistic Risk Management) the ultimate focus is management of all significant risks faced by the organization. Risk is an integral part of each and every action of the organization in the sense that an organization is a basket of contracts associated with risk (in terms of losses and opportunities). The idea of ERM is simple and logical, but implementation is difficult. This is because its involvement with a wide stakeholder community, which in turn involves groups from different disciplines with different beliefs and understandings. Indeed, ERM needs theories (which are the interest of academics) but a grand theory of ERM (which invariably involves an interdisciplinary concept) is far from having been achieved.

D.L. Olson, D. Wu (eds.) *New Frontiers in Enterprise Risk Management*,

Consequently, for practical proposes, what is needed is the development of a framework (a set of competent theories) and one of the key challenges of this thesis is to establish the key features of such a framework to promote the practice of ERM.

Multidisciplinary Views of Risk

The objective of the research is to study the ERM of insurance companies. In line with this it is designed to investigate what is happening practically in the insurance industry at the current time in the name of ERM. The intention is to minimize the gap between the two communities (i.e., academics and practitioners) in order to contribute to the literature of risk management.

In recent years ERM has emerged as a topic for discussion in the financial community, in particular, the banks and insurance sectors. Professional organizations have published research reports on ERM. Consulting firms conducted extensive studies and surveys on the topic to support their clients. Rating agencies included the ERM concept in their rating criteria. Regulators focused more on the risk management capability of the financial organizations. Academics are slowly responding on the management of risk in a holistic framework following the initiatives of practitioners. The central idea is to bring the organization close to the market economy. Nevertheless, everybody is pushing ERM within the scope of their core professional understanding. The focus of ERM is to manage all risks in a holistic framework whatever the source and nature. There remains a strong ground of knowledge in managing risk on an isolated basis in several academic disciplines (e.g., economics, finance, psychology, sociology, etc.). But little has been done to take a holistic approach of risk beyond disciplinary silos. Moreover, the theoretical understanding of the holistic (i.e., multidisciplinary) properties of risk is still unknown. Consequently, there remains a lack of understanding in terms of a common and interdisciplinary language for ERM.

Risk in Finance

In finance, risky options involve monetary outcomes with explicit probabilities and they are evaluated in terms of their expected value and their riskiness. The traditional approach to risk in finance literature is based on a mean-variance framework of portfolio theory, i.e., selection and diversification.[1] The idea of risk in finance is understood within the scope of systematic (non-diversifiable) risk and unsystematic (diversifiable) risk.[2] It is recognized in finance that systematic risk is positively correlated with the rate of return.[3] In addition, systematic risk is a non-increasing function of a firm's growth in terms of earnings.[4] Another established concern in finance is default risk and it is argued that the performance of the firm is linked to the firm's default risk.[5] A large part of finance literature deals with several techniques of measuring risks of firms' investment portfolios (e.g., standard deviation, beta, VaR, etc.).[6] In addition to the portfolio theory, Capital Asset Pricing Model (CAPM) was discovered in finance to price risky assets on the perfect capital markets.[7] Finally, derivative markets grew tremendously with the recognition of option pricing theory.[8]

Risk in Economics

Risk in economics is understood within two separate (independent) categories, i.e., endogenous (controllable) risk and background (uncontrollable) risk. It is recognized that economic decisions are made under uncertainty in the presence of multiple risks.[9] Expected Utility Theory argues that peoples' risk attitude on the size of risk (small, medium, large) is derived from the utility-of-wealth function, where the utilities of outcomes are weighted by their probabilities.[10] Economists argue that people are risk averse (neutral) when the size of the risks is large (small).[11] Prospect theory provides a descriptive analysis of choice under risk.[12] In economics, the concept of risk-bearing preferences of agents for independent risks was described under the notion of "standard risk aversion."[13] Most of the economic research on risk is originated on the study of decision making behavior on lotteries and other gambles.

Risk in Psychology

While economics assumes an individual's risk preference is a function of probabilistic beliefs, psychology explores how human judgment and behavior systematically forms such beliefs.[14] Psychology talks about the risk taking behavior (risk preferences). It looks for the patterns of human reactions to the context, reference point, mental categories and associations that influence how people make decisions.[15] The psychological approach to risk draws upon the notion of loss aversion[16] that manifests itself in the related notion of "regret." According to Willett[17]; "risk affects economic activity through the psychological influence of uncertainty." Managers' attitude of risk taking is often described from the psychological point of view in terms of feelings.[18] Psychologists argue that risk, as a multidisciplinary concept, can not be reduced meaningfully by a single quantitative treatment. Consequently, managers tend to utilize an array of risk measurers to assist them in the decision making process under uncertainty.[19] Risk perception plays a central role in the psychological research on risk, where the key concern is how people perceive risk and how it differs to the actual outcome.[20] Nevertheless, the psychological research on risk provides fundamental knowledge of how emotions are linked to decision making.[21]

Risk in Sociology

In sociology risk is a socially constructed phenomenon (i.e., a social problem) and defined as a strategy referring to instrumental rationality.[22] The sociological literature on risk was originated from anthropology and psychology[23] is dominated by two central concepts. First, risk and culture[24] and second, risk society.[25] The negative consequences of unwanted events (i.e., natural/chemical disasters, food safety) are the key focus of sociological researches on risk. From a sociological perspective entrepreneurs remain liable for the risk of the society and responsible to share it in proportion to their respective contributions. Practically, the responsibilities are imposed and actions are monitored by state regulators and supervisors. Nevertheless, identification of a socially acceptable threshold of risk is a key challenge of many sociological researches on risk.

Convergence of Multidisciplinary Views of Risk

Different disciplinary views of risk are obvious. Whereas, economics and finance study risk by examining the distribution of corporate returns,[26] psychology and sociology interpret risk in terms of its behavioral components. Moreover, economists focus on the economic (i.e., commercial) value of investments in a risky situation. In contrast, sociologists argue on the moral value (i.e., sacrifice) on the risk related activities of the firm.[27] In addition, sociologists' criticism of economists' concern of risk is that although they rely on risk, time, and preferences while describing the issues related to risk taking, they often miss out their interrelationships (i.e., narrow perspective). Interestingly, there appears some convergence of economics and psychology in the literature of economic psychology. The intention is to include the traditional economic model of individuals' formal rational action in the understanding of the way they actually think and behave (i.e., irrationality). In addition, behavioral finance is seen as a growing discipline with the origin of economics and psychology. In contrast to efficient market hypothesis behavioral finance provides descriptive models in making judgment under uncertainty.[28] The origin of this convergence was due to the discovery of the prospect theory[29] in the fulfillment of the shortcomings of von Neumann-Morgenstern's utility theory for providing reasons of human (irrational) behavior under uncertainty (e.g., arbitrage). Although, the overriding enquiry of disciplines is the estimation of risk, they comparing and reducing into a common metric of many types of risks are there ultimate difficulty. The key conclusion of the above analysis suggests that there exist overlaps on the disciplinary views of risk and their interrelations are emerging with the progress of risk research. In particular, the central idea of ERM is to obscure the hidden dependencies of risk beyond disciplinary silos.

Insurance Industry Practice

The practice of ERM in the insurance industry has been drawn from the author's PhD research completed in 2006. The initiatives of four major global European insurers (hereinafter referred as "CASES") were studied for this purpose. Out of these four insurers one is a reinsurer and the remaining three are primary insurers. They were at various stages of designing and implementing ERM. A total of fifty-one face-to-face and telephone interviews were conducted with key personnel of the CASES in between the end of 2004 and the beginning of 2006. The comparative analysis (compare-and-contrast) technique was used to analyze the data and they were discussed with several industry and academic experts for the purpose of validation. Thereafter, a conceptual model of ERM was developed from the findings of the data.

Findings based on the data are arranged under five dimensions. They are understanding; evaluation; structure; challenges, and performance of ERM.

Understanding of ERM

It was found that the key distinction in various perceptions of ERM remains between risk measurement and risk management. Interestingly, tools and processes are found complimentary. In essence, meaning that a tool can not run without a process and vice versa. It is found that the people who work with numbers (e.g., actuaries, finance people, etc.) are involved in the risk modeling and management (mostly concerned with the financial and core insurance risks) and tend to believe ERM is a tool. On the other hand internal auditors, company secretaries, and operational managers; whose job is related to the human, system and compliance related issues of risk are more likely to see ERM as a process.

ERM: A Process

Within the understanding of ERM as a process, four key concepts were found. They are harmonization, standardization, integration and centralization. In fact, they are linked to the concept of top-down and bottom-up approaches of ERM.

The analysis found four key concepts of ERM. They are harmonization, standardization, integration and centralization (in decreasing order of importance). It was also found that a unique understanding of ERM does not exist within the CASES, rather ERM is seen as a combination of the four concepts and they often overlap. It is revealed that an understanding of these four concepts including their linkages is essential for designing an optimal ERM system.

Linkages Amongst the Four Concepts

Although harmonization and standardization are seen apparently similar respondents view them differently. Whereas, harmonization allows choices between alternatives, standardization provides no flexibility. Effectively, harmonization offers a range of identical alternatives, out of which one or more can be adopted depending on the given circumstances. Although standardization does not offer such flexibility, it was found as an essential technique of ERM. Whilst harmonization accepts existing divergence to bring a state of comparability, standardization does not necessarily consider existing conventions and definitions. It focuses on a common standard, (a "top-down" approach). Indeed, integration of competent policies and processes, models, and data (either for management use, compliance and reporting) are not possible for global insurers without harmonizing and standardizing them. Hence, the research establishes that a sequence (i.e., harmonization, standardization, integration, and then centralization) is to be maintained when ERM is being developed in practice (from an operational perspective). Above all, the process is found important to achieve a diversified risk culture across the organization to allocate risk management responsibilities to risk owners and risk takers.

ERM: A Tool

Viewed as a tool, ERM encompasses procedures and techniques to model and measure the portfolio of (quantifiable) enterprise risk from insurers' core disciplinary perspective. The objective is to measure a level of (risk adjusted) capital (i.e., economic capital) and thereafter allocation of capital. In this perspective ERM is thought as a sophisticated version of insurers' asset-liability management. Most often, extreme and emerging risks, which may bring the organization down, are taken into consideration. Ideally, the procedure of calculating economic capital is closely linked to the market volatility. Moreover, the objective is clear, i.e., meeting the expectation of shareholders. Consequently, there remains less scope to capture the subjectivity associated with enterprise risks.

ERM: An Approach

In contrast to process and tool, ERM is also found as an approach of managing the entire business from a strategic point of view. Since, risk is so deeply rooted in the insurance business, it is difficult to separate risk from the functions of insurance companies. It is argued that a properly designed ERM infrastructure should align risk to achieve strategic goals. Alternatively, application of an ERM approach of managing business is found central to the value creation of insurance companies. In the study, ERM is believed as an approach of changing the culture of the organization in both marketing and strategic management issues in terms of innovating and pricing products, selecting profitable markets, distributing products, targeting customers and ratings, and thus formulating appropriate corporate strategies. In this holistic approach various strategic, financial and operational concerns are seen integrated to consider all risks across the organization.[30]

It is seen that as a process, ERM takes an inductive approach to explore the pitfalls (challenges) of achieving corporate objectives for broader audience (i.e., stakeholders) emphasizing more on moral and ethical issues. In contrast, as a tool, it takes a deductive approach to meet specific corporate objectives for selected audience (i.e., shareholders) by concentrating more on monitory (financial) outcomes. Clearly, the approaches are complimentary and have overlapping elements.

The Evaluation of ERM

In the survey suggested 82% suggested the leadership of CEO as being the key driving force. In addition, Solvency II, Corporate Governance, Leadership of CRO, and Changing Risk Landscape, are rated as the leading motivating forces for developing ERM.

The analysis establishes leadership of the CEO and regulations (Solvency II and Corporate Governance) as the key driving forces of motivation towards insurers' ERM.

Leadership

It is interesting to explore why leadership of the CEO is regarded as a key driver for developing ERM. In fact, the ideas of leadership vary and they depend on the level of management in the hierarchy.[31] The analysis suggests that the CEO was influenced to encourage ERM by a number of factors as discussed below.

It is seen that the markets of the CASES are global and insurance and solvency capital regulations are becoming more global. Moreover, rating agencies (who eventually fill up the gaps between the regulators and insurance companies) are increasingly focusing on ERM. Practically, ratings influence the decisions of insurers' customers (i.e., policyholders) and shareholders. In addition, a major factor influencing the CEOs was the fact that shareholders were unhappy with the massive reduction in the value of companies' shares 2000 and 2003, when most shareholders in the insurance sector lost a substantial percentage of their investments and they held management accountable. This ultimately influenced the board of directors of all CASES to change their CEOs during this period of time.

The analysis however finds other factors which influenced the leaders (CEO, CRO and Board of Directors) to think about ERM. They are profit stream, the economic environment, regulations, and the dynamic nature of risks. However, these factors of motivation are seen interrelated but difficult to prioritize. It was revealed that their resultant consequence influences the leaders to implement an aggressive business drive to manage their risks holistically. In fact, all these factors have led CASES to be aware of the dynamics of the global marketplace in which they operate. In turn, the CASES were motivated to think about the adequacy of their level of capital to protect them from any potential economic downturn.

Regulations

In addition to leadership, solvency regulation and the initiative of rating agencies were also found as the key drivers of ERM in the CASES. Clearly, the new regime of risk-based regulations forced the CASES to accelerate and reshape their decentralized risk management systems in a more holistic framework. Interestingly, a voice was also noted from the respondents about their intention of going ahead above of the regulatory curve. This means that in some CASES, regulations guide but they do not necessarily drive their ERM initiatives. In other words, regulation can be seen as a key driving force of ERM for some CASES but for others regulation simply provides guidance to the internal motivation.

In summary, the leadership of CEO and CRO were found as a key motivation towards ERM within CASES. However, such leadership was not an isolated issue but essentially driven by many economic and political factors (e.g., market volatility, competition, globalization, etc.). All these sub factors effectively influence the CEOs (and the top management) to add more value in the firm in order to remain solvent and beat the competition. In addition, regulation was also found as a key factor towards the motivation of insurers' ERM.

Structure of ERM

The study revealed four key stages (i.e., identification, quantification, assessment, and implementation), which build the structure of insurers' ERM. In essence, they are understood as the core management process of any organizational function.

Four Essential Stages

The ERM design, as seen in the CASES, has four common stages: identification, quantification, implementation and monitoring. The first stage involves an identification of the risks faced by the organization. This is not just an identification of risks for purposes of compliance but necessarily for strategic decision making. The second important stage of ERM involves analysis and quantification of risks. The third stage of ERM involves assessing what can be done about the risk that is now understood. The key managerial concern is to determine the amount of chance (i.e., opportunity) that an organization assumes in a certain level of loss. The initial analysis assesses the capacity (or ability) of the organization in terms of available resources. This gives insurers an understanding of their capability, which then helps to find insurers' current position and to decide where they want to be at a certain time of future. Finally, the fourth stage is for actual implementation and ongoing execution of the ERM process. So ERM, in a very broad sense, in the CASES involves with these four stages. However, it is noticed that each CASE undertakes different specific activities under each of these stages. However, in all four key stages, organizational structure plays an important role. The following paragraph discusses its various aspects as seen in the study.

The Structure of Risk Governance

The study revealed a three line organizational structure. The structure distinguishes risk observing as an independent function from risk taking. However, risk taking was found as a management function. The first line of defence takes owns and manages risks in accordance with the set guidelines (e.g., Group Risk Policy). Although the group CEO holds the overall responsibility for the management of risks faced by the group, as the owner of risk, the primary responsibility of managing risks goes to individual business units (or local units). The second line of defence (constituting a part of central office) is often led by the CRO, who acts as risk observer and facilitator, with primarily responsible for providing technical (and logistic) support to the first line of defence. The second line of defence however does not incur any management responsibility. Consequently, it was not found directly liable for mismanagement of risks. The third line of defence, often led by a group internal auditor (who directly reports to the board), provides independent assurance on the effectiveness of risk management (carried out by the first line of defence) and efficiency of technical support (offered by the second line of defence). Since both the second and the third lines of defence do not hold any risk management responsibility (they perform an advisory function), their functions (e.g., operational risk) sometimes coincide. However, it is found that the objective of these two lines of defence in relation to operational risk is distinct. In one hand, the group internal auditors look at operational risks around the area of non-compliance of Group Risk Policy (for example). On the other hand, the CRO is keen to develop tools and techniques to manage large-scale operational risks and monitor the efficiency of the tools and provide alternative solutions, where necessary, in association with the relevant technical people. Alternatively, the job of CRO under ERM is found more creative and innovative.

Challenges of ERM

The challenges of implementing ERM were found into two separate phases, i.e., operational and technical. The former (i.e., operational) is linked to the process and the latter (i.e., technical) is linked to the tools as discussed earlier.

Operational Challenges

In the survey, 82% respondent identified the development of a common risk language in communication issues as the key operational challenge. This is followed by several other factors, i.e., a common culture and risk awareness (i.e., identifying and studying the risk prior to the happening of the event), etc. In addition, the accuracy, consistency and adequacy of data were found as the key challenges.

Discussion

It is important to discuss why the identified issues, e.g., data accuracy, risk communication, risk awareness, a common risk language, and a common risk culture as derived from the above process are perceived as the key challenges facing the

CASES in implementing ERM. The discussion establishes that communication is the overriding operational challenge of ERM. It is important to note that all the issues are closely linked to each other. Whereas risk awareness is a potential barrier to effective communication of risk, a common language of risk facilitates communication. While economic capital provides a common language of risk[32] across the financial community, it is not so well understood by other respondents. As such, effective communication of risk across the organization suffers. Since people understand and judge risks in terms of locally defined values and concerns, communication is found to be a major problem. Moreover, because of the lack of communication and awareness, people focus on their own risk (which remains under their individual domain) thus providing inadequate knowledge of risk sharing between members of the organization. Consequently, the enterprise risk remains hidden, and ultimately becomes large, complex and costly over time.[32] It is understood that risk communication, culture, and awareness of risk need to be aligned within a common language. The study finds that such a common language of risk is often attempted by the organizations through developing a unique and consistent Group Risk Policy. The central point of all of these discussions focuses to a point, which suggests that insurers should always hold a balance on the portfolio of its risks.

Technical Challenges

The analysis indicated that the CASES struggle significantly with technical challenges in implementing ERM. In the survey 71% respondents ranked the measurement of operational risk as the top technical challenge. This was followed by several other factors, e.g., measuring correlation of risk among risk types and lines of businesses and risk profiling at the corporate level.

Measurement of Operational Risk

It was found that the management of operational risk within ERM in the CASES has particular interest to calculate an amount of (economic) capital as necessary for solvency requirements. Consequently, the management of operational risk has evolved as a quantitative exercise beyond the traditional aspects of operating errors. Recalling the previous discussion it is understood that the two dimensions of ERM, i.e., organizational (process) and technical (tool) are complimentary. In essence, operational risk arises from both dimensions (i.e., tool and process) but they have different characters. Nevertheless, operational risk is not new in the insurance industry but the study discovered that measurement of operational risk in numerical terms is a new idea. Therefore, conceptualizing and defining operational risk, and identifying a complete list of risk indicators (which may include purchasing inadequate reinsurance, incorrect data, and loss of reputation) is problematic.[33] Consequently, measurement of operational risk is a major technical challenge, although the recent regulatory constraints for measuring operational risk have given initial momentum to the insurers' ERM initiatives.

Risk Correlations

The issue regarding correlation (or dependency) comes with the complexity of quantifying total risks of insurers. In order to combine the different parts of the business it is important to consider correlations between risks (across types and business lines). This arises because the capital charges for risks may not be accurate (often it is higher) if the proper correlations are not considered. This is also found as an important issue for diversification of risks. In addition to the appropriate model, the key challenge to calculating correlations is accurate and adequate data.

Risk Profiling and Modeling

In order to increase the visibility of risk, risk profiling is found as a challenging issue. A risk profile was established as the key to the accuracy of all risk management functions and strategic decisions in the CASES. Alternatively, the risk profile is considered a primary support tool for their ERM, including risk identification and managing risk tolerances. Risk modeling is also regarded as a core of function of ERM in the CASES. However, it is closely related to other issues (e.g., risk quantification, risk correlations, and risk profiling) as identified earlier. CASES were found to be well developed in modeling financial risks, but they struggled to model operational risk within ERM. However, it was noted that CASES have taken the modeling of operational risks seriously because of the regulatory constraints. Still the adequacy, accuracy and consistency of data are found to be the key concerns of all CASES.

Performance of ERM

The analysis finds that CASES do not use any specific framework or technique to evaluate the performance of their ERM. The evaluation of companies' performance by key stakeholders (credit rating agencies, financial analysts, and regulators) is generally considered as crude benchmarking criteria. The analysis finds that the execution of ERM is complex, time-consuming and costly. This is because ERM depends on the company's specific business model (retail or wholesale), its culture, the depth of knowledge of its staff in handling risks and also the size of the organization. It is concluded that organizations having less (or more) volatile profit streams have less (or more) structured ERM systems in place. In addition, the effort of reinsurers towards developing ERM is seen to be greater than that of primary insurers.

The analysis suggests that the benefits that managers find while practicing ERM are general in nature. They include improved risk assessment in terms of understanding, identifying and prioritizing risks. Through risk mapping, management has a better knowledge of the critical risks and their potential impact on the company. It is argued that the organization through ERM will be better prepared to manage its risks and maximize its opportunities within the acquisition, product, and funding programs. In addition, the practice of ERM could provide a common language for describing risks and its potential effects, which could improve general communication. Better knowledge of risk, in particular, the emergent risks, could enable management to handle them more efficiently and effectively in terms of quantification and modeling; which may help the efficient pricing of risk. The development of risk awareness could mitigate the level of risk, thus requiring less capital, which would ultimately reduce the cost of capital. Above all, the practice of ERM may enable insurers to maintain competitive advantage. In addition, the research finds that industry managers apparently do not see any disadvantages arising from ERM. Although the centralization (as opposed to harmonization) of risk and capital management issues in the framework of ERM could cause a systemic failure in the future.[34]

A Conceptual Model of ERM

Until now the findings of the study were discussed under five headings, i.e., understanding, evolution, structure, challenges, and performance of ERM. The following paragraphs will develop a model of ERM out of the above findings. The model represents several internal risk models designed for several significant risks (i.e., market risk, credit risk, investment risk, insurance risks, operational risk, etc.) The separate models are used, in aggregation, to estimate economic capital for three purposes, i.e., compliance of solvency regulations; achieving targeted ratings; and driving the business in the competitive market.

The study found that insurance companies are increasingly using the ERM model as an essential part of making corporate decisions and delivering strategies. One of the key characteristic of the model is that it discusses ERM both as a process and a tool simultaneously.

The study noted two technical aspects of the ERM model. They are estimation of the probability of default (or failure) and deployment of (economic or risk-adjusted) capital on the basis of this estimation. However, the requirements of the governance issues have emerged distinctly in relation to the components.

Five Stages of the ERM Model

Stage 1: The model theoretically suggests that ERM should consider all risks irrespective of source and nature. Risks captured in an (imaginary) radar screen are separated through a filter into numerically quantifiable and unquantifiable components. The quantifiable risks, which contain financial (i.e., market (stock, FX, interest rate), core business (insurance), credit (counterparty), and operational (system and human error)) are then identified. Thereafter, a risk landscape (risk register or profile) is opened to track the quantifiable risks. Even all quantifiable risks are not considered for the purpose of ERM; rather a chunk of large risks including emergent risks (which are best described as the unknown of known risks, e.g., natural catastrophes, human pandemics, etc.) are there considered for the next stage of ERM. The choice of significant risk is purely a unique exercise for any organization because organizations' corporate objectives and strategies are distinct in the competitive marketplace. A second radar screen always remains in operation to capture the new statistical correlations within the portfolio of significant risks.

Stage 2: The significant risks are then modeled numerically in a predetermined probability of default (failure) over a certain period of time. In addition, the efforts remain always live to measure the unquantifiable risks as much as possible. Another filter (imaginary) is then used to calculate total acceptable risks, which are essentially linked to the risk appetite of the firm. In fact, the risk appetite is a complex issue as it includes many subjective factors like organizational culture, customers' preference, market environment, shareholders expectations, organization's past experience, etc. They are very specific to the firm and difficult to quantify numerically. In effect, the organizations often exhibit inconsistent risk preferences. Ideally, risk appetite should reflect a clear picture of the current level of business risk of the firm. Organizations' risk tolerance is then determined numerically based on its risk appetite. In essence, the risk tolerance of a firm drives its corporate strategies. One of the complex tasks in ERM is the aggregation of various risk models. Several reasons lead such complexities, i.e., non-linearity among the lines of business, different risk class and inconsistent risk measures, etc.[35] Indeed, selection of the level of tolerance (i.e., acceptable impacts or confidence level) and determination of time horizon depends on the prudent judgment of the insurers.

Stage 3: Various techniques, including both the insurance market and capital market are used to transfer and finance the total acceptable risk. A variable (risk-adjusted) amount of capital is then deployed to finance these total acceptable risks. These actions illustrate that the CASES deal with risks by first calculating and then choosing from the available and alternative risk-return combinations.[36] A third radar screen comes into operation at this stage to observe the changes in the total acceptable risks (including potential unexpected losses) and this information is then deployed to adjust the amount of capital. This is commonly known as economic capital.[37] There always remains a residual risk (= liabilities – economic capital), which insurers always to carry. At this stage risks are also reduced through additional mitigation measurers (e.g., improve controls).

Stage 4: Upon determining the economic capital the next step is to allocate risks into different risk types and lines of businesses. The objective is to ensure the proportional contribution of each line of business on the overall cost of capital of the firm.[38] Furthermore, determining the size of the economic capital and its breakup of the subsidiaries is problematic because of the inconsistencies of regulations among geographical locations. The idea of an economic balance sheet (in contrast to statutory accounting balance sheet) is to reflect the forecasted market volatility in the return taking the time value of money into account. This in turn is linked to the calculation of shareholder (firm) value at a particular point (or period) of time in order to derive future business strategies.

Stage 5: The performance of risk management is then disclosed (reported) to the stakeholders (i.e., shareholders, bondholders, and policyholders). The policyholders and shareholders have different interests in insurers' performance in terms of the economic balance sheet. Ideally, policyholders want to see that the organization operates with the maximum amount of capital but the shareholders prefer the opposite. Third parties, i.e., government regulatory agencies, and rating agencies play an influential role to monitor the performance of the insurers. Regulators are there to maintain the interest of the policyholders and rating agencies provide their opinion on the financial strength of the organizations, which interests both policyholders and shareholders. The objective of the organization is to comply with the (solvency) regulations and meeting the criteria of the rating agencies to achieve or maintain a targeted level of rating. Finally, the system needs to repeat continually with necessary adjustments in line with the corporate objectives and strategies.

It is important to mention here that the five-stage model is not unique but a benchmark of managing insurers' enterprise (i.e., all significant) risks. Indeed, the execution could vary at the operational stage from one company to another. For example, risk tolerances may be established in Stage 1 instead of Stage 2 to see of the potential impact of various risks during identification phase in line with corporate objectives.

Conclusion

The objective of the research was to study the ERM in the insurance industry empirically. Leadership and regulations were found the key motivation of ERM in insurance. Moreover, the understanding of ERM is uneven. ERM is understood both as a tool (objective view) and a process (subjective view). Four key stages of the process, i.e., centralization, integration, standardization, and harmonization were discovered. In addition, ERM was seen as an approach of managing business holistically. There appears a need of close integration of the process oriented knowledge of risk (i.e., corporate governance in terms of the fluctuation of performance) with the subject oriented expertise of ERM (i.e., opportunity). The central idea of the discussions suggests two perspectives of risk management. First, risk as insurers' core business functions (i.e., underwriting, investment, finance) and second risk arising from the fluctuation of performance while performing the core business functions. The former views risk management as a tool and the latter as a process. At the corporate level, ERM combines both toll and process views of risk management and suggests an approach of managing the total risks of the organization in a single framework.

The design and implementation of ERM was found inconsistent across the industry mainly because of the different level of risk appetite. The value of ERM still remains as a speculation for the absence of concrete evidence. Nevertheless,

ERM is an evolving concept and there need more research on the topic from multi-disciplinary perspective. Practically, insurers' internal risk models are regarded as a part of Solvency II framework. Principally, thinking widely on the sources of risk and deploying appropriate mitigation tools/strategies will reveal opportunities. Despite the complexity of integrating the objective and subjective concepts of risk, the study reveals that insurance companies will increasingly use ERM system to support their future growth opportunities (in line with corporate objectives) by maintaining targeted level of capital. The central idea of virtually all functions within ERM is to secure maximum profit (i.e., shareholder value) at the minimum (i.e., lowest) level of risk. However, incorporating the benefits of business mix and geographical diversification into the ERM model will remain an ongoing debate between the organization and regulators and rating agencies.

Finally, the evolution of ERM is a part of firms' initiative towards establishing a market-oriented organizational culture to generating, disseminating, and responding appropriately to market requirements. The challenge is however to maximize the link between the demand of the market (i.e., external requirements) and competency of the organization (i.e., internal requirements). Ideally, risk (i.e., the volatility) is the key component of such a complex link and ERM has been evolved to minimize the total risk of the firm. Consequently, ERM is a value adding function. In particular, it is important to remember that similar to other process/system, an ERM, even robust, can not always guarantee the efficient and effective management of risk of the origination. The success essentially depends on the dedication and attitude of users (i.e., both at individual and group levels) towards identifying and managing risks in their everyday functions for the best interest of their organizations.

Acknowledgements The author gratefully acknowledges the contribution of Professor Johnnie Johnson for the supervision of the doctoral thesis. Special thanks to Professor Gerry Dickinson, Professor Stella Fearnley, Dr. Geoff Willcocks and John R. S. Fraser for their helpful comments and feedback. The support of the interviewees and their employers are also acknowledged gratefully.

End Notes

1. Markowitz, H. (1952). Portfolio selection, *The Journal of Finance* 7:2, 77–91.
2. Beja, A. (1972). On systematic and unsystematic components of financial risk, *The Journal of Finance* 27:1, 37–45.
3. Gehr, A.K. (1979). Risk and return, *The Journal of Finance* 34:4, 1027–1030.
4. Turnbull, S.M. (1977), Market value and systematic risk, *The Journal of Finance* 32:4, 1125–1142.
5. Shapiro, A.C., and Titman, S. (1986). An integrated approach to corporate risk management. In Stern, J.M., and Chew, D.H. (eds.). The Revolution in Corporate Finance, Blackwell, Oxford: 215–229.
6. Babcock, G.C. (1972). A note on justifying Beta as a measure of risk, *The Journal of Finance* 27:3, 699–702.

7. Sharpe, W.F. (1964). Capital asset prices: A theory of market equilibrium under conditions of risk, *The Journal of Finance* 19(3): 425–442; Lintner, J. (1965). The valuation of risk assets and the selection of risky investments in stock portfolios and capital budgets, *The Review of Economics and Statistics* 47:1, 13–37; Mossin, J. (1966). Equilibrium in a capital asset market, *Econometrica* 34:4, 768–783.
8. Black, F., and Scholes, M. (1972). The valuation of option contracts and a test of market efficiency, *The Journal of Finance* 27:2, 399–417; Black, F., and Scholes, M. (1973). The pricing of options and corporate liabilities, *The Journal of Political Economy* 81:3, 637–654.
9. Eeckhoudt, L., Gollier, C., and Schlesinger, H. (1996). Changes in background risk and risk taking behavior, *Econometrica* 64:3, 683–689.
10. Neumann, J., and Morgenstern, O. (1944). Theory of Games and Economic Behaviour. 2nd edn., Princeton University Press, New Jersey.
11. Friedman, M., and Savage, L.J. (1948). The utility analysis of choices involving risk, *The Journal of Political Economy* 56:4, 279–304.
12. Kahneman, D., and Tversky, A. (1979). Prospect theory: An analysis of decision under risk, *Econometrica* 47:2, 263–292.
13. Kimball, M.S. (1993). Standard risk aversion, *Econometrica* 61:3, 589–611.
14. Rabin, M. (2000). Risk aversion and expected-utility theory: A calibration theorem, *Econometrica* 68:5, 1281–1292.
15. Shiller, R.J. (2003). From efficient markets theory to behavioral finance, *The Journal of Economic Perspectives* 17:1, 83–104.
16. Tversky, A., and Kahneman, D. (1991). Loss aversion in riskless choice: A reference-dependent model, *The Quarterly Journal of Economics* 106:4, 1039–1061.
17. Willett, A. (1951). The Economic Theory of Risk and Insurance, Columbia University Press, Philadelphia, Pennsylvania.
18. March, J.G., and Shapira, Z. (1987). Managerial perspectives on risk and risk taking, *Management Science* 33:11, 1404–1418; Loewenstein, G.F., Weber, E.U., Welch, N., and Hsee, C.K. (2001). Risk as feelings. *Psychological Bulletin* 127:2, 267–286.
19. Rippl, S. (2002). Cultural theory and risk perception: A proposal for a better measurement, *Journal of Risk Research* 5:2, 147–165.
20. Weber, E.U., Blais, A.-R., Betz, N.E. (2002). A domain-specific risk-attitude scale: measuring risk perceptions and risk behaviors, *Journal of Behavioral Decision Making* 15:4, 263–290.
21. Slovic, P, Finucane, M.L., Peters, E., and MacGregor, D.G. (2004). Risk as analysis and risk as feelings: Some thoughts about affect, reason, risk, and rationality, *Risk Analysis* 24:2, 311–322.
22. Peter, T.-G., and Zinn, J.O. (2006). Current directions in risk research: New developments in psychology and sociology, *Risk Analysis* 26:2, 397–411.
23. Tierney, K.J. (1999). Toward a critical sociology of risk, *Sociological Forum* 14:2, 215–242.
24. Douglas, M., and Wildavsky, A. (1982). Risk and Culture: An Essay on the Selection of Technical and Environmental Dangers. University of California Press, Berkeley; Lash, S. (2000). Risk culture. In: Adam, B., Beck, U., and Loon, J.V. (eds.). The Risk Society and Beyond: Critical Issues for Social Theory. Sage, London: 47–62.
25. Beck, U. (1992). Risk Society: Towards a New Modernity. Sage, London.
26. Fisher, I.N., and Hall, G.R. (1969). Risk and corporate rates of return, *The Quarterly Journal of Economics* 83:1, 79–92.
27. Perry, R.B. (1916). Economic value and moral value, *The Quarterly Journal of Economics* 30:3, 443–485.
28. Shiller, R.J. (2003). The New Financial Order: Risk in the 21st Century. Princeton University Press, New York.
29. Kahneman and Tversky (1979), op cit.
30. Olson, D.L., and Wu, D. (2008). Enterprise Risk Management. World Scientific, Hackensack, NJ.
31. Avery, G.C. (2003). Understanding Leadership: Paradigms and Cases. Sage, London.

32. Shiller. (2003). op cit.
33. Tripp, M.H., Bradley, H.L., Devitt, R., Orros, G.C., Overton, G.L., Pryor, L.M., and Shaw, R.A. (2004). Quantifying Operational Risk in General Insurance Companies. Institute of Actuaries, London.
34. Bate, O., Plato, P., and Thallinger, G. (2006). Stochastic modelling – Boon or bane for insurance industry capital regulation? *Geneva Paper on Risk and Insurance: Issues and Practice* 31:1, 57–82.
35. Myers, S.C., and Read, J.A., Jr. (2001). Capital allocation for insurance companies, *The Journal of Risk and Insurance* 68:4, 545–580; Dhaene, J., Goovaerts, M.J., and Kaas, R. (2003). Economic capital allocation derived from risk measures, *North American Actuarial Journal* 7:2, 44–59; Goovaerts, M.J., Borre, E.V., and Laever, R.J.A. (2005). Managing economic and virtual economic capital within financial conglomerates, *North American Actuarial Journal* 9:3, 44–59; Sherris, M., and Hock, J. (2006). Capital allocation in insurance: Economic capital and the allocation of the default option value, *North American Actuarial Journal* 10:2, 39–61.
36. March and Shapira. (1987). op cit.
37. Belmont, D.P. (2004). Value Added Risk Management, Wiley, Singapore.
38. Cummins, J.D. (2000). Allocation of capital in the insurance industry, *Risk Management and Insurance Review* 3:1, 7–28.

Chapter 5
Supply Chain Risk Management

D.L. Olson and D. Wu

Global competition, technological change, and continual search for competitive advantage have motivated risk management in supply chains.[1] Supply chains are often complex systems of networks, reaching hundreds or thousands of participants from around the globe in some cases (Wal-Mart or Dell). The term has been used both at the strategic level (coordination and collaboration) and tactical level (management of logistics across functions and between businesses).[2] In this sense, risk management can focus on identification of better ways and means of accomplishing organizational objectives rather than simply preservation of assets or risk avoidance. Supply chain risk management is interested in coordination and collaboration of processes and activities across functions within a network of organizations. Tang provided a framework of risk management perspectives in supply chains.[3] Supply chains enable manufacturing outsourcing to take advantages of global relative advantages, as well as increase product variety. There are many risks inherent in this more open, dynamic system.

Supply Chain Risk Management Process

One view of a supply chain risk management process includes steps for risk identification, risk assessment, risk avoidance, and risk mitigation.[4] These structures for handling risk are compatible with Tang's list given above, but focus on the broader aspects of the process.

Risk Identification

Risks in supply chains can include operational risks and disruptions. Operational risks involve inherent uncertainties for supply chain elements such as customer demand, supply, and cost. Disruption risks come from disasters (natural in the form of floods, hurricanes, etc.; man-made in the form of terrorist attacks or wars) and from economic crises (currency reevaluations, strikes, shifting market prices).

D.L. Olson, D. Wu (eds.) *New Frontiers in Enterprise Risk Management*,

Most quantitative analyses and methods are focused on operational risks. Disruptions are more dramatic, less predictable, and thus are much more difficult to model. Risk management planning and response for disruption are usually qualitative.

Risk Assessment

Theoretically, risk has been viewed as applying to those cases where odds are known, and uncertainty to those cases where odds are not known. Risk is a preferable basis for decision making, but life often presents decision makers with cases of uncertainty. The issue is further complicated in that perfectly rational decision makers may have radically different approaches to risk. Qualitative risk management depends a great deal on managerial attitude towards risk. Different rational individuals are likely to have different response to risk avoidance, which usually is inversely related to return, thus leading to a tradeoff decision. Research into cognitive psychology has found that managers are often insensitive to probability estimates of possible outcomes, and tend to ignore possible events that they consider to be unlikely.[5] Furthermore, managers tend to pay little attention to uncertainty involved with positive outcomes.[6] They tend to focus on critical performance targets, which makes their response to risk contingent upon context.[7] Some approaches to theoretical decision making prefer objective treatment of risk through quantitative scientific measures following normative ideas of how humans should make decisions. Business involves an untheoretical construct, however, with high levels of uncertainty (data not available) and consideration of multiple (often conflicting) factors, making qualitative approaches based upon perceived managerial risk more appropriate.

Because accurate measures of factors such as probability are often lacking, robust strategies (more likely to enable effective response under a wide range of circumstances) are often attractive to risk managers. Strategies are efficient if they enable a firm to deal with operational risks efficiently regardless of major disruptions. Strategies are resilient if they enable a firm to keep operating despite major disruptions. Supply chain risk can arise from many sources, including the following:[8]

- Political events
- Product availability
- Distance from source
- Industry capacity
- Demand fluctuation
- Changes in technology
- Changes in labor markets
- Financial instability
- Management turnover

Risk Avoidance

The oldest form of risk avoidance is probably insurance, purchasing some level of financial security from an underwriter. This focuses on the financial aspects of risk, and is reactive, providing some recovery after a negative experience. Insurance is not the only form of risk management used in supply chains. Delta Airlines insurance premiums for terrorism increased from $2 million in 2001 to $152 million in 2002.[9] Insurance focuses on financial risks. Other major risks include loss of customers due to supply change disruption.

Supply chain risks can be buffered by a variety of methods. Purchasing is usually assigned the responsibility of controlling costs and assuring continuity of supply. Buffers in the form of inventories exist to provide some risk reduction, at a cost of higher inventory holding cost. Giunipero and Al Eltantawy compared traditional practices with newer risk management approaches.[10] The traditional practice, relying upon extra inventory, multiple suppliers, expediting, and frequent supplier changes suffered from high transaction costs, long purchase fulfillment cycle times, and expensive rush orders. Risk management approaches, drawing upon practices such as supply chain alliances, e-procurement, just-in-time delivery, increased coordination and other techniques, provides more visibility in supply chain operations. There may be higher prices incurred for goods, and increased security issues, but methods have been developed to provide sound electronic business security.

Risk Mitigation

Tang provided four basic risk mitigation approaches for supply chains.[11] These focus on the sources of risk: management of uncertainty with respect to supply, to demand, to product management, and information management. Furthermore, there are both strategic and tactical aspects involved. Strategically, network design can enable better control of supply risks. Strategies such as product pricing and rollovers can control demand to a degree. Greater product variety can strategically protect against product risks. And systems providing greater information visibility across supply chain members can enable better coping with risks. Tactical decisions include supplier selection and order allocation (including contractual arrangements); demand control over time, markets, and products; product promotion; and information sharing, vendor managed inventory systems, and collaborative planning, forecasting, and replenishment.

Supply Management

A variety of supplier relationships are possible, varying the degree of linkage between vendor and core organizations. Different types of contracts and information exchange are possible, and different schemes for pricing and coordinating schedules.

Supplier Selection Process

Supplier (vendor) evaluation is a very important operational decision. There are decisions selecting which suppliers to employ, as well as decisions with respect to quantities to order from each supplier. With the increase in outsourcing and the opportunities provided by electronic business to tap world-wide markets, these decisions are becoming ever more complex. The presence of multiple criteria in these decisions has long been recognized.[12] A probabilistic model for this decision has been published to include the following criteria:[13]

1. Quality personnel
2. Quality procedure
3. Concern for quality
4. Company history
5. Price relative to quality
6. Actual price
7. Financial ability
8. Technical performance
9. Delivery history
10. Technical assistance
11. Production capability
12. Manufacturing equipment

Some of these criteria overlap, and other criteria may exist for specific supply chain decision makers. But clearly there are many important aspects to selecting suppliers.

Supplier Order Allocation

Operational risks in supply chain order allocation include uncertainties in demands, supply yields, lead times, and costs. Thus not only do specific suppliers need to be selected, the quantities purchased from them needs to be determined on a recurring basis.

Supply chains provide many valuable benefits to their members, but also create problems of coordination that manifest themselves in the "bullwhip" effect.[14] Information system coordination can reduce some of the negative manifestations of the bullwhip effect, but there still remains the issue of profit sharing. Decisions that are optimal for one supply chain member often have negative impacts of the total profitability of the entire supply chain.[15]

Demand Management

Demand management approaches include using statistics in models for identification of an optimal portfolio of demand distributions[16] and economic models to select strategies using price as a response mechanism to change demand.[17] Other strategies include shifting demand over time, across markets, or across products. Demand management of course is one of the aims of advertising and other promotional activities. However, it has long been noted as one of the most difficult things to predict over time.

Product Management

An effective strategy to manage product risk is variety, which can be used to increase market share to serve distinct segments of a market. The basic idea is to diversify products to meet the specific needs of each market segment. However, while this would be expected to increase revenues and market share, it will lead to increase manufacturing costs and inventory costs. Various ways to deal with the potential inefficiencies in product variety include Dell's make-to-order strategy.

Supply Chain Disruption

Tang classified supply chain vulnerabilities as those due to uncertain economic cycles, customer demand, and disasters. Land Rover reduced their workforce by over one thousand when a key supplier went insolvent. Dole was affected by Hurricane Mitch hitting their banana plantations in Central America in 1998. September 11, 2001 suspended air traffic, leading Ford Motor Company to close five plants for several days.[18] Many things can disrupt supply chains. Supply chain disruptions have been found to negatively impact stock returns for firms suffering them.[19]

Supply Chain Risks

Recent research into supply chain risk covers many topics.

New Technology Risk

Golda and Phillipi[20] considered technical and business risk components of the supply chain. Technical risks relate to science and engineering, and deal with the uncertainties of research output. Business risks relate to markets, human responses to products and/or related services. At Intel, three risk mitigation strategies were considered to deal with the risks associated with new technologies:

1. Partnerships, with associated decisions involving who to partner with, and at what stage of product development

2. Pursue extendable solutions, evolutionary products that will continue to offer value as new technical breakthroughs are gained
3. Evaluate multiple options to enable commercialization

Partner Selection Risk

Partner (to include vendor) evaluation is a very important operational decision. Important decisions include which vendors to employ and quantities to order from each vendor. With the increase in outsourcing and the opportunities provided by electronic business to tap world-wide markets, these decisions are becoming ever more complex. The presence of multiple criteria in these decisions has long been recognized.[21]

Outsourcing Risks

Other risks are related to partner selection, focusing specifically on the additional risks associated with international trade. Risks in outsourcing can include:[22]

- Cost – unforeseen vendor selection, transition, or management
- Lead time – delay in production start-up, manufacturing process, or transportation
- Quality – minor or major finishing defects, component fitting, or structural defects

Outsourcing has become endemic in the United States, especially information technology to India and production to China.[23] Risk factors include:

- Ability to retain control
- Potential for degradation of critical capability
- Risk of dependency
- Pooling risk (proprietarial information, clients competing among themselves)
- Risk of hidden costs

Ecological Risks

In our ever-more complex world, it no longer is sufficient for each organization to make decisions in light of their own vested self-interest. There is growing concern with the impact of human decisions on the state of the earth. This is especially true in mass production environments such as power generation,[24] but also is important in all aspects of business. Cruz (2008) presented a dynamic framework for modeling and analysis of supply chain networks in light of corporate social responsibility.[25] That study presented a framework multiple objective programming model with the criteria of maximizing profit, minimizing waste, and minimizing risk.

Multiple Criteria Selection Model

A number of methodologies are applied in practice, to include simple screening and scoring methods,[26] supplier positioning matrices to lay out risks by vendor, with associated ratings,[27] and a combination of sorts combining risk categorization with ratings of opportunity, probability, and severity.[28] Traditional multiple criteria methods have also been applied, to include analytic hierarchy process.[29] The simple multiattribute rating theory (SMART)[30] model bases selection on the rank order of the product of criteria weights and alternative scores over these criteria, and will be used here. Note that we are demonstrating, and are not claiming that the orders and ratings used are universal. We are rather presenting a method that real decision makers could use with their own ratings (and even with other criteria that they might think important in a given application).

Options

There are various levels of outsourcing that can be adopted. These range from simply outsourcing particular tasks (much like the idea of service oriented architecture), co-managing services with partners, hiring partners to manage services, and full outsourcing (in a contractual relationship). We will use these four outsourcing relationships plus the fifth option of doing everything in-house as our options.

Criteria

We will utilize the criteria given below:

- Cost (including hidden)
- Lead time
- Quality
- Ability to retain control
- Potential loss of critical capability
- Risk of dependency
- Risk of loss of proprietarial information
- Risk of client contention

The SMART method begins by rank ordering criteria. Here assume the following rank order of importance:

1. Ability to retain control
2. Risk proprietarial information loss
3. Quality of product and service
4. Potential loss of critical capability
5. Risk of dependency
6. Cost
7. Lead time
8. Risk of client contention

The next step is to develop relative weights of importance for criteria. We will do this by assigning the most important criterion 100 points, and give proportional ratings for each of the others as given in Table 5.1:
Weights are obtained by dividing each criterion's assigned point value by the total of points (here 435). This yields weights shown in Table 5.2:

Scoring of Alternatives over Criteria

The next step of the SMART method is to score alternatives. This is an expression by the decision maker (or associated experts) of how well each alternative performs on each criterion. Scores range from 1.0 (ideal performance) to 0 (absolute worst performance imaginable). This approach makes the scores independent of scale, and independent of weight. Demonstration is given in Table 5.3:

Table 5.1 Assignment of points to criteria

Rank	Criterion	Points
1	Ability to retain control	100
2	Risk proprietarial information loss	90
3	Quality of product and service	85
4	Potential loss of critical capability	60
5	Risk of dependency	40
6	Cost	30
7	Lead time	25
8	Risk of client contention	5

Table 5.2 Weight development

Rank	Criterion	Points	Weights
1	Ability to retain control	100	0.230
2	Risk proprietarial information loss	90	0.207
3	Quality of product and service	85	0.195
4	Potential loss of critical capability	60	0.138
5	Risk of dependency	40	0.092
6	Cost	30	0.069
7	Lead time	25	0.057
8	Risk of client contention	5	0.011

Table 5.3 Scores

Criteria	Out-tasking	Co-managed	Managed	Contract	In-house
Ability to retain control	0.9	0.6	0.3	0.0	1.0
Risk proprietarial information loss	0.8	0.5	0.2	0.0	1.0
Quality of product and service	0.3	0.4	0.6	0.9	0.7
Potential loss of critical capability	0.3	0.2	0.2	0.0	1.0
Risk of dependency	0.8	0.4	0.3	0.0	1.0
Cost	0.3	0.5	0.7	1.0	0.2
Lead time	0.8	0.3	0.5	0.7	0.4
Risk of client contention	0.0	0.2	0.3	1.0	0.3

Table 5.4 Value functions

Alternative	Out-tasking	Co-managed	Managed	Contract	In-house
	0.613	0.438	0.363	0.297	0.844
	2	3	4	5	1

Once weights and scores are obtained, value functions for each alternative are simply the sum products of weights times scores for each alternative. The closer to 1.0 (the maximum value function), the better. Table 5.4 shows value scores for the five alternatives:

The outcome here is that in-house operations best satisfy the preference function of the decision maker. Obviously, different weights and scores will yield different outcomes. But the method enables decision makers to apply a sound but simple analysis to aid their decision making.

Conclusions

Supply chains have become important elements in the conduct of global business. There are too many efficiency factors available from global linkages to avoid. We all gain from allowing broader participation by those with relative advantages. Alliances can serve as safety nets by providing alternative sources, routes, or products for its members. Risk exposure within supply chains can be reduced by reducing lead times. A common means of accomplishing lead time reduction is by collocation of suppliers at producer facilities.

This chapter has discussed some of the many risks associated with supply chains. A rational process of dealing with these risks includes assessment of what can go wrong, quantitative measurement to the degree possible of risk likelihood and severity, qualitative planning to cover a broader set of important criteria, and contingency planning. A wide variety of available supply chain risk-reduction strategies were reviewed, with cases of real application.

While no supply chain network can expect to anticipate all future disruptions, they can set in place a process to reduce exposure and impact. Preplanned response is expected to provide better organizational response in keeping with organizational objectives.

End Notes

1. Ritchie, B., and Brindly, C. (2007). Supply chain risk management and performance: A guiding framework for future development, *International Journal of Operations and Production Management* 27:3, 303–322.
2. Mentzer, J.T, Dewitt, W., Keebler, J.S., Min, S., Nix, N.W., Smith, C.D., and Zacharia, Z.G. (2001). *Supply Chain Management*. Thousand Oaks, CA: Sage.
3. Tang, C.S. (2006). Perspectives in supply chain risk management, *International Journal of Production Economics* 103, 451–488.
4. Chapman, P., Cristopher, M., Juttner, U., Peck, H., and Wilding, R. (2002). Identification and managing supply chain vulnerability, *Logistics and Transportation Focus* 4:4, 59–64.
5. Kunreuther, H. (1976). Limited knowledge and insurance protection, *Public Policy* 24, 227–261.
6. MacCrimmon, K.R., and Wehrung, D.A. (1986). *Taking Risks: The Management of Uncertainty*. New York: Free Press.
7. March, J., and Shapira, Z. (1987). Managerial perspectives on risk and risk taking, *Management Science* 33, 1404–1418.
8. Giunipero, L.C., and Aly Eltantawy, R. (2004). Securing the upstream supply chain: A risk management approach, *International Journal of Physical Distribution and Logistics Management* 34:9, 698–713.
9. Rice, B., and Caniato, F. (2003). Supply chain response to terrorism: Creating resilient and secure supply chains, *Supply Chain Response to Terrorism Project Interim Report*. Cambridge, MA: MIT Center for Transportation and Logistics.
10. Giunipero and Aly Eltantawy. (2004). op cit.
11. Tang (2006), op cit.
12. Dickson, G.W. (1966). An analysis of vendor selection systems and decisions, *Journal of Purchasing* 2, 5–17.
13. Moskowitz, H., Tang, J., and Lam, P. (2000). Distribution of aggregate utility using stochastic elements of additive multiattribute utility models, *Decision Sciences* 31, 327–360.
14. Sterman, J.D. (1989). Modeling managerial behavior: Misperceptions of feedback in a dynamic decision making experiment, *Management Science* 35, 321–339.
15. Bresnahan, T.F., and Reiss, P.C. (1985). Dealer and manufacturer margins, *Rand Journal of Economics* 16, 253–268.
16. Carr, S., and Lovejoy, W. (2000). The inverse newsvendor problem: Choosing an optimal demand portfolio for capacitated resources, *Management Science* 47, 912–927.
17. Van Mieghem, J., and Dada, M. (2001). Price versus production postponement: Capacity and competition, *Management Science* 45, 1631–1649.
18. Tang (2006), op cit.
19. Hendricks, K., and Singhal, V. (2005). An empirical analysis of the effect of supply chain disruptions on long-run stock price performance and equity risk of the firm, *Production and Operations Management* 25–53.
20. Golda, J., Philippi, C. (2007). Managing new technology risk in the supply chain. *Intel Technology Journal* 11:2, 95–104.
21. Dickson, G.W. (1966). op cit.; Weber, C.A., Current, J.R., and Benton, W.C. (1991). Vendor selection criteria and methods, *European Journal of Operational Research*, 50, 2–18; Moskowitz, H., et al. (2000). op cit.

22. Wellborn, C. (2007). op cit.
23. Sanders, N.R., Locke, A., Moore, C.B., and Autry, C.W. (2007). A multidimensional framework for understanding outsourcing arrangements. *Journal of Supply Chain Management: A Global Review of Purchasing and Supply* 43:4, 3–15.
24. Sheu, J.-B. (2008). Green supply chain management, reverse logistics and nuclear power generation. *Transportation Research: Part E* 44:1, 19–46.
25. Cruz, J.M. (2008). Dynamics of supply chain networks with corporate social responsibility through integrated environmental decision-making. *European Journal of Operational Research* 184, 1005–1031.
26. Golda and Philippi. (2007). op cit.
27. Chou, S.-Y., Shen, C.-Y., and Chang, Y.-H. (2007). Vendor selection in a modified re-buy situation using a strategy-aligned fuzzy approach. *International Journal of Production Research* 45:14, 3113–3133.
28. Wellborn, C. (2007). Using FMEA to assess outsourcing risk. *Quality Progress* 40:8, 17–21.
29. Levary, R.R. (2007). Ranking foreign suppliers based on supply risk. *Supply Chain Management: An International Journal* 12:6, 392–394; Balan, S., Brat, P., Kumar, P. (2008). A strategic decision model for the justification of supply chain as a means to improve national development index. *International Journal of Technology Management* 40:1/3, 69–86.
30. Edwards, W., and Barron, F.H. (1994). SMARTS and SMARTER: Improved simple methods for multiattribute utility measurement, *Organizational Behavior and Human Decision Processes* 60, 306–325; Olson, D.L. (1996). *Decision Aids in Selection Problems*. New York: Springer.

Chapter 6
Two Polar Concept of Project Risk Management

S.M. Seyedhoseini, S. Noori, and M. AliHatefi

The state-of-the art of Risk Management Process (RMP) has primarily relied on two main phases, (a) Risk Assessment and (b) Risk Response. Most of these studies have had a significance emphasis on risk assessment but we can find a limited study on the subject of risk response. So, the main objective of this research study is to emphasize on the indispensable shift of our perspectives at the present time to a more "Equilibrant" RMP, both for risk assessment and risk response. Based on this view, this paper proposes a two-polar generic RMP framework for projects and introduces some new elements. It can be concluded that a two-polar perspective proposed in this research study can be used for risk management projects in most effective and productive manner in real world's problems.

We require managing risks, related to our projects. The need for project risk management has been widely recognized[1] but it is generally overlooked, from concept to completion. "Sadly, many organizations do not know much about risk management and do not even attempt to practice it."[2] Project risk management has been defined as the art and science of identifying, assessing, and responding to project risk throughout the life of a project and in the best interests of its objectives.[3]

The main objective of this chapter is to emphasize on the indispensable shift of our perspectives at the present time to a more "Equilibrant RMP." For this purpose, after looking at some RMPs in the state-of-the art, the paper introduces the concept of "Equilibrium" in RMP and proposes a two-polar generic framework for RMP.

Risk Management Processes

Many studies have introduced risk management processes (RMPs), but there is more work needed. Most studies proposing RMP applied in the project environment belong to one of the contexts given below:

- Project management context
- Civil engineering context

D.L. Olson, D. Wu (eds.) *New Frontiers in Enterprise Risk Management*,

- Software engineering context
- Public application context

Almost all conventional RMPs have a similar framework. In many cases there are differences in the way of structuring the process. The series of steps in the process tends to reflect the view of the author but the overall approaches tend to be similar; however there are detail differences. In some RMPs there are scope differences. One of the biggest differences through common RMPs being discovered is some kind of planning which is included in the process.[4] Furthermore, conventional RMPs, usually, consist of three to nine phases. Within the research by present paper, we have studied and compared most of RMPs in the literature. Some typical RMPs are presented in Table 6.1.

Equilibriant RMPs and Related Gaps

There has been some discussion about the relative importance of different phases of RMP. The assumption would thus be that all phases support equally but in different ways the overall goal of improving project performance.[21] We define the critical success factor of the "Equilibrium" as due attention to all phases of RMP which are important in turn. There is a consensus that the RMP must be comprised of two main phases.[22] The first phase is risk assessment including risk identification and risk analysis, which is analytical in nature. The second phase is risk response, which is synthetic. The critical success factor of the "Equilibrium" expresses that the initial phases of RMP play a fundamental role and the tail end

Table 6.1 Typical RMPs

RMP name	Author	Context	Year	Description
Construction risk management system (CRMS)	Al-Bahar and Crandall[5]	Civil Engineering	1990	This RMP provides an effective and systematic framework for quantitatively identifying, evaluating, and responding to risk in construction projects
RISKMAN	Carter et al.[6]	Project Management	1996	It has a practical approach to the management of risk. The purpose of the RISKMAN methodology is to provide a general framework for professional project RM, and guidance for its implementation

(continued)

Table 6.1 (continued)

RMP name	Author	Context	Year	Description
Risk analysis and management for projects (RAMP)	UK Institution of Civil Engineers et al.[7]	Civil Enginee ring	1998	The RAMP has four phases and thirteen sub-phases specifically conceived for capital investment projects
Continuous risk management (CRM)	Rosenberg et al.[8]	Software Engineering	1999	This methodology was developed in conjunction with the Software Engineering Institute (SEI) at Carnegie Mellon University and tailored to the NASA systems community
Department of defense (DoD)	U.S. Department of Defense (DoD) et al.[9]	Public Application	2000	The DoD is a product of a joint effort by the under secretary of defense. This RMP includes risk planning, assessing, handling and monitoring steps with feedback from monitoring and documentation for all process steps
Capability matur ity model integration (CMMI)	Software Engineering Institute (SEI)[10]	Software Engineering	2001	It is the updated revision of the CMM, Capability Maturity Model, by SEI and Humphrey (1990)
RISKIT (Risk Kit)	Kontio[11]	Software Engineering	2001	It is based on a graphical modeling formalism. The RISKIT method supports multiple stakeholder views to risks by considering their potential utility losses. Kontio developed the concept of risk scenario within the RISKIT. Also a process improvement framework and some empirical evaluations support the RISKIT
Management of risks (MoR)	Office of Government Commerce (OGC)[12]	Public Application	2002	The MoR is a guide which; defines the best practice in the implementation of RMP. It takes a corporate governmental focused approach to the development of an organizational framework for managing risk from strategic level to operational level

(continued)

Table 6.1 (continued)

RMP name	Author	Context	Year	Description
Risk filtering, rank-ing and management (RFRM)	Haimes, et al.[13]	Public Application	2002	The RFRM identifies, prioritizes, assesses, and manages risks to complex, large-scale systems. It encapsulates the six questions of risk assessment and management, thereby adhering to a comprehensive risk analysis process. The RFRM consists of eight phases
Project uncertainty management (PUMA)	Del Cano and De la Cruz[14]	Civil Engineering	2002	The PUMA is a hierarchically structured, flexible, and generic methodology that has been applied to construction projects. This methodology is proposed based on professional experience of the authors, an analysis of the previously published RMP of project environment and Interviews to professionals
Shape, harness, and manage project uncertainty (SHAMPU)	Chapman and Ward[15]	Project Management	2003	The SHAMPU is a generic RMP consisting of nine steps. It is explicitly defined to be iterative with the level of detail
Project management body of knowledge (PMBoK)	Project Management Institute (PMI)[16]	Project Management	2004	The first versions of PMBoK released in 1996, which; included four phases. In the next version, the 2000 edition, the PMBOK presented six processes. The 2004 edition is developed version of the 2000 edition
Project risk analysis and management (PRAM)	Simon et al.[17]	Project Management	2004	In the PRAM all phases are defined in detail, including flowcharts covering the different activities in each phase. The process is designed for the largest projects and the authors provide simplifications for specific cases

(continued)

Table 6.1 (continued)

RMP name	Author	Context	Year	Description
Multi-party risk management process (MRMP)	Pipattanapiwong[18]	Civil Engineering	2004	The MRMP considers several parties' views involved in project. It consists of three main systematic and logical processes which; is shown in input-process-output flow diagram
AS/NZS 4360	Australian New Zealand Standard[19]	Public Application	2004	This standard was developed in 1996 to accommodate public sectors and private organizations on risk management. Its risk management approach is very generic and can be used in any projects
RISKAID	Risk Reasoning Ltd.[20]	Project Management	2005	The RISKAID includes a methodical process for identifying and assessing risks, identifying actions and assessing their effects on risks, then managing the risks throughout the project lifecycle. It supported by a software toolset, a training guideline and a backup service

phases of RMP play a throughout role. Focusing on one and ignoring the other misleads RMP. Indeed, one can assume that risk assessment and risk response are poles of RMP in which; risk assessment is a decision-making tool and risk response is the decision made and put in practice. It should be noted that, ignoring the concept of the "Equilibrium" causes problems in design of and/or implementation of RMP. One of the biggest problems with many RMPs is that one or more process steps are missing, weakly implemented, or out of order. "All RMP steps are equally important. If you do not do one or more steps, or you do them poorly, you will likely have an ineffective RMP."[23]

Importance of Risk Assessment and Risk Response

The primary phase in RMP is risk assessment, so any faults and defections on this phase are extends and accumulated to the next phases. So, effective RMP begins with effective risk assessment.[24] In the other words, one cannot manage risks if one does not characterize them to know what they are, how likely they are, and what their impact might be.[25] On the other hand, one can consider that risk response phase has a throughout role in RMP. Kliem and Ludin maintained that good risk management requires good decision-making.[26] Some investigators assert that importance of risk response is premier than importance of risk assessment. They believe that it is risk response which; really leads RMP toward the final results. Hillson stated "Identification and assessment will be worthless unless responses can be developed and implemented which really make a difference in addressing identified risks."[27] Fisher also stated that all of the risk management activities are meaningless if they do not produce information based on which the decision maker makes decisions for the benefit of the program.[28] Williams asserted that the purpose of risk analysis is always providing input for an underlying decision problem.[29]

A Significant Gap

In the traditional view, initial phases of RMP are more significant cause they are more fundamental. Based on this view, Elkjaer and Felding stated, "If risks are not identified, they cannot be managed thus giving greatest weigh to the risk identification phase."[30] This view has directed most risk management researches toward risk assessment. This subject has originated a significant gap in the related researches in the literature. Undoubtedly, we can assert that the main recent gap in RMP is in the subject of risk response. Many researchers stress the mentioned gap while the following statements confirm it:

- "Yet risk response development is perhaps the weakest part of RMP, and it is here that many organizations fail to gain the full benefits of RMP."[31]
- "Although there is wide agreement that the development of risk response plans is an important element of project risk management, few solutions have been proposed and there are no widely accepted processes, models or tools to support the cost-effective selection of risk responses."[32]
- "Risk response planning is far more likely to be inadequately dealt with, or overlooked entirely, in the management of project risk."[33]
- "A few specific tools have been suggested in the literature for determining risk responses."[34]
- "There are several systematic tools and techniques available to be promptly used in risk identification; several quantitative and qualitative techniques also are available for risk analysis; but, in risk response process, less systematic and well-developed frameworks have been provided."[35]

The above statements emphasize that existing RMPs are directed toward focusing on risk assessment and neglecting risk response. Table 6.2, introduced by Pipattanapiwong, supports the above statements.

Table 6.2 Summary of risk management research in construction

RMP			
Area of risk management research	Risk identification	Risk analysis	Risk response
Risk category			
Economic, financial, bidding risk	Medium	High	Low
Estimating, scheduling related risk	Low	High	Low
Managerial risk	Medium	Medium	Low
Political and legal risk	Medium	Low	Low
Cultural related risks	Medium	Low	Low
Health and safety risk	Low	Low	High
Social, design, force major risk	Low	Low	Low
RM Development	**High**	**High**	**Low**
Subjective issues			
Subjective assessment	Low	Medium	Low
Risk perception	Low	Low	Low
Risk attitude	Low	Low	Low
Risk communication	Low	Low	Low
Survey of risk management practice	**Low**	**Medium**	**Medium**
Type of application project			
Build, Operate, Transfer (BOT)	Medium	Low	Low
Infrastructure project	Low	Medium	Low

A Two Polar RMP Framework for Projects

Regarding the critical success factor of "Equilibrium" in RMP, the two-polar perspective expresses that RMP has two main equivalent poles or columns including risk and response. Here, we propose a two-polar RMP, which is compatible to project environment. This RMP commences with the box of "RMP start up" and finishes with the box of "RMP shut down." Table 6.3, shows the breakdown of our proposed RMP.

The proposed RMP has the following main properties:

- The proposed RMP is designed based on a two-polar concept. In deed, we have designed all elements of our RMP, in respect with two main equivalent poles or columns including risk and response.
- The proposed RMP is generic. This means that risk management analysts must generate a RMP to match the size and complexity of their project.
- Our RMP is integrated to the overall project plan.
- The proposed RMP could be applied to each given level of project work breakdown structure (WBS). Project WBS is a top-down hierarchical chart of tasks and subtasks required for completing the project.[36]
- The skeleton of our proposed RMP is based on the view of Plan-Do-Check-Action (PDCA)[37] (Kleim and Ludin 1997). The iteration loop consists of

Table 6.3 Breakdown of the proposed RMP

PDCA view (Plan-do-check-action)	Level-1	Level-2	Level-3
	RMP start up		
Action	Actuation		
Plan	Risk assessment	Risk identification	
		Risk analysis	Risk measurement
			Risk processing
			Risk classification
	Response assessment	Response identification	
		Response analysis	Response measurement
			Response processing
			Response classification
Do and Check	Implementation and control		
	RMP shut down		

Acuation, Risk Assessment, Response Assessment, and Implementation and Control. The most overriding core of this process is "Plan" which; will be established based on a two-polar concept because it contains risk assessment and response assessment.

Conceptual Framework

To establish a powerful RMP, the risk management analyst must define project, risks and responses and distinguishes clear relationship among them. So the conceptual model presented here is structured based on three pivotal elements i.e. project, risks and responses. The key concepts are defined as following:

Project measure: The project scope is split into three key success factors including project time, project quality and project cost (see Table 6.4). These factors could be named as project measures. In principle, reaching the project scope requires us to get the targets related to these three project measures.

Project ultimacy: It is the ultimate state of project in terms of project measures.

Risk event: It is a discrete occurrence that if it occurs, has a positive (opportunity) or negative (threat) effect on the project measures (Simon et al. 2004).[38] Indeed, risks affect on schedule, quality and cost of project work elements and these affections generalizes to the project scope.

Risk measure: Risks have several characteristics, which could be used to characterize risk events. We name these characteristics as risk measures, which are described in Table 6.5.

Table 6.4 Project measures

No.	Project measure	Description
1	Project time	The project plan on schedule
2	Project quality	The specifications of the project product
3	Project cost	The planned cost of project

Table 6.5 Risk measures

Risk measure	Description
Risk probability	The likelihood of occurring risk event (risk event occurrence probability)
Risk impact	When an event occurs, it impacts on the project measures. Therefore, risk event impact could be stated in terms of schedule, quality and cost
Risk detection	The degree of easiness of detection of risk.[39] This measure is developed based on Risk Priority Number (RPN) that is a failure assessment criterion in Failure Mode and Evaluation Analysis (FMEA)
Risk manageability	It refers to degree of influence on the controlling of the risk.[40] Indeed this measure is concerned with this question: "Can anything be done about risk?"
Risk effect delay	This measure, which sometimes is named timeframe,[41] describes the time of latency between the event occurring time and the actual impact of damage[42]
Risk proximity	Some risks occur early in the project cycle and others late in the cycle. Risk proximity is the period of time within which the risk is expected to occur
Risk predictability	This measure determines where and when in the project, risk might occur[43]
Risk growth	The variation of risk measures along time, if it is left unattended[44]
Risk uncertainty	Risk uncertainty refers to the lack of information about the nature of probabilistic distribution function of risk measures. This measure brings the risk classification including known, unknown known and unknown unknowns[45]
Risk uniqueness	Sometimes, dealing with a special subject, a risk may receive attention. For example, a special marketing situation guides the risk management analyst to give high weigh to a risk
Risk coupling	The effect, which a risk would have on measures of other risks

Risk class: Risk class implies typology of risk. A risk, from different views, belongs to different classes.

Response action: Response action is a discrete activity that when carried out, has a positive (ameliorator) or negative (deteriorator) effect on the risks measures.

Response measure: Similar to those of risk, there are some measures to characterize response actions. These characteristics could be named as response measures. Response measures are explained in Table 6.6.

Response class: Response class implies typology of response. A response, from different views, belongs to different classes.

The conceptual framework to clarify the relationships among project, risks, responses and their measures contains five important scenarios as follows:

- Implementing of response actions affects the risk measures
- Occurrence of risk events affects the project measures
- Response measures are used to characterize response actions
- Risk measures are used to characterize risk events
- Project measures are used to characterize project ultimacy

RMP Start up

Our proposed RMP begins with phase of starting up. In this phase, organization/project management board decides about applying RMP for project and appoints the leader of risk management. Then, the most important tasks are establishing the organizational chart of risk management, constructing team of risk management and training RMP team and project members. Here, some critical success factors are as following:

- *Early starting up*: It should be noted that risk management researchers emphasize that RMP should start in a very early stage of the project process. Naturally, when risk management is started early it is more difficult but more useful.[51]
- *Teamwork*: Most authors of risk literature think that risk management is essentially a team effort.[52] Also consider that leadership is a key.[53] It is recommended to demonstrate a visible and continuous senior leadership for the RMP.[54]
- *Training*: An organizational focus for training about risk management is essential. So, project members must receive sufficient training in risk management to implement RMP effectively.[55]
- *Organizational position*: Risk management must have a suitable position in the organizational chart of project organization. One of the major choices is whether to have a centralized or decentralized risk management organization. The decentralized risk management organization is the recommended approach, and generally results in an efficient use of personnel resources.[56]

Actuation

This phase is designed as an extended form of the phase of "risk management planning" in PMI (2000) or the phase of "establish the context" in standard AS/NZS 4360 (2004). The major activities of this phase are presented in Table 6.7. Some of these activities will be explained in the next sections. It should be noted that actua-

Table 6.6 Response measures

Response measure	Description
Response probability	The likelihood of success response action (response action success probability)
Response impact	When a response action is applied, it impacts on the measures of risk events. Therefore, response action impact could be stated in terms of risk measures
Response resources	This response measure focuses on the resources, which response action will take to address the risk. Simply, one can state this measure in term of response action cost
Response capacity	This response measure focuses on the availability of resources to implement response action.[46] Kontio (2001) states that the resource constraints may rule out some effective response actions
Response duration	Similar to the work elements in a project, response actions also take time. This measure could be mapped in scheduling tools such as risk and response Gantt chart[47]
Response effect delay	It describes the time of latency between the implementation of response action and the actual impact of response action. In the other words, response effect delay is the time period which risks will be impacted by response action
Response urgency	A risk should be addressed so as to have the desired effect.[48] Therefore, response urgency is the measure of how imperative or critical it is to address the risk.[49] According to PMI (2000), the time-criticality of response actions may magnify the importance of a risk
Response uncertainty	It is about the lack of information about the nature of probabilistic distribution function of response measures
Response uniqueness	Sometimes, dealing with a special subject, a response action may receive priority. For instance, stakeholder perspectives may influence the priority of a response action[50]

tion phase is repeated in each round of the proposed RMP. In deed, this phase is the core part of "Action" within the loop of PDCA

Assessment of Project, Risks and Responses

"Assessment" is an activity, which contains two phases of identification and analysis. We prefer to use the term "Assessment" for project, risks and responses. Before the

Table 6.7 The major activities in the phase of "Actuation"

Activity	Description	Application
Regarding the project WBS, the level of RMP should be clarified.	Determining what level of the project WBS to be applied to RMP	Determining level of efforts on RMP
Determining possible classes of risks	It includes determining the hierarchical or dimensional structures for risk classification	Priorizing risks
Assigning weighted factors to risk classes	For each identified class, the risk management analysts may assign a coefficient	Formulating risk level function
Determining possible classes of responses	It includes determining the hierarchical or dimensional structures for response classification	Priorizing responses
Assigning weighted factors to response classes	For each identified class, the risk management analysts may assign a coefficient	Formulating response level function
Selecting risk measures.	Risk measures are risk characteristics such as risk probability etc	Priorizing risks.
Assigning weighted factors to selected risk measures	For each selected risk measures, the risk management analysts should assign a coefficient.	Formulating risk level function
Selecting response measures.	Risk measures are response characteristics such as response cost etc.	Priorizing responses.
Assigning weighted factors to selected response measures	For each selected response measures, the risk management analysts should assign a coefficient	Formulating response level function
Defining the formulation of risk level function	In comprehensive view, this function includes all risk measures and risk classes	Priorizing risks.
Defining the formulation of response level function	In comprehensive view, this function includes all response measures and response classes	Priorizing responses.
Selecting tools and techniques	It includes determining all tools and techniques, which will be used in steps of the RMP	
Clarifying conditions of beginning next periods of the RMP	The conditions may be time-bases, optimality-based, etc	Specifying when the next round of the RMP should be commenced
Establishing the RMP success measurement indicators	To determine the amount of success in each round, we require establishing some indicators	This indicators guide the risk analysts to measure the effectiveness of RMP on achieving the project scope

phase of project/risk/response analysis, the analyst must identify project work elements/risks/responses.

We encapsulate all conventional project-planning activities into the box of project assessment. In fact, project assessment includes identifying work elements and analyzing of them. This box contains steps such as creating WBS, resources assignment, project scheduling and project costing. Risk assessment phase contains two stages of risk identification and risk analysis. Also, response assessment phase includes response identification and response analysis. As mentioned previously, risk and response assessment constitute the part of "Plan" within the loop of PDCA. Risk analysis stage, have two steps. Firstly, risk measures should be determined (risk measurement) and secondly, risks should be classified (risk classification). Through these two steps, the risk management analysts may process risks. The next step is to determine risk level and then risk priority. Responses, also, require to the go through all the above-mentioned processes (response measurement, response classification, response processing, response level specification and response priority determining).

Risk and Response Identification

We believe that almost, all of the techniques, which could be used in risk identification, also, could be applied in response identification. Some of those techniques are brainstorming, brain writing, interviewing, checklists, panel sessions, Delphi technique, etc.[57] In addition to these techniques, we recommend using risk/response classes and project WBS. However, the output of risk identification and response identification are, respectively, serial lists of risks and responses.

Risk and Response Measurement

Traditionally, most RMPs consider two risk measures: risk probability and risk impact that is a two-dimensional notion.[58] For example, Kerzner defines risk as *f(likelihood, impact)*.[59] These two risk measures are both descriptive of the risk event. This means that other risk measures are not addressed at all.[60] We believe that to have more complete simulation of risks, the risk management analyst is required to consider not only these two measures, but also all pivotal risk measures as Table 6.5. Also, regarding the two-polar perspective, the risk management analyst can use response measures to model responses. Risk measures focus on the potential risk event itself but response measures focus on the ability to address response actions. Here, the next step to establish the measurement system is to scale the above measures. For example, some instance scaled measures are presented in Tables 6.8–6.11.

Risk and Response Classification

Hillson (2002) states that risk identification often produces nothing more than a long list of risks, which can be hard to understand or manage.[61] The list does not provide any insight into the class of risk. The best way to deal with a large amount

Table 6.8 Scaling the measure of risk effect delay

No.	Qualitative scale	Synonym term	Quantitative scale	Weighted factor
1	Very low	Near term	<1 months	0.1
2	Low	Short term	1–2 months	0.2
3	Moderate	Medium term	2–4 months	0.4
4	High	Long term	4–6 months	0.7
5	Very high	Far term	>6 months	0.8

Table 6.9 Scaling the measure of risk manageability

No.	Qualitative scale	Synonym term	Weighted factor
1	Very low	Largely uncontrollable	0.1
2	Low	Uncontrollable	0.4
3	Moderate	Moderate controllable	0.5
4	High	Highly controllable	0.8
5	Very high	Essentially manageable	0.9

Table 6.10 Scaling the measure of response capacity

No.	Qualitative scale	Synonym term	Weighted factor
1	Very low	No capacity available	0.1
2	Low	Available with low resource	0.2
3	Moderate	Available with moderate resource	0.6
4	High	Available with high resource	0.7
5	Very high	Free available	0.8

Table 6.11 Scaling the measure of response urgency

No.	Qualitative scale	Synonym term	Weighted factor
1	Very low	Can be addressed at a later stage	0.9
2	Low	Must be addressed in the near future	0.9
3	Moderate	Must be addressed immediately to avoid adjustments to project plan	0.7
4	High	Must be addressed immediately but will require minor adjustment to project plan	0.4
5	Very high	Must be addressed immediately but will require major adjustment to project plan	0.3

of data is to structure the information to aid comprehension. This function is one of the main steps of risk analysis in some RMPs. For example RISKIT method calls it as "risk clustering" and RISKAID calls it as "risk structuring." Apart from terminology, the classification could be accessed through the classification of data into the hierarchical or dimensional structures. In a hierarchical structure, classes are organized in a tree format and in dimensional structures classes are formed into matrix templates. Based on the two-polar perspective, we believe that these structure models should be considered for both risks and responses. For classification in the hierarchical structure, we recommend the terms event taxonomy structure (ETS) and action taxonomy structure (ATS) respectively for risks and responses (Note that the hierarchical structure is related to typology of risk events rather than breakdown of a unique phenomenon, therefore, we prefer to use ETS instead of risk breakdown structure (RBS) that is used in the existent literature). Table 6.8, presents a sample ETS in software engineering projects, which is proposed by the software engineering institute (SEI) (Table 6.12).

One can create dimensional structures by placing some hierarchical structures in the dimensions of a matrix. For classification in the dimensional structure, we recommend the terms event structuring matrix (ESM) and action structuring matrix (ASM) respectively for classification of risks and responses. Table 6.13 shows a sample ESM, which is introduced in the RISKAID. For instance the event "Delay in consultant presence at work" falls in a type of human and category of consortium. Also, regarding this matter and category of actions based on project resources, a sample ASM could be created as Table 6.14. For example, the action "Incrementing the number of labors for an activity" to accelerate the pace falls in type of reducing and category of manpower.

Risk and Response Processing

During risk measurement and risk classification, the risk management analyst may do some process on risks. The aim of risk processing is to better risk analysis through decreasing complexity and size or increasing accuracy and precision. Regarding risk measures and risk classes, one may do one of the following processes:

- Risk screening: Removing risks
- Risk bundling: Combining some risks to one
- Risk adding: Adding new risks
- Risk refracting: Decomposing one risk to some risks

The risk management analyst can considers similar processes to the above mentioned ones for responses, which are response screening, response bundling, response adding and response refracting.

Risk and Response Prioritization

Risk level is an index that indicates risk magnitude which; could be used to determine the priority of risks. For an assumed work element, a risk with higher level is more critical. Traditionally, to determine risk level, the risk management analysts use two risk measures including risk probability and risk impact as Fig. 6.1. A requirement for using most measures is to project them on a one-dimensional scale.[63] Therefore, the risk management analyst may establish a function for determining risk level. For instance, according to Wideman (1992), the standard perception

Table 6.12 A sample ETS[62]

	Class	Element	Attribute
Project	Product engineering		Stability
		Requirements	…
			Scale
			Functionality
		Design	…
			Non-development SW
			Feasibility
		Code and unit test	…
			Coding/implementation
			Environment
		Integration and test	…
			System
			Maintainability
		Engineering specialties	…
			Specifications
	Development Environment		Formality
		Development process	…
			Product control
			Capacity
		Development system	…
			Deliverability
			Planning
		Management process	…
			Program interfaces
			Monitoring
		Management methods	…
			Configuration Mgt
			Quality attitude
		Work environment	…
			Morale
	Program constrains		Schedule
		Resources	…
			Facilities
			Type of contract
		Contract	…
			Dependencies
			Customer
		Program interfaces	…
			Politics

Table. 6.13 A sample ESM to class risk events

	Type		
ESM	Technical	Human	Politic/economic
Category	Project		
	Consortium		
	External		

Table 6.14 A sample ASM to class response actions

		Type				
	ASM	Remove	Reduce	Avoid	Transfer	Accept
Category	Management					
	Money					
	Manpower					
	Machinery					
	Method					
	Material					

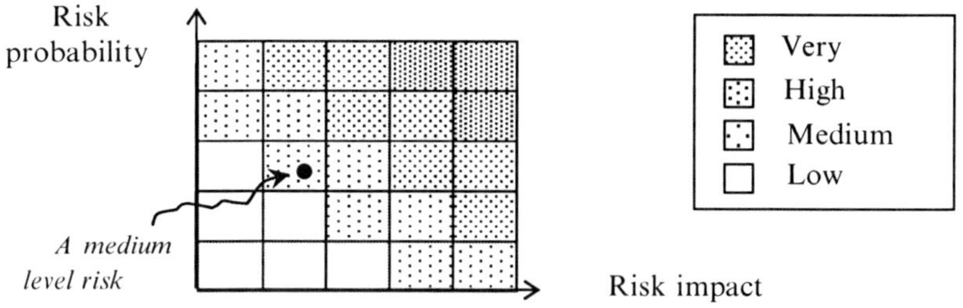

Fig. 6.1 Risk level (traditional view)

is that risk probability multiplied by risk impact results in risk level [(1)]. Conrow (2003) has put more functions forward.[64]

Regarding the two-polar perspective, response level is an index that presents its magnitude that could be applied to determine the priority of responses. In other words, for an assumed risk, a response with higher level is better than a response with lower level. Within a simple view, similar to the above risk level, we can determine response level by response probability multiplied by response impact divided by response resources, (see Fig. 6.2 and (2). The fraction of response impact divided by response resources indicates efficiency of response.

In a comprehensive view, one could benefit from more risk measures to establish a function for determining risk level. Based on the two-polar idea, a function which; includes more response measures could be used to specify response level. The terms (3) and (4), respectively, show these functions.

$$Risk\ level = f\,(Risk\ mesure) \tag{3}$$
$$Response\ level = f\,(Response\ measure) \tag{4}$$

As mentioned earlier, one of the aims of risk classification may be to assign weighted factor to classes. Therefore, (3) and (4) could be influenced by weighted factor associated with risk and responses classes. Consequently, risk and response level functions might be termed as (5) and (6).

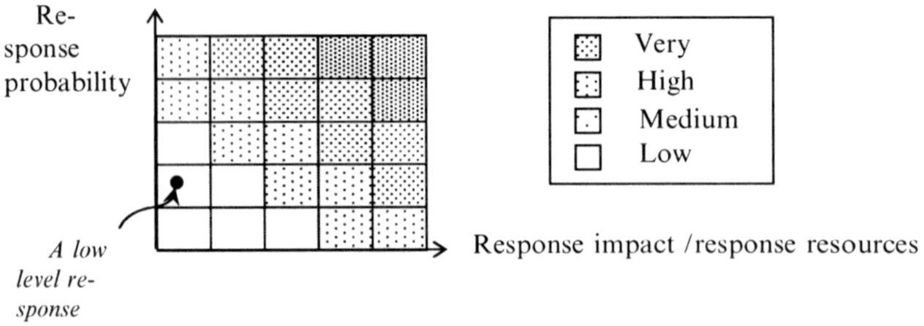

Fig. 6.2 Response level

$$\textit{Risk level} = f(\textit{Risk measure, Risk classes}) \quad (5)$$
$$\textit{Response level} = f(\textit{Response measure, Response classes}) \quad (6)$$

Downside or Upside Risk/Response

According to Hillson (2001), there is no doubt that common usage of the word "risk" sees only the downside.[65] This is reflected in the traditional definitions of the word, both in standard dictionaries and in some technical definitions (for example standard of CAN/CSA-Q850-97 (1997)).[66] However, some professional bodies and standard organizations have gradually developed their definitions of "risk" to include both upside and downside (for example standard of AS/NZS 4360 (2004)). One can consider that the concepts of downside risk (threat) and upside risk (opportunity) are integrated in a risk spectrum. As mentioned previously, risk has positive or negative effect on measures of projects. Also, as discussed in the previous section, this effect could be stated as risk level. Therefore, by mapping risk level in risk spectrum as Fig. 6.3, one can determine that if risk is downside or upside.

Regarding the two-polar view, we define the concepts of downside response (deteriorator) and upside response (ameliorator). As mentioned previously, response has positive or negative effect on measures of risks. Thus downside response includes action with negative effect on risk measures and upside response includes action with positive effect on risk measures. Now, by mapping response level in response spectrum as Fig. 6.4, one can determine that if response is downside or upside. Naturally, downside responses are not favorable and must be crossed out from responses list.

Secondary Risks and Responses

Regarding the two subjects of secondary risk and secondary response, one can observe a tow-polar concept. Secondary risks are created after implementing responses

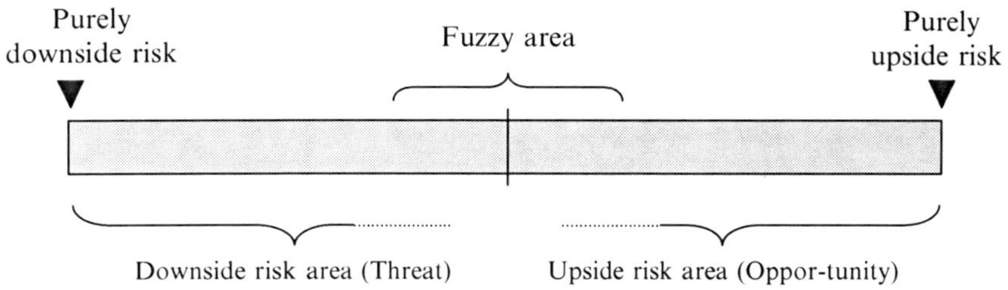

Fig. 6.3 Risk spectrum

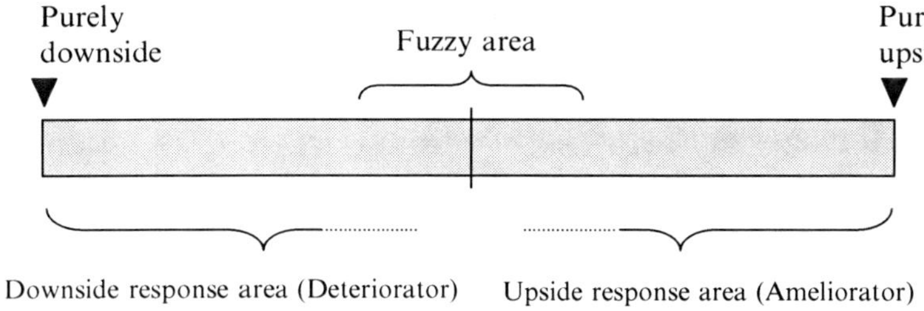

Fig. 6.4 Response spectrum

and secondary responses are those that are planned for secondary risks. The risk management analysts may consider these items through assessment phases.

Implementation and Control

For an assumed round of the proposed RMP, at the end of the response assessment phase, the planned responses should be executed. Therefore, implementation and control are parts of "Do" within PDCA. To implement and control risks, all risks and responses must have ownership. The task of risk ownership is risk control. Risk control includes tracking risk statement and monitoring it. The task of response ownership is response control. Response control contains tracking response implementation and monitoring it. As a useful guideline, to assign risk/response ownerships, the risk management analysts may consider the previously classified risk/response in the phase of risk/response analysis. However, it is very important that each person's responsibility and authority regarding all the risks and responses be determined. Continuous application of control indicators, tools and forms, also, is a critical subject. To control risks and responses, different indexes, tools and techniques are developed which have already been specified in the phase of actuation and are put in practice in this phase. The essential conditions to begin new round of the RMP are determined in the phase of actuation. These conditions may be open-loop control (for example a six-month period) or closed-loop control (for example while having an index reached a particular threshold). Before starting the next round, it requires us to calculate success measurement indicators for the previous round. Also it is useful to record all "lesson learned" which could be valuable to be applied in the next rounds. However, this is the part of "Check" within PDCA.

RMP Shut Down

This final phase guarantees that the RMP completes its mission. It should be noted that the RMP is shut down after closing the project. In shut down phase, some major activities should be carried out as the following. Firstly, it should be cleared that if risk management has been successful or not. As mentioned before, the RMP success measurement indicators are established in the phase of actuation. Secondly, it requires recording all data, information, knowledge, experiences and "lesson learned" which; are earned during the RMP periods. This is a very useful input to the next projects and can be a channel to integrate knowledge management programs of organization. Thirdly, regarding the models of Risk Maturity Model (RMM)[67] (Hillson 1997) and regarding the recent implemented RMP, the risk management analysts can distinguish the level of RMM of the project or the organization and can use it as a useful guideline for the next projects.

Comparison

In this section, to emphasize the two-polar concept of our proposed RMP, some of related aspects are compared, as in Table 6.15. According to the proposed RMP, it is apparent that importance of risk is equal to importance of response. This is a hint to considering the critical success factor of the "Equilibrium" for RMP.

Conclusion

Our investigations depicted that most of risk management studied researches and consequently most of conventional RMPs have had a significance emphasis on risk assessment but we found a limited study on the subject of risk response. To emphasize on the indispensable shift of our perspectives at the present time to a more "Equilibrant" RMP, both for risk assessment and risk response, in this research study we proposed a two-polar generic RMP framework for projects and introduced some response related aspects such as response measures, response level, response spectrum, etc. We conclude that a two-polar perspective proposed in this research study can be used for risk management projects in most effective and productive manner in real world's problems. We hope that taking this perspective directs the risk management researchers toward developing more and more methods, tools and techniques in the field of risk response.

Table 6.15 Some aspects of the two-polar concept of the proposed RMP

Risk related items	Response related items
Risk	Response
Risk event	Response action
Risk measure	Response measure
Risk class	Response class
Risk level	Response level
Risk priority	Response priority
Risk event occurrence probability	Response action succession probability
Risk event Impact	Response action impact
Risk effect delay	Response effect delay
Risk uncertainty	Response uncertainty
Risk uniqueness	Response uniqueness
Risk assessment	Response assessment
Risk identification	Response identification
Risk analysis	Response analysis
Risk measurement	Response measurement
Risk classification	Response classification
Risk priorization	Response priorization
Risk screening	Response screening
Risk bundling	Response bundling
Risk adding	Response adding
Risk refracting	Response refracting
Risk event taxonomy structure (ETS)	Response action taxonomy structure (ATS)
Risk event structuring matrix (ESM)	Response action structuring matrix (ASM)
Risk level function	Response level function
Risk spectrum	Response spectrum
Downside risk (threat)	Downside response (Deteriorator)
Upside risk (opportunity)	Upside response (Ameliorator)
Secondary risk	Secondary response
Risk ownership	Response ownership
Risk control	Response control
Risk tracking	Response tracking
Risk monitoring	Response monitoring

Acknowledgement We are grateful to chief and experts of the Project Management Research and Development Center for theirs assistance in executing present study. This center is commissioned to accelerate the proceduralization of Iranian Petrochemical projects (http://www.PMIR.com).

End Notes

1. Williams, T.M. (1995). A classified bibliography of recent research relating to project risk management, *European Journal of Operational Research*, 85:1, 18–38.
2. Hulett, D.T. (2001). Key Characteristics of a Mature Risk Management Process, Fourth European Project Management Conference, PMI Europe, London UK.
3. Wideman, R.M. (1992). Project and Program Risk Management: A Guide to Managing Project Risks and Opportunities, Project Management Institute, Upper Darby, Pennsylvania, USA.
4. Saari, H.-L. (2004), Risk Management in Drug Development Projects, Helsinki University of Technology, Laboratory of Industrial Management.

5. Al-Bahar, J., and Crandall, K.C. (1990). Systematic risk management approach for construction projects, *Journal of Construction Engineering and Management*, 116:3 533–546.
6. Carter, B., Hancock, T., Marc Morin, J., and Robins, N. (1996). Introducing RISKMAN: The European Project Risk Management Methodology, Blackwell, Cambridge, Massachusetts 02142, USA.
7. Institution of Civil Engineers, Faculty of Actuaries, Institute of Actuaries. (1998). Risk Analysis and Management for Projects (RAMP), Thomas Telford, London, UK.
8. Rosenberg, L., Gallo, A., and Parolek, F. (1999). Continuous Risk Management (CRM) Structure of Functions at NASA, AIAA 99-4455, American Institute of Aeronautics and Astronautics.
9. U.S. DoD (Department of Defense), Defense Acquisition University, Defense Systems Management College, (2000), Risk management guide for DoD Acquisition, Defense Systems Management College Press, Fort Belvoir, Virginia, USA.
10. Humphrey, W.S. (1990). Managing the Software Process, Addison Wesley; Software Engineering Institute (SEI), (2001), CMMI – Capability Maturity Model Integration, version 1.1 Pittsburgh, PA, Carnegie Mellon University. USA.
11. Kontio, J. (2001). Software Engineering Risk Management: A Method, Improvement Framework, and Empirical Evaluation, Nokia Research Center, Helsinki University of Technology, Ph.D. Dissertation.
12. Office of Government Commerce (OGC). (2002). Management of Risk (MOR): Guide for Practitioners, London.
13. Haimes, Y.Y., Kaplan, S., and Lambert, J.H. (2002). Risk filtering, ranking and management framework using hierarchical holographic modeling, *Risk Analysis*, 22:2, 381–395.
14. Del Cano, A., and De la Cruz, M.P. (2002). Integrated methodology for project risk management, *J. Construction Engineering and Management*, 128:6, 473–485.
15. Chapman, C.B., and Ward, S.C. (2003). Project risk Management, Processes, Techniques and Insights, 2nd edn., Wiley, Chichester, UK.
16. Project Management Institute (PMI). (2004). A guide to the project management body of knowledge (PMBOK guide), Newtown Square, Pennsylvania, USA.
17. Simon, P., Hillson, D., and Newland, K. (2004). PRAM project risk analysis and management guide, The Association for Project Management (APM), High Wycombe, UK.
18. Pipattanapiwong, J. (2004). Development of Multi-party Risk and Uncertainty management process for an Infrastructure project, Dissertation submitted to Kochi University of Technology for Degree of Ph.D.
19. AS/NZS 4360. (2004). Risk Management, Strathfield, Standards Associations of Australia, www.standards.com.au.
20. Swabey, M. (2004). Project Risk Management, An Invaluable Weapon in any Project Manager's Armoury, White Paper, Aspen Enterprises Ltd.
21. Saari, H.-L. (2004). op cit.
22. Miler, J. (2005). A Method of Software Project Risk Identification and Analysis, Ph.D. Thesis, Gdansk University of Technology, Faculty of Electronics, Telecommunications and Informatics.
23. Conrow, E.H. (2003). Effective Risk Management: Some Keys to Success, 2nd edn. American Institute of Aeronautics and Astronautics, Reston.
24. Rosenberg, et al. (1999). op cit.; U.S. DoE (Department of Energy). (2005). The Owner's Role in Project Risk Management, ISBN: 0-309-54754-7.
25. US DOE. (2005). op cit.
26. Kleim, R.L., and Ludin, S. (1997). Reducing Project Risk, Gower.
27. Hillson, D. (1999). Developing Effective Risk Response, Proceeding of the 30th Annual Project Management Institute, Seminars and Symposium, Philadelphia, Pennsylvania, USA.
28. Fisher, S. (2002). The SoCal Risk Management Symposium – It Made Me Think, *Risk Management Newsletter*, 4:4.
29. Williams. (1995). op cit.

30. Elkjaer, M., and Felding, F. (1999). Applied Project Risk Management – Introducing the Project Risk Management Loop of Control, *Project Management*, 5:1, 16–25.
31. Hillson. (1999). op cit.
32. Ben, D.I., and Raz, T. (2001). An integrated approach for risk response development in project planning, *Operational Research. Society*, 52, 14–25.
33. Gillanders, C. (2003). When Risk Management turns into Crisis Management, AIPM National Conference, Australia.
34. Saari. (2004). op cit.
35. Pipattanapiwong. (2004). op cit.
36. Olson, D.L. (2004). Introduction to Information Systems Project Management, McGraw-Hill.
37. Kleim and Ludin. (1997). op cit.
38. Simon, et al. (2004). op cit.
39. Santos, S.D.F.R., and Cabral, S. (2005). FMEA and PMBoK Applied To Project Risk Management, International Conference on Management of Technology, Vienna.
40. Elkjaer and Felding. (1999). op cit.
41. Garvey, P.R. (2001). Implementing a Risk Management Process for a Large Scale Information System Upgrade – A Case Study, *Incose Insight*, 4:1.
42. Sandy, M., Aven, T., and Ford, D. (2005). On Integrating Risk Perspectives in Project Management, *Risk Management: An International Journal*, 7:4, 7–21.
43. Charette, R. (1989). Software Engineering Risk Analysis and Management, McGraw Hill.
44. Clayton, J. (2005). West Coast CDEM Group Operative Plan, Civil Defense & Emergency Management Group for the West Coast.
45. Wideman. (1992). op cit.
46. Labuschagne, L. (2003). Measuring Project Risks: Beyond the Basics, Working paper, Rand Afrikaans University, Johannesburg.
47. Swabey. (2004). op cit.
48. Labuschagne. (2003). op cit.
49. Clayton. (2005). op cit.
50. Hillson. (1999). op cit.
51. Saari. (2004). op cit.
52. U.S. Department of Defense. (2000). op cit.
53. Chadbourne, S.B.C. (1999). To the Heart of Risk Management: Teaching Project Teams to Combat Risk, Proceedings of the 30th Annual Project Management Institute, Seminars and Symposium, Philadelphia, Pennsylvania, USA.
54. Graham, A. (2003)., Risk Management: Moving the Framework to Implementation: Keys to a Successful Risk Management Implementation Strategy, A Report by the Graham and Deloitte and Touche Site.
55. Chadbourne. (1999). op cit.; Graham. (2003). op cit.
56. U.S. Department of Defense. (2000). op cit.
57. Del Cano and de la Cruz. (2002). op cit.
58. Williams, T.M. (1996). The two-dimensionality of project risk, *International Journal of Project Management*, 14:3.
59. Kerzner, H. (2003). Project Management: A Systems Approach to Planning, Scheduling, and Controlling, 8th edn. Wiley.
60. Labuschagne. (2003). op cit.
61. Hillson, D. (2002). The Risk Breakdown Structure (RBS) as an Aid to Effective Risk Management, Fifth European Project Management Conference, PMI Europe, Cannes, France.
62. Dorofee, A.J., Walker, J.A., Alberts, C.J., Higuera, R.P., Murphy, R.L., and Williams, R.C. (1996). Continuous Risk Management (CRM) Guidebook, Carnegie Mellon University Software Engineering Institute (SEI), US.
63. Porthin, M. (2004). Advanced Case Studies in Risk Management, Thesis for Master of Science in Technology, Helsinki University of Technology, Department of Engineering Physics and Mathematics.

64. Wideman. (1992); Conrow. (2003). op cit.
65. Hillson, D. (2001). Extending the Risk Process to Manage Opportunities, Fourth European Project Management Conference, PMI Europe, London UK.
66. CAN/CSA-Q850-97. (1997). Risk Management: Guidelines for Decision Makers, Ontario, National Standards of Canada, Canadian Standard Association.
67. Hillson, D. (1997). Towards a Risk Maturity Model, *International Journal of Project and Business Risk*, spring, 35–46.

Part III
ERM Technologies

Chapter 7
The Mathematics of Risk Transfer

M. Escobar and L. Seco

Hedge Funds of the Twenty-First Century

Canadian winters are extreme: cold and snow are a fact of everyday life. Canada spends over $1Bn every year removing snow. As one example, consider the city of Montreal. The city spends over $50M every year removing snow, about 3% of its total budget. It does that through a fixed-price contract agreement with a third party, which starts on November 15 and ends in April 15 – the snow season. During this time, the city's exposure to snow removal costs are – to a large degree – predictable. However, snow precipitation outside of this period can become very costly: it is outside of the contractual arrangement, and the city may incur into expenses which may, on a relative basis, exceed the ones during the snow season. The city is exposed to snow financial risk. But snow financial risk affects also other corporations, such as ski resorts. For them, the snow financial risk is opposite: low precipitation during the late part of the fall or early spring will yield operational losses compared to years when snow fall is ample early in the fall or late into the spring. They also face snow financial risk.

Sometime ago, a proposal was launched to partially mitigate this: a snow swap. In this, a city will pay a premium to a dealer when snow is scarce outside the snow season, and receive a premium if snow appears. Similarly, a ski resort will receive payments if snow is scarce and will pay if snow is plentiful. The dealer arranges this, and collects a commission for its services. The dealer has no risk exposure to snow precipitation because it is exchanging offsetting payments between the two parties. The snow swap did not succeed, however, because there was no agreement as to where the measurements for snow precipitation were to occur. The snow financial risk seemed to be solved by the snow swap, but the geographical spread risk could not be absorbed by anyone.

Let us consider the hypothetical following proposition: a group of investors (a fund) gets together, puts up some money upfront (merely as collateral), and decides to take the geographical spread risk. It will pay the city in the case of out-of-season snow falls in the city, and will pay the ski resort in case of no out-of-season snow falls at the resort. By contrast, it will receive payments from both if the opposite occurs. With a nominal payment of $1M, and a nominal fee of 10% ($100,000), the deal will look as follows (Table 7.1):

D.L. Olson, D. Wu (eds.) *New Frontiers in Enterprise Risk Management*,

Table 7.1 Cash flows for the snow swap

Payments	Snow	No-snow
City	–$1M	$1M
Ski resort	$1M	–$1M

Table 7.2 Cash flows for the fund

Event	Cash flow	Probability (%)
Offset payments	$200,000	75
Pays both	–$1,800,000	12.5
Receives from both	$2,200,000	12.5

The difference with the previous, unsuccessful snow swap is that in this case, both the city as well as the ski resort gets to measure the snow precipitation at the place of their choice, with the fund taking the geographical risk. To move ahead with our example, let us assume the snow events in both places are correlated at 50%, and the fund will charge a $200,000 fee for its risk: this means that the cash-flows for the fund will be (Table 7.2):

To get an idea of the quality of these funds, note that the expected return for the $2M the fund had to invest to participate in the swap is $200,000, or 10%, comparable to an investment in the stock market. The standard deviation, however, is 50%, which is more or less comparable to a game of poker. From an investment viewpoint, this is not a very good proposition, as the risk is too high for the expected return. Things become more interesting if the fund decided to do similar swaps in other cities. If 100 independent swaps are considered, for a total of $200M invested, the expected return continues to be 10%, but the standard deviation, as a measure of risk, now drops to 5%. As an investment, this is now better than investing in the stock market and the fund has a future.

But things are slightly better. In our snow fund, we raised $200M to post as collateral for 100 different swap agreements. This was to give rise to an expected return of 10% ($20M) for the period (6 months), with a standard deviation of 5%. Note that in calculating our cash flows, we have neglected the fact that the collateral ($200M) was not to be used except as a guarantee to the counterparties – cities and ski resorts – that our fund would be able to honor its payment obligations even when all deals may turn against the fund. In other words, the collateral is there just to enable the fund to have the right credit rating for the deal. The fund would obtain a rating of AAA, the best possible. But there is no reason to hold the $200M in cash, one could easily invest them in T-Bills (short term interest notes issued by the government of the United States), and hence earn LIBOR, the on-going risk-free interest rate. In this way, our return will be LIBOR+10%, with a standard deviation almost unchanged.

Situations such as this one are becoming common at the beginning of the twenty-first century: a certain investment partnership takes on some risk, in an effort to obtain a return. The risk is often times the result of providing risk mitigation to a third party, but the fund absorbed residual risk, which is often times hard to deal with but it may be diversifiable, such as in our example. These funds, which often times operate in areas where the traditional financial companies (banks, insurance companies, etc.) do not operate, and are sometimes based in domiciles with allow unregulated activities (Cayman, Bermuda, etc.), are generally called hedge funds.

But is this type of activity new? From an abstract point of view, financial activity is an affair in risk transfer. Stocks and bonds, the financial instruments of the nineteenth century, are designed to allow investors to participate in commercial enterprises; stock holders assume market risk, i.e., the risk that the firm does not meet profitability expectations; bond investors are not exposed to that market risk, and only assume default risk, i.e., the risk that the issuing entity cannot meet its financial obligations. This is also called credit risk, and losses can also occur without the company defaulting: a mere credit downgrade will lead to a decrease in the market value of the bond, and hence a loss, realized or not.

In the latter part of the twentieth century, market risk was traded massively through the derivatives market. Investors could buy price protection related to stocks, currencies, interest rates or commodities by purchasing options or other derivatives; some are standard, others are tailor-made and labelled "over-the-counter." At the same time, default (or credit) risk was considered through ad hoc considerations, but was not part of a quantitative treatment, and hence risk transfer of credit risk was not common. Towards the end of the twentieth century, events such as the Russian default, Enron and Worldcom, and the demise of Long Term Capital Management, put credit risk at the forefront of financial institutions, and credit transfer emerged.

Today, credit risk has been regulated in BIS-II, the resolution of the Bank for International Settlements, but the credit market has just started (although at the present time its volumes are very high). A host of new credit products are created everyday. Later in the paper we will explore some of the newest ones, the Collateralized Fund Obligations, or CFOs, designed to provide financing to investors in hedge funds. What is interesting, from a mathematical viewpoint, is that the arrival of new credit-sensitive products is accompanied with new risks, which need to be determined, and priced.

We will review some of the earlier properties of financial risk, and we will focus on the analysis of CFOs as a means to highlight some of the new paradigms that we will likely face in the near future.

Pricing Risk

There are three types of risk: diversifiable risk, tradable risk (or hedgeable risk), and systemic risk. The first type of risk is the one we considered in the snow swap. There was nothing we could do to mitigate it, but building a portfolio of independent risks allowed us to diversify it to the point that it was worth taking. The second type of risk is tradable risk, best explained through the following example. The main difference with respect to our previous example is that, in this case, we will be able to price the risk accurately, as described below.

Imagine the following a very simple hypothetical situation (see Fig. 7.1).

There is an asset (a stock, a home, a currency, etc.) trading today at \$1, which can only be worth \$2 or \$0.50 next year, with equal probability; interest rates are 0%, i.e., borrowing is free. Consider also an investor who may need to buy this asset next year and is therefore concerned with increase in value; for that reason decides to buy insurance in the following form: if the asset raises to \$2, then the insurance policy will pay \$1. If the asset drops in price however, the policy pays nothing. This situation is summarized in Fig. 7.1. One would be tempted to price this insurance policy with a premium obtained through probabilistic considerations, and it would seem that \$0.50 is the price that makes sense.

However, the following argument shows that this is not the case: if the investor paid \$0.50, then the seller of the policy could do implement the following investment strategy: she borrows an additional \$0.10, and buys 60% of the stock. If the stock raises in value, after paying the \$1 and returning the loan, she would make a profit of \$0.10. If, however, the stock drops in price, she will make a net profit of \$0.20, as the policy pays nothing and they only need to return the loan. In other words, \$0.50 is too much, as the issuer of the option will always make a profit: this phenomenon is called arbitrage, and it is a fundamental assumption for pricing theories that arbitrage should not exist (market design assumes that any chance of making free money will be eliminated from the market from smart traders, affecting the price which will immediately reach a non-arbitrage equilibrium.) A simple calculation will show that the no-arbitrage price is exactly \$1/3. As opposed to traditional insurance premiums, financial insurance for tradable risks is not based merely on probabilistic considerations.

This simple example (a "call option") is the basis of the no-arbitrage pricing theory,[1] and we can quickly learn a few things from it. First, the price of a contract that depends on market moves may be replicated with buy/sell strategies, which mimic the contract pay-out but can be carried out with fixed, pre-determined costs. Second, there is a probability of events which is implied by their price, and is perhaps independent of historical events. In our example above, the implied probability of an up-move has to be 66%, and the probability of a down-move is 33%, because with those probabilities we can price the contract taking simple expectations. However, a more profound revision of the previous example will convince the reader with a background in diffusion processes that, if one takes the simple one-step

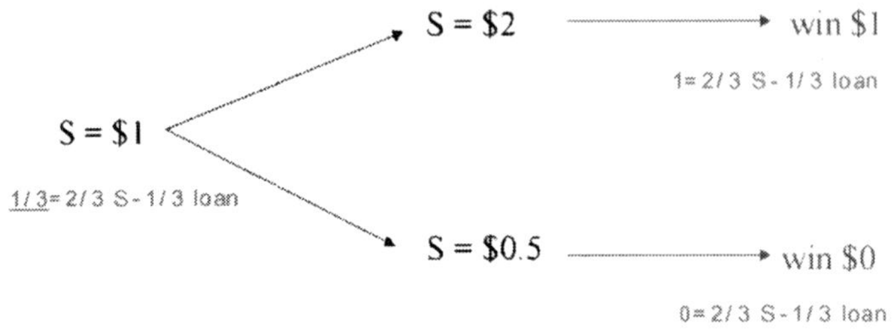

Fig. 7.1 Pricing Fundamentals

example into a continuum of infinitesimal time/price increments, one ends with Brownian motion and associated Kolmogorov forward operator: the heat equation. One will also have a diffusion process for the asset or stock, and an associated diffusion process implied by market prices.

Black, Scholes[2] and Merton[3] derived the analogue of the heat equation and Brownian motion for the case of an option with an underlying stock price that follows the Ito process given by

$$dS = \mu S\,dt + \sigma S\,dW^{P}$$

Where here S denotes the stock price, μ denotes the drift, σ is the volatility, and dW are infinitesimal Brownian increments. An option on a stock is as a contract that will pay a future value at expiration: the payoff depends on the value of the underlying stock S, and will be denoted by $f_0(S)$. We denote by T the expiration time. Note the similarity with our simple example above (in Fig. 7.1), the main difference being that in our case now the stock trades continuously and we could therefore replicate our option by trading the stock continuously. In this case, the Black–Scholes–Merton theory shows that the price of the option contract is obtained by solving the following backward parabolic Partial Differential Equation, or PDE, for all times $t<T$ prior to expiration:

$$\begin{cases} \dfrac{\partial f}{\partial t} + \dfrac{\sigma^2}{2} S^2 \dfrac{\partial^2 f}{\partial S^2} + rS\dfrac{\partial f}{\partial S} - rf = 0 \\ f(S,T) = f0 \end{cases}$$

At first sight, this expression has two counterintuitive features: the absence of μ and the presence of the interest rate r in the PDE. A moment's reflection however, will convince us that this is not entirely surprising: after all, in our example in Fig. 7.1 we already saw that the price of that option is independent of the probabilities of up and down moves of the stock, and it will only depend on the cost of borrowing. This was forced on us by our no-arbitrage assumption.

In more general terms, it turns out that option pricing can be established by taking expectations with respect to a "risk neutral" measure Q, which is perhaps different from the historical measure P. In our particular case, this implies that the solution to the PDE is given by

$$f(S,t) = \frac{1}{\sqrt{2\pi(T-t)}\sigma}\int_0^{\infty} f(u)\exp\left\{\frac{\left(\ln\left(\dfrac{u}{s(L)}\right)-\left(r-\dfrac{\sigma^2}{2}\right)(T-t)\right)^2}{2(T-t)\sigma^2}\right\}du$$

which is easily checked? From this perspective, pricing becomes equivalent to finding risk neutral probabilities and their pay-off expectations, and the PDE above is nothing but the Feynmann–Kac formula for this expectation.

The Black–Scholes–Merton theory also shows that one can replicate the option pay-off by continuously trading the stock so that we always own $-\partial_S f$ units of it.

This signified a tremendous revolution, that won Black and Scholes the Nobel prize for Economics in 1997, as it not only established a pricing mechanism for the booming options and derivative markets, but because it established certainty where there was risk: derivatives could be replicated by buy/sell strategies with predetermined costs.

Their discovery revolutionized market risk perspectives. But Merton, who had re-derived their pricing formalism using stochastic control theory, used this advance to start the modern theory of credit risk. His viewpoint, which we present below, was just as revolutionary.

Merton viewed a firm as shareholders and bond-holders. Bond-holders lent money to the firm, and the firm promised to pay back the loan, with interest. Shareholders own the value of the assets of the firm, minus the value of the debt (or liabilities); but firms have limited liability, which means that if the value of the assets falls below the value of the liabilities, in Merton's view, the firm defaults, shareholders owe nothing and the bond-holders use the remaining value of the assets to recover a portion of their loan. In other words, the shareholders own a call option on the value of the assets of the firm, with a strike price given by the value of the liabilities at the given maturity time of the loan. The timing of his theory, which dates back to 1974, was perfect as the theory of option pricing had just been developed one year earlier, and this opened the ground for credit risk pricing and credit risk derivatives.

Strictly speaking, the Merton approach assumes that the liabilities of a firm (its debt) expire at a certain time, and default could occur only at that time. Black and Cox conceptually refined Merton's proposal by allowing defaults to occur at anytime within the life of the option, creating the "first passage default models."[4] The reason for this modification is that, according to Merton's model, the firm value could dwindle to nearly nothing without triggering a default until much later; all that matters was its level at debt maturity and this is clearly not in the interest of the bond holders. Bond indenture provisions therefore often include safety covenants providing the bond investors with the right to reorganize or foreclose on the firm if the asset value hits some lower threshold for the first time. This threshold could be chosen as the firm's liabilities.

But the largest event in the credit market still had to wait until 1998, when the default of Russia and the menace of the impeachment of President Clinton over the Monica Lewinsky affair threw financial markets into disarray; the Russian default, and worries about the political stability of the United States created a credit crunch as bond investors fled from corporate debt for the more secure treasury bill market, introducing credit spread dislocations of historical proportions. This situation culminated with the collapse of Long Term Capital Management, a multi-billion dollar hedge fund that, anecdotally, had lured Scholes and Merton to their board of directors.

The result of these massive historical events was the explosion of the credit market. In it, financial players seek to buy and sell credit risk, either for insurance and protection in the case of default or bankruptcy of their counter-parties, or to take risk exposure which are considered either cheap or advantageous, and therefore earn above average returns. The financial instruments, which are used in the credit market, are numerous, but two are especially noteworthy: credit default swaps (CDS), and collateralized debt obligations (CDO).

A credit default swap (CDS, see Fig. 7.2) is a contract that provides insurance against the risk of a default by particular company (known as the reference entity). The buyer of the insurance obtains the right to sell a particular bond issued by the company for its par value when a credit event occurs. The bond is known as the reference obligation and the total par value of the bond that can be sold is known as the swap's notional principal. The buyer of the CDS makes periodic payments to the seller until the end of the life of the CDS or until a credit event occurs. A credit event usually requires a final accrual payment by the buyer.

A collateralized debt obligation (CDO) provides a way of creating securities with different risk characteristics from a portfolio of debt instruments. A general example would be, M types of securities are created from a portfolio of N bonds. The first tranche of securities has p_1 of the total bond principal and absorbs all credit losses from the portfolio during the life of the CDO until they have reached p_1 of the total bond principal. The second tranche has p_2 of the principal and absorbs all losses during the life of the CDO in excess of p_1 of the principal up to a maximum of p_1+p_2 of the principal. The last tranche has p_M of the principal absorbs all losses in excess of $p_1+p_2+\ldots+p_{M-1}$ of the principal. The reason these instruments exist is that banks with large loan books, can use CDO's to effectively slice the default risk in those portfolios with credit-linked securities (the different tranches) and sell them to investors (who are often times hedge funds) in packets which exhibit very different risk profiles: from the highly risk of the top – mezzanine – tranche (which will earn a higher fee spread), to the very secure last tranche, which will earn perhaps a minimal fee. One can also easily imagine similar situations where the underlying securities for the tranches are mortgages, not bonds. Many hedge funds are active participants

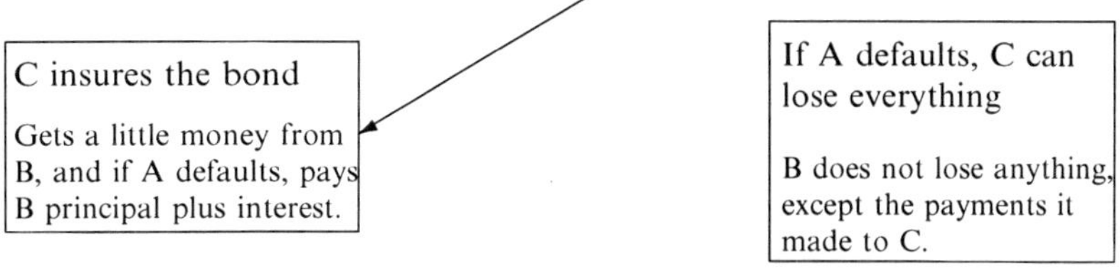

Fig. 7.2 A credit default swap

as counterparties to these type of deals, and the hedge fund style that does this is called mortgage arbitrage (here, the term arbitrage is abused, in the sense that there is no real arbitrage, just a statistical arbitrage as the tranches pay more on average than other instruments with similar risk profiles.)

The valuation of such structures is based on computing the probability distribution of the event "*m*th default." This is technically difficult because it requires one to handle the multivariate distribution of defaults, and generally most credit models fail to reliably capture multiple defaults. There are basically two procedures for evaluating these basket derivatives, multifactor copula models[5] and intensity models.[6]

Escobar and Seco present a partial differential equation (PDE) procedure for valuing a family of credit derivatives work within the structural framework, where the default event is associated to whether the minimum value of an stochastic processes (firm's asset value) have reached a benchmark, usually the firm's liabilities.[7] More precisely, they assume:

- The interest rate, r is constant
- The value of the assets, $V_i(t)$, follows an Ito process with constant drift r and volatility $\sigma_i^2(t)$:

$$dV_i = rV_i dt + \sigma_i(t)\, V_i dW_i(t).$$

- Firm i defaults as soon as its asset value $V_i(t)$ reaches the liabilities, denoted as $D_i(t)$. This is the definition of default within the structural framework.[8]

Define $X(t)=ln\ V(t)$ as the n-dimensional Brownian motion vector with drift $\mu = (\mu_{1,\ldots,}\mu_n)$, $\mu_1 = r-\sigma_i^2(t)/2$ and co-variances $\sigma_{i,j}(t)$. The running minimum is defined as:

$$\underline{X}_i(t) = \min_{0 \le s \le t} X_i(s)$$

They show that the price is a function of the multivariate density p of the vector of joint Brownian motions and Brownian minimums (it can be easily extended to maximums)

$$\begin{aligned} &P(X_1(t)\in dx_1,\ldots,X_n(t)\in dx_n, \underline{X}_1(t) > m_1,\ldots,\underline{X}_n(t) > m_n) \\ &= p(x_1,\ldots,x_n,t,m_1,\ldots,m_n,\mu,\Sigma)dx_1\ldots dx_n, \end{aligned}$$

For the case of more than two underlying components, p is the solution of a PDE with absorbing and boundary conditions (a Fokker–Planck equation) given by

$$\begin{cases} \dfrac{\partial p}{\partial t} = -\sum_{i=1}^{n} \mu_i(t) \bullet \dfrac{\partial p}{\partial x_i} + \sum_{i,j=1}^{n} \dfrac{\sigma_{ij}(t)}{2} \bullet \dfrac{\partial^2 p}{\partial x_i \partial x_j} \\ p(x,t=0) = \Pi_{i=1}^{n} \delta(x_i) \\ p(x_i,\ldots,x_i = m_i,\ldots,x_n,t) = 0, \qquad i = 1,\ldots,n \\ x_i > m_i, m_i \le 0, \qquad i = 1,\ldots,n \end{cases}$$

In a one-dimensional setting, assuming constant drift and volatility, the solution is closely related to the inverse Gaussian distribution

$$p(\underline{X}_1(t) \geq m_1) = \Phi\left(\frac{m_1 - \mu t}{\sigma\sqrt{t}}\right) - \exp\left\{\frac{2m_1\mu}{\sigma^2}\right\}\Phi\left(\frac{-m_1 - \mu t}{\sigma\sqrt{t}}\right).$$

He, Keastead and Rebholz provided an explicit formula for the joint density for the case of two Brownian motions, or two underlying stocks.[9] Formulas for the general n-dimensional case remain unknown.

Collateralized Fund Obligations

Let us consider now our next, and final, example, which will bring together the hedge fund example of Sect. 1, and the credit derivatives of the previous one.

There are over 10,000 hedge funds in the world. Many of them try to obtain returns independent of market directions but the majority of them, unlike our snow fund example; they try to do it through financial instruments which are traded in the financial exchanges: equities, bonds, derivatives, futures, etc. They often times try to extract return from situations of inefficiency: for example, they would buy a stock – also termed "taking a long position" – which they perceive is undervalued with respect to the value of its underlying assets, and would sell short – borrow, or "take a short position" – a stock they perceive is overvalued with respect to the value of their assets, expecting a convergence to their fair price, hence obtaining return in the long term, and not being subject to the direction of the stock markets, which will probably affect their long and short stock portfolio the same way. Others may do the same with bonds: there will be bonds which will earn slightly higher interest than others, simply because there are less numbers of them, and hence trade slightly cheaper than other bond issues, large and popular. Other funds, will monitor mergers between companies and try to benefit from the convergence in equity value and bond value that takes place after a merger by taking long and short positions in the companies' stocks and/or bonds. And we already mentioned those funds who try to benefit from the slightly higher interest earning properties of tranches of mortgage pools with respect to borrowing interest rates.

All of this gives investors with a wide universe to make investment choices. Let us imagine that each of those funds gives us returns similar to the snow fund: LIBOR+10% expected return, and 5% standard deviation. A portfolio of such investments will give us the same expected return, but the standard deviation is likely to decrease, because their return streams will be uncorrelated with each other. These investments, at least on paper, look extremely attractive. However, for the risk diversification to truly exist, one need to invest in a sufficiently large number of them; there is always the possibility of fraud – these funds are largely unregulated and unsupervised-, convergence-based trades may take a long time before they work, and deviations from our mathematical expectations may occur in the short term, etc. And, unlike stocks, or mutual funds, these funds often require minimum investments of the order of $1M. That means that diversifying amongst them will require substantial amounts of money.

There are several ways to invest in hedge funds: the three more frequent ones are:

- Fund of funds. They are simple portfolio of hedge funds. The assets of the fund-of-funds are invested in a number of hedge funds (from 10 to 100). The chosen hedge funds are usually of a variety of different trading styles to achieve maximum diversification.
- Leveraged products. Imagine an investor has $10M to invest in hedge funds. Instead of allocating $1M to a portfolio of ten different hedge funds, they may borrow an additional $30M from lenders, and invest the total amount $40M, in 40 different hedge funds. The investor pays interest to the lenders, and keeps the remaining gains. We will describe these types of investments in higher detail below.
- Guaranteed products. They are term products, issued at maturities of 5 years, for example. The investor is guaranteed their money back after that period – 5 years – with no interest of course. In lieu of interest, they will receive a variable amount, which will be linked to the performance of the hedge fund portfolio. If the performance is good, the payment may be very large. If not, they simply get their money back, without interest. They are issued by a high-quality institution, who will take the investor's assets, invest a portion on a bond that will guarantee the principal at maturity of the note, and invest the rest – the interest earnings that the investor gives up – in a leveraged product we described earlier, to maximize the return of the investor's assets. They are very popular with retail products, as well as for institutions who can only invest in bonds, as these can be structured as a bond (Fig. 7.3).

Leveraged products are attractive because of the following. Back in our snow swap example, expected return was LIBOR+10%. LIBOR is the base lending rate. With proper collateral, lending at LIBOR+1% is very feasible. That means that we can borrow at LIBOR+1%, and invest at LIBOR+10%. In other words, for every dollar we borrow we will make 9 cents for free, after paying all fees. Therefore, investors should want to borrow as much as possible and invest all the borrowed amounts. If it was not for the standard deviation, indeed that would be fantastic. The standard deviation, as well as other risks, limits the borrowing capacity and appetite of investors.

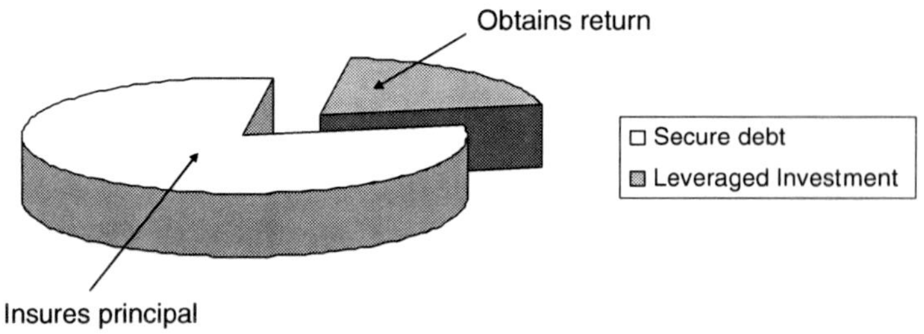

Fig. 7.3 Anatomy of a guarantee

Leverage products are most often offered by banks; they lend to investors, investors take the first risk that the funds do not perform as expected, but the banks face the secondary risk that the losses exceed the equity provided by the investors and a portion of the lent amount may also be lost. Let us just mention that a number of safety measures are put in place by the banks to prevent this from happening, such as partial liquidation of the investments as the performance deviates from expectations. Recently, leverage products are organized by banks, but the borrowed amount is done through outside investors, through bond tranches very similar to the CDO structures we reviewed in our previous section. To explain how it works, we consider the case of the Diversified Strategies CFO SA, launched in 2002. Investors provided equity worth $66.3M, which supported an investment of $250M in hedge funds. The additional funds ($183.70M) were raised through three bond tranche issues, as follows:

- AAA tranche ($125M)
- A tranche ($32.5M)
- BBB tranche ($26.2M)

We are not going to go in great detail into the details of the transaction; we will simply mention that the tranche structure is similar to a CDO; the bond investors provide the capital, and upon maturity get their principal and interest. In the case the CFO structure fails to have enough assets to pay back its debts; the CFO will enter into default. In that scenario, the AAA-tranche investors are first in line to get their money back (principal plus interest). Next in line will be the A tranche, and the BBB tranche will be last in line. In a default situation, the equity investors would have lost all their assets. Because of the difference in default risk, each of the bond investors receives different interest payments, highest for the BBB tranche, lowest for the AAA investors.

The interest payment their risk is worth – a credit spread – is a very interesting risk pricing problem. It is easier than the CDO pricing problem we described earlier, since here we only need to look at the performance of the entire fund performance, and we do not need to enter into individual default numbers. In fact, with the assumption that the fund returns are normally distributed, it is very easy to determine the credit spread. The probability of default will be given by the quantile of a normally distributed Ito process, which has a simple risk-neutral analog, and we just price that using expectation under the risk neutral measure. In the case of the Diversified Strategies CFO, the respective interest rates were as follows:

- AAA tranche. LIBOR+0.60%
- A tranche: LIBOR+1.60%
- BBB tranche: LIBOR+2.80%

Non-Gaussian Returns

Many of the mathematical theories that study financial problems make a fundamental assumption: returns are normally- or log normally-distributed. It is a reasonable assumption that permits robust mathematical modeling. However, non-Gaussian properties of real market data are a fact, and considerable effort goes into the mathematical modeling of such situations that relaxes the Gaussian assumptions. In our context, the non-Gaussian nature of real markets exhibits itself in two main ways:

Non-Gaussian marginal distributions. The graph below depicts the monthly return frequency of a hedge fund index, the CSFB fixed income arbitrage index (Fig. 7.4):

There are clear non-Gaussian features, for example, fat tails, also called Kurtosis, which in this case we can trace back to the events of 1998, and asymmetry, also know as skewness. This second feature comes naturally for most series, as return can not go below-1, event of total lost, but still could theoretically be as positive as wanted. This left-bounded range, together with the drive of companies to emphasize above average growth, leads to asymmetric distributions for the returns. Other common but difficult to graph marginal features are: time dependent return volatilities, trends in the return's mean as well as cycles, just to mention a few Non-Gaussian dependence structures. If one tries to determine the dependence amongst several assets fitting it to a correlation matrix, one often finds that at certain times, the simultaneous occurrence of certain events does not correspond to a correlation measure.

This is a high-dimensional phenomenon, which is not so easy to describe graphically, but we will try to explain with the following sets of pictures (Fig. 7.5).

In the first one, we see the correlation matrix of a hedge fund universe. The matrix is read from left to right and from the bottom to the top, and numbers close to +1 or −1 are represented with a dark pixel, whereas numbers close to 0 are represented with a light pixel. We see that correlations are mostly low, with few instances of high correlations. This is consistent with our view of hedge funds.

The second picture represents the correlations taking into account only months of unusual returns; say months where the returns exceed the Gaussian safety band of 2 standard deviations from the mean. We see a very different correlation struc-

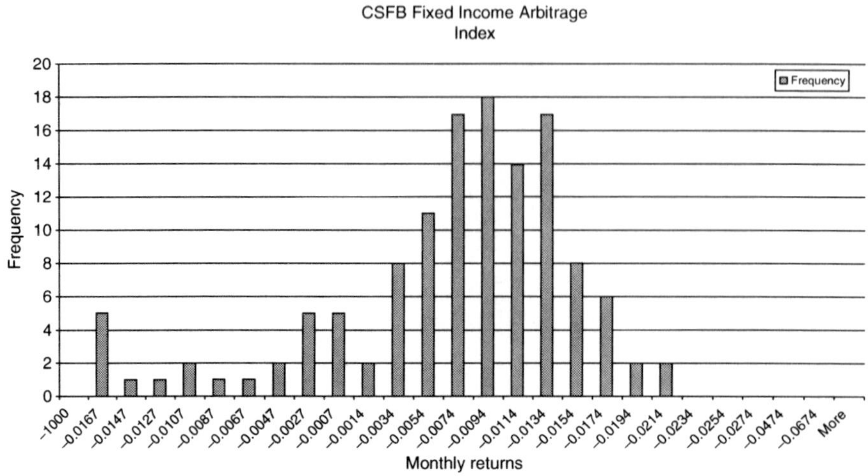

Fig. 7.4 Histogram

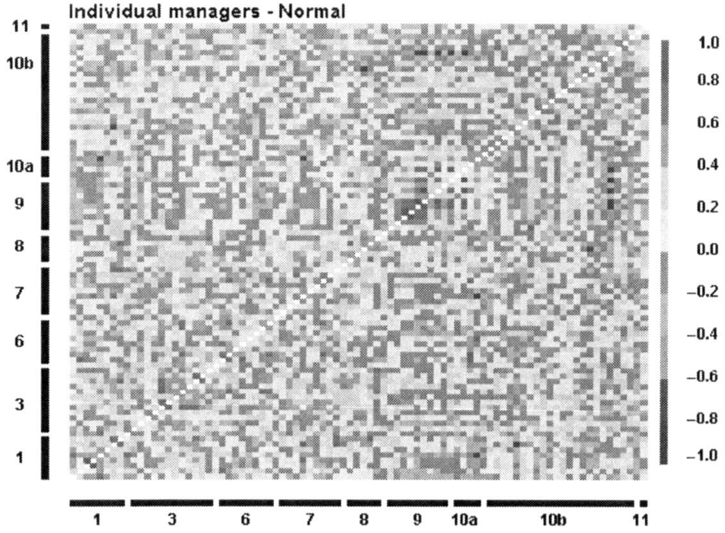

Fig. 7.5 Correlations – normal

ture, with increased high correlation numbers. We denote this as correlation risk, or correlation breakdown phenomena (Fig. 7.6).

Given that correlation is one of the fundamental properties of hedge fund investing-remember our snow fund, correlation breakdown is a very damaging non-Gaussian effect for hedge fund portfolios and related structures.

This previous presentation assumed correlation as the right measure to describe dependence. The very emphasize in the correlation as "the measure" to describe dependence structures has been strongly challenge since the nineties by the mathematically more general notion of Copulas, for which the Gaussian correlation is a particular case.[10] This area of research is quite complex from a mathematical viewpoint and at the same time is difficult to provide a meaning and a reliable estimation framework to the various parameters that appear; therefore it is still very much under development.

These non-Gaussian dependence structure features have an important impact all over mathematical finance, leading to interesting results on apparently unrelated issues like Portfolio theory and Derivative Pricing. On the former, Buckley–Saunders–Seco studied the implications for Portfolio Theory of assuming multidimensional Gaussian-mixture distributions for the underlying returns[11]

The following feature shows contour plots of probability density functions when working with multidimensional Gaussian Mixtures. The top row contains two bivariate Gaussian distributions potentially for the tranquil (left) and distressed (right) regimes. The bottom row illustrates the composite Gaussian mixture distribution obtained by mixing the two distributions from the top row (left) and a bivariate normal distribution with the same means and variance/covariance matrix as the composite (right).

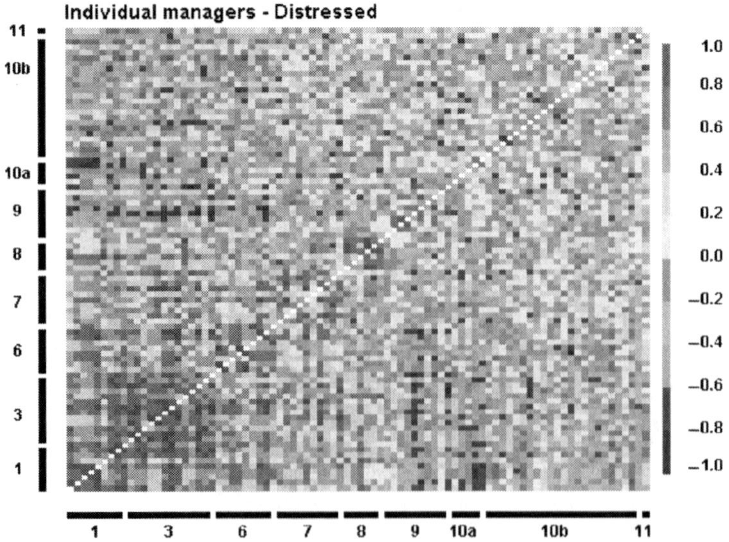

Fig. 7.6 Correlations – distress

Investment opportunity sets for the tranquil and distressed regimes superimposed onto the same plot. The axes are the portfolio mean and variance (Fig. 7.7).

Typically the Gaussian Mixture approach optimal portfolio will be sub-optimal with respect to both the tranquil and distressed mean-variance objectives

On the later, its effect on the default probabilities, and associated credit spreads for CFO tranches has been studied in Ansejo et al.[12] More precisely, it is shown there that the credit ratings of CFO tranches are sensitive to the correlation breakdown probability, as summarized by Figs. 7.8 and 7.9. Figure 7.8 shows that the probabilities of default spread over a substantial range when changing the probability of a distress month 1-p (market conditions). For example the mezzanine tranche probability of default could go from 2 to 9%. Figure 7.9 shows the sensitivities of the spread yield to the market condition parameter p, which present a similar behavior to probabilities of default.

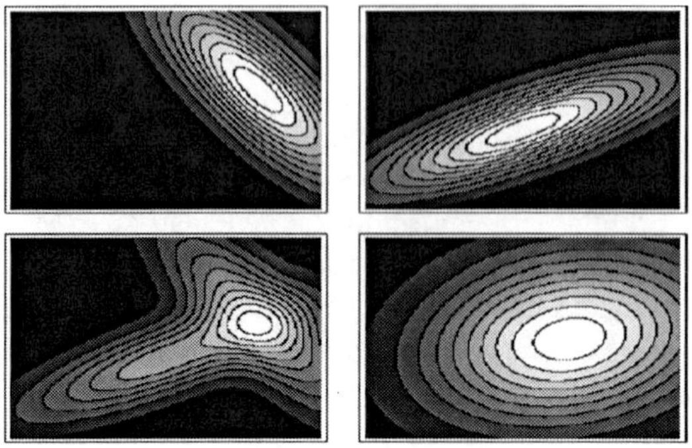

Fig. 7.7 Non Gaussian multivariate

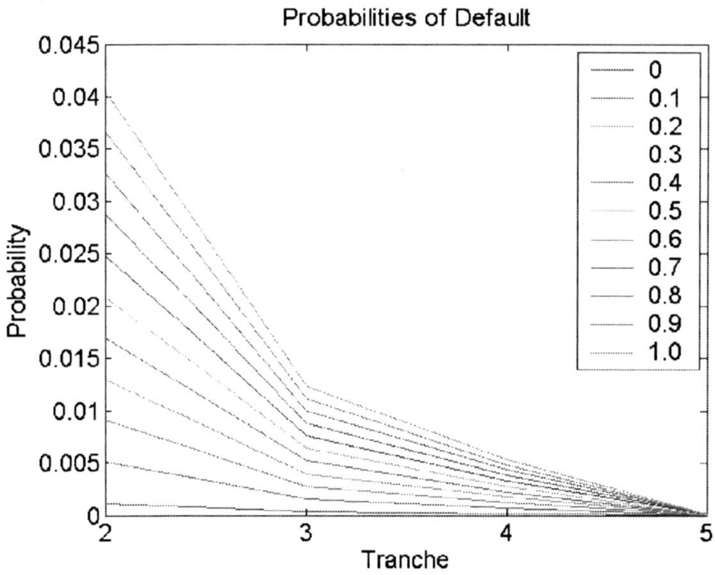

Fig. 7.8 Probability of default

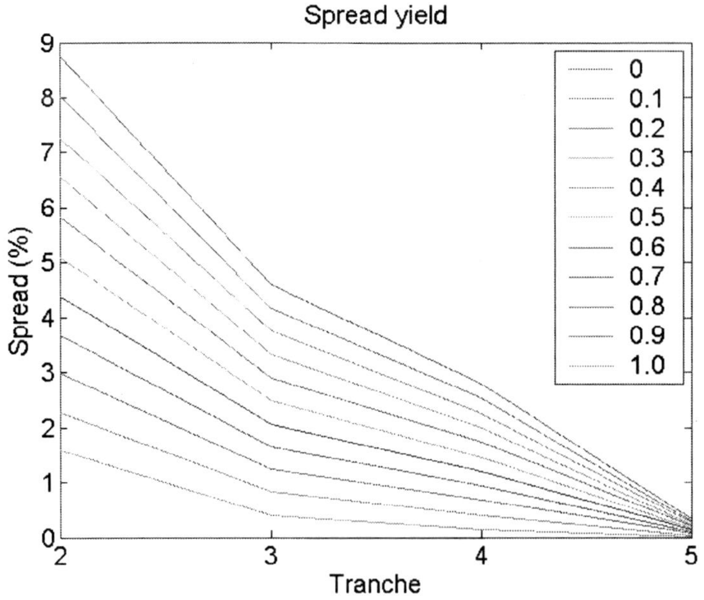

Fig. 7.9 Spread yield

Challenges in the New Century

There are important challenges ahead for academics and practitioners in the mathematics of risk transfer, some of which are causing distress in financial markets everywhere since the very beginning of the century. A whole book would be a minimum to explain in detail the nature of such challenges; here we aim at exposing them as well as mentioning some of the recent works on those issues.

The Curse of Dimensionality

The curse of dimensionality is a term coined by Richard Bellman to describe the problem caused by the increase in volume associated with adding extra dimensions to a (mathematical) space. For example, 100 evenly-spaced sample points (i.e., from daily stock prices) suffice to sample a unit interval with no more than 0.01 distance between points; an equivalent sampling of a ten-dimensional unit hypercube with a lattice with a spacing of 0.01 between adjacent points would require $10^{2}0$ sample points: thus, in some sense, the ten-dimensional hypercube can be said to be a factor of 10^{8} "larger" than the unit interval.

Another way to realize the "vastness" of high-dimensional Euclidean space is to compare the size of the unit sphere with the unit cube as the dimension of the space increases: as the dimension increases, the unit sphere becomes an insignificant volume relative to that of the unit cube; thus, in some sense, nearly all of the high-dimensional space is "far away" from the centre, in other words, the high-dimensional unit space can be said to consist almost entirely of the "corners" of the hypercube, with almost no "middle."

The curse of dimensionality is a significant obstacle for modeling and pricing financial products. The reasons are various, in first place, no amount of available data points could fill up the vastness of the space implied by the joint behavior of hundreds (as in the case of a CFO), sometime thousands (common for CDO squares and portfolio theory), of companies. On top of this space-curse, there is the time factor effect. The stochastic nature of financial products leads to a second direction of dimensionality: time. Unfortunately, the time component has been downplayed for ages by relying on first and/or second moment autoregressive processes. Nowadays there is enough evidence to show the richness of time behavior is far more complex and it requires extending the ideas of Copulas to the very time relationship within stock prices. These matricial (dynamic) copulas (columns and rows denoting space and time respectively) are being studied and they are in a very initial stage of development.

An even more serious issue comes into play when trying to calibrate the parameters of even very simple models like the discrete-time multivariate Garch or the continuous-time Wishart processes. Calibration is a statistical exercise that requires consistency (eventual convergence to the actual unknown parameters) but more vital for multidimensional problems, efficiency (a quick convergence to the true parameters). It is well known since the beginning of the twentieth century that the most efficient calibration method the maximum likelihood. The drawback, the speed of its convergence depends on the number of parameters to be estimated. In other words, when calibrating multidimensional models, the sample size needed to achieve the desire closeness to the true parameters has to be larger than what is needed to achieve the same level for unidimensional data. The reason being that not only the parameters describing the marginal have to be calibrated but also those describing the dependence structure (Copula). For example, in the simple case of a Gaussian multivariate, the total marginal parameters are 2n while the copula parameters are $n(n-1)/2$, order n^2.

Too Many Features as Sources of Randomness

Exacerbating both the difficulty for proper estimation and the lack of data due to dimensionality is the richness of financial data features. Since the 1980s for discrete-time models and popular on the 1990s for continuous-time model is the feature of stochastic volatility. A purely unidimensional problem but with enough complexity to keep pushing publications decades to come. Some of the difficulties come from the unobservable nature of the volatility, which implies not only estimating parameters but also requiring filtering to obtain the hidden process.

From the very beginning of the new century a new breed of stochastic unobservable features have been nurtured by the academic and backed up by evidence from practitioners. Among these stochastic correlations, the one among stock prices is currently the most popular, but notice that it involves a whole set of, roughly, n^2 hidden processes which require calibration and filtration. Some new stochastic features have been listed quite recently, these are: stochastic covariation and correlation between volatilities, between stock prices and cross volatilities and between stock prices and correlations themselves. The next figure shows these features in the context of two well known stock prices.

Each of those stochastic features has various implications not only for risk management objectives but also in the pricing of risk-oriented derivatives as those explained in this document. Failure to proper model stocks and therefore to price financial products inevitably leads to market unexpected adjustment with the corresponding chaos implied. This is one of the main reasons for the big losses in the credit market during the year 2007; at the core of these losses was the mismanagement of complex but popular products like CDOs and CFOs. These products depend on hundred of companies for which no model has been found capable of being simple and, at the same time, explaining their joint behavior.

End Notes

1. Hull, J., and White, A. (2004). Valuation of a CDO and nth to default CDS without Monte Carlo simulation, *Journal of Derivatives* 12:2, 8–23.
2. Black, F., and Scholes, M.S. (1973). The pricing of options and corporate liabilities, *JPE* 81, 81–98.
3. Merton, R.C. (1974). On the pricing of corporate debt: The risk structure of interest rate, *Journal of Finance*, 29, 449–470.
4. Black, F., and Cox, J.C. (1976). Valuing corporate securities: some effects of bond indenture provisions, *AFAJ* 31, 351–367.
5. Li, D.X. (2000). On default correlation: A copula approach, *Journal of Fixed Income,* 9, 43–54; Laurent, J.P., and Gregory, J. (2003). Basket default swaps, CDO's and factor copulas, Working Paper, ISFA Actuarial School, University of Lyon.
6. Duffie, D., and Garland, N. (2001). Risk and valuation of CDO, *Financial Analysts J.* 57:1, 41–59.
7. Escobar, M., and Seco, L. (2006). A partial differential equation for credit derivatives pricing, *Centre de Recherches Mathematiques*, 41, Winter.
8. Merton, R. (1974). On the pricing of corporate debt: the risk structure of interest rates, *Journal of Finance* 29, 449–470; Black and Cox. (1976). op cit.; Giesecke, K. (2003). Default and information, Working paper.
9. He, H., Keirstead, W., and Rebholz, J. (1998). Double lookbacks, *Journal of Mathematical Finance,* 8, 201–228.
10. Harry, J. (1997). Multivariate Models and Dependence Structures. Chapman and Hall/CRC.
11. Buckley, I.R.C., Saunders, D., and Seco, L. (2008). Portfolio optimization when assets have the Gaussian mixture distribution, *European Journal of Operations Research*, 185:3, 1434–1461.
12. Ansejo, U., Bergara, A., Escobar, M., and Seco, L. (2006). Correlation breakdown in the valuation of collateralized debt obligations, *Journal of Alternative Investments*, Winter.

Chapter 8
Stable Models in Risk Management

P. Olivares

Introduction

It is a well known fact that the Gaussian assumption on market data is not supported by empirical evidence. Particularly, the presence of skewness and a large kurtosis can dramatically affect the risk management analysis, specially, the Value at Risk (VaR) calculation through quantile estimators.

In this context stable, generalized hyperbolic and Gaussian mixing distributions have been used with considerable success in order to explain asymmetry and heavy tail phenomena.

The presence of heavy tails also affects standard estimation and model testing procedures, due to the frequent presence of "outliers," calling for more robust methods.

In the 1960s Mandelbrot and Fama[1] applied α-stable laws to the modeling of financial data. The family of stable distributions not only describes heavy tails and asymmetric behavior but also, the dependency on four parameters allows more flexibility in the fitting and testing of stable models to empirical data.

Another nice property is that stable laws have domain of attraction, i.e., limits of sums of independent identically distributed random variables, under mild assumptions are also stables after a suitable renormalization.

The stable distribution has nevertheless two major drawbacks: the density probability function has no explicit form except in the cases of the Cauchy and the Normal laws. Numerical methods are needed to compute it. Also, second and higher moments do not exist; which constitutes a challenge to most statistical methods.

In the next section the family of stable laws and its properties are introduced. The next section reviews some calibration and simulation methods for stable distributions. Next, a maximum likelihood approach (m.l.e.) is considered under the framework of ARMA processes driven by stable noises. Asymptotic properties are studied and numerical methods are discussed. Finally, we present some simulation results for stable GARCH processes. The Value at Risk (VaR) for these stable models is calculated and compared with its Gaussian counterpart, revealing important differences between them. The procedure is also illustrated in real financial data.

D.L. Olson, D. Wu (eds.) *New Frontiers in Enterprise Risk Management*,

Stable Laws: Simulation and Calibration

In this section we introduce the stable distribution, some of its properties, different parameterizations and simulation techniques.

A stable random variable X can be defined as follows:

Let a and b be two real positive numbers and X_1 and X_2 be independent random variables equally distributed to X. There exist $c \in \mathbf{R}^+$ and $d \in \mathbf{R}$ such that $aX_1 + bX_2 = cX + d$ in distribution. Equivalent characterizations are also possible.

A random variable X with stable distribution and parameters $(\alpha, \beta, \sigma, \mu)$ is denoted as $S(\alpha, \beta, \sigma, \mu)$.

The interpretation of the parameters is as follows: α is a tail parameter,[2] β is a coefficient of skewness, σ is a scale parameter and μ is a location parameter.

The tail property is expressed for $\alpha \in (0, 2)$ as:

$$\lim X^{\alpha} P(X > x) = C_{\alpha}(1+\beta)\sigma^{\alpha} \tag{1}$$

where the limit is taken when x goes to infinity. C_α is a constant depending on α. In particular this property implies that moments of order smaller than α do not exist.

Another interesting property stable laws have is self-similarity. Namely, a change in the time scale at which we observe a sequence of stable random variables still produces a stable distribution. It is particularly useful to treat financial data under different time scales. Note also that the Gaussian law is included in the family of stable laws.

The characteristic function (CF) of stable laws is not continuous with respect to the parameters at $\alpha = 1$. A useful parameterization solves this problem.[3] The tail index and the location parameter in this approach coincide with the standard parameterization. A Monte Carlo generation of stable random numbers is given by means of a suitable nonlinear transform of a pair of independent uniform and exponentially random variables.[4] In Fig. 8.1 it is shown a empirical density function obtained from simulated data vs. the density function obtained by inverting the characteristic function. Note that both functions are reasonably close.

The density of a stable law is calculated using the inverse Fourier transform. As it is a peaked function, the computation of the cumulative function requires some care. A numerical method is applied in order to compute the corresponding area under the curve after dividing this area into two parts by the point where the density function attains its maximum value.

In order to estimate the parameters of stable distributions several methods are available. We group them according to the criterion used in the estimation. An extensive review on the methods, comparison performance and application to financial series is available.[5]

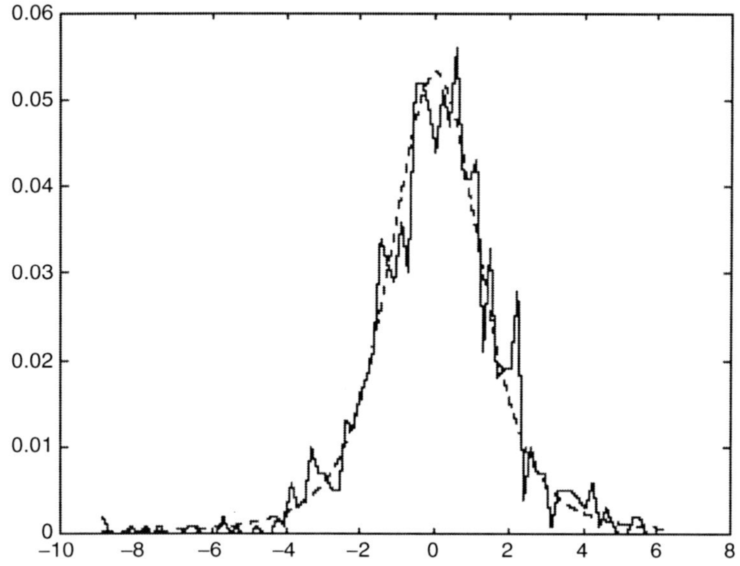

Fig. 8.1 In *continuous line* an empirical stable density with $\alpha = 1.5$ is obtained from simulated data using Weron's technique. In *discontinuous line* the approximated density function using Nolan's approach

Tail Based Methods

Tail estimation methods estimate the tail index α by using the information about the behavior of extreme data.

A simple approach is to consider, taking into account (1), the regression equation:

$$\log P(X > x) = K_{\alpha}(1+\beta)\sigma - \alpha \log x \tag{2}$$

for x large enough. Then the slope α is estimated using standard least squares technique. Expression (1) is true only for large values of x, hence, in practice, it is difficult to assess whether we are in the tail of the distribution. Moreover it depends on the value of the unknown parameter α. On the other hand, if we go farther in the tail fewer points are available for the estimates. In this sense, empirical studies suggest to start from the 90% quantile. In simulation studies the method is reported to overestimate α for values larger than 1.5, especially when the data achieve an asymmetric behavior. The Hill estimator is based on the differences between logarithms of the order statistics is also considered.[6] Its asymptotic confidence interval is known. A critical issue is the choice of the window size k. It is a compromise between the position in the extreme of the tail and the variance of the estimator. Indeed, the window size needs to be small enough to capture the tail position and large enough to control the variance. Numerical studies report the need of large sizes to achieve accurate results.

Quantile and Moment Methods

The method is based on quantile estimation. The main idea is to use differences in the quantile distribution properly normalized in order to get rid dependence on location and scale parameters. Then, two functions on α and β are numerically calculated from the sample quantiles values and inverted to get the corresponding parameter estimates.

An interpolation algorithm allows to get more precise functional values. The idea goes back to McCulloch (1986).[7]

A critical point here is the procedure established in order to calculate the in verse function on the index set into the parametric space. Tables are available to this end.[8] Proceeding by bilinear interpolation the estimates are obtained. A simpler alternative to DuMouchel tables is to construct a grid of 100×100 points with the values of the indices.

Once the sample index is calculated, the nearest tabulated index is taken and its corresponding parameter is chosen. For more precision, a rather sophisticated inversion method is implemented. It consists in finding the solution by moving through segments of the grid of points (α, β). Precise tabulated values of ν require a large amount of computation, though it is processed only once.

Method of L-Moments

The method of l-moments consists in matching sample weighted quantiles to the theoretical one. Moments put a greater weight in the tails of the distribution; therefore they are more affected by the heavy tail phenomena, which is not the case of l moments. That is particularly true for stable laws where some moments do not exist. Moreover l-moments exist when the mean of the distribution is finite, which seems to be the case in most stable financial applications.

L-moments are defined, for a random variable X with cumulative distribution function F, as:

$$M_{p,r,s} = EX^p[F(X)]^r[1-F(X)]^s$$

L-moments can be viewed as conventional moments weighted by polynomials on u and 1 - u.[9]

L-moments themselves are difficult to interpret, however certain linear combinations of them can be viewed in terms of a location parameter $\lambda_1 = \alpha_0$, a scale parameter $\lambda_2=\alpha_0-2\alpha_1$ or $2\beta_1-\beta_0$, a skewness parameter $\lambda_3 = 6\beta_2 \_ 6\beta_1 + \beta_0$ and a kurtosis parameter $\lambda_4=\alpha_0-12\alpha_1+30\alpha_2-20\alpha_3$.

A natural estimator for the parameters is constructed. Though exact distributions of the estimators are difficult to obtain, and confidence intervals are not, in general available, they can be obtained for large sample approximation using asymptotic theory. For most standard distributions, L-moments estimators and quantiles are asymptotically normal, hence we can find standard errors and confidence intervals.

For stable distributions only approximated theoretical l-moments can be obtained. The difference with the general procedure is that equations matching theoretical and sample moments should to be solved numerically As in the McCulloch case a table is constructed relating parameters α and β with the theoretical l-moments for $\mu = 0$ and $\sigma = 1$. To summarize, the steps in the calculation of l-moments are:

- Calculate sample probability weighted moments
- Calculate sample l-moments
- For a given set of parameters (α, β, μ, σ) calculate the approximated density function by inversion in a suitable grid of points
- Calculate the corresponding cumulative distribution function and the corresponding quantile function
- Calculate numerically, by a trapezoidal method, the expected values $E(X_{r:k})$

For applications to Risk Management and quantile estimation based on l-moments have been studied.[10] Theoretical optimal properties of l – moment estimators have been studied.[11]

Maximum Likelihood Method

Classical m.l.e. has long been implemented for stable distributions.[12] The main difficulty in the estimation is that a closed form of the density is unknown. Probability density function (p.d.f.) can be approximated by inverting the characteristic function via Fast Fourier Transform. Other related method relies in the Zolotarev's integral representation. Once the p.d.f. is calculated on a grid, a quasi-Newton method is implemented to maximize the likelihood:

$$l(\alpha,\beta,\theta,\zeta) = \sum \log f(X_i;\alpha,\beta,\theta,\zeta)$$

in the corresponding four dimensional parametric space.

As most quasi-Newton methods, the idea is to construct an approximation of the inverse Hessian using the information gathered at the descent process, driven by the gradient. The current approximation converges to the inverse of the Hessian like in the classical Newton method but without the necessity to calculate it at every point, which has a high computational cost. Two stopping criteria are used; a limited number of evaluations and the amount of the increment in the likelihood. McCulloch estimators are considered for a starting point. Consistency, asymptotic normality and efficiency are well known properties of the m.l.e.

Monte Carlo Markov Chain Simulated Annealing Method

An alternative to ascent methods is the Monte Carlo Markov Chain (MCMC) simulated annealing approach. The main idea involved is to construct a grid on the parametric space and find the maximum by moving through neighbor points in the grid. The dynamic in moving from one point to another is as follows:

Starting from any point, among its neighbors, it is chosen at random with equal probability one of them and, if the likelihood evaluated at this point is greater than the previous one, the system will move to it with a certain probability. Repeating the process, a reversible Markov Chain is constructed whose stationary probability law is the desired one. This can be done using the Hansting Metropolis Algorithm. It turns out that the limit probability law depends on a parameter called temperature. In order to assure the probability law charges only optimum points the temperature is raised slowly to infinity. The maximum of the log-likelihood given in (1.2) is calculated now on the set of points in the parametric space belonging to the grid.

Sample Characteristic Function Methods

The main idea is to minimize the distance between the CF and the empirical characteristic function (ECF) on an appropriate norm. While the minimization procedure implies a lot of calculations, some simpler variants, exploiting particular relations derived from CF in stable laws have been used. By the Law of Large Numbers the ECF is a consistent estimator of the theoretical CF.

The method finds the minimum of the difference between both functions on the parametric space on a weighted given norm. Optimal selection of discrete points t_1, $t_2, \ldots, t_p$ have been discussed.[13] A weighting function W(t) with density w(t) with respect to the Lebesque measure, typically an exponential law, is selected. Another advantage of ECF methods is that they can be extended to non i.i.d. cases, particularly to dynamic models with heteroscedastic volatility, by considering a multivariate or conditional CF instead. Asymptotic properties as consistency and normality still hold in this general case.

Regression Method

A regression type method is available.[14] From the general expression of the CF a linear expression is obtained between certain functionals of the CF and the parameters α and σ, then, using the ECF, it is fitted a linear regression to estimate α which is precisely the slope of the straight line and then σ. Another linear expression is obtained from the CF relating the parameters β and μ together with nonlinear relationship on α and σ, then once the later are estimated we proceed to estimate the first ones by fitting a linear regression. The first adjustment can be repeated a number of times to achieve better precision in the estimation. We applied a variant, consisting in a recursive estimation of parameters, once an estimation set is obtained; the data are standardized by subtraction of the location parameter and dividing by the scale parameter. A first equation is obtained from general expression of the stable CF namely:

$$\log(\log\varphi(t)^2) = \log(2\sigma^\alpha) + \alpha\log|t|$$

A linear regression is fitted at some conveniently selected K points, where the value of K, ranging from 9 to 134, is determined empirically following Koutrouvelis' proposal. We have found, for simulated and real financial data, Monte Carlo Markov Chain m.l.e. performs the best as expected, but at a high computational cost. Regression and McCulloch estimators offer a reasonable compromise between speed and accuracy.

Autoregressive Moving Average (ARMA) Process with Stable Noises

We consider now an ARMA process with stable noises, to simplify let us first study an autoregressive process of order one(AR(1)) given by:

$$X_t = aX_{t-1} + \sigma\varepsilon_t \qquad (3)$$

where (ε_t) are independent random variables with symmetrical stable distribution $S(\alpha, 0, 1, 0)$. Its density is denoted by f_α. The likelihood function based on observations $X_1, X_2, \ldots, X_n$ and assuming the initial distribution does not depends on the parameter is given by:

$$L_n(\alpha) = \prod f(X_k / X_{k-1}),$$

where $f(x/X_{k\_1})$ is the density of X_k conditionally to X_{k_1}, corresponding to a stable distribution with parameters $\mu = aX_{k\_1}$, σ and α. The product runs from k = 1 to n, the sample size.

We study the consistency and asymptotic normality of the m.l.e. given by a parametric space such that (a, α, σ) is constrained to closed intervals.

Remark 1. Note that the parametric space is a compact set. The assumption that $\alpha > 1$ is not very restrictive in the financial context, the bounds on σ can be made as large as necessary for practical proposes.

We denote by $\theta_0 = (a_0, \alpha_0, \sigma_0)$ the true value of the parameter. Also we have $\theta_m = (a_M, \alpha_m, \sigma_m)$ and $\theta_M = (a_M, \alpha_M, \sigma_M)$.

First, we give some technical results about the uniform control of the density and its derivatives, their proofs have been given.[15]

Lemma 1. *For every x∈**R***

$$(i) \sup / \log f_{\theta}(X) / \leq h_1(x)\, for\, \alpha \in [\alpha_m, \alpha_M]$$

$$(ii) \sup \partial^2 \log f_{\theta}(x) / \partial \alpha^2 \leq h_2(x)\, for\, \alpha \in [\alpha_m, \alpha_M]$$

are P_θ*-integrable functions.*

Lemma 2. *For r > 0 and || θ - θ' ‖ < r we have sup 1/n (ln(θ) - ln(θ')) converges to zero as n goes to infinity* $P_{\theta 0}$ *a.s.*

The consistency and asymptotic normality of the m.l.e. is obtained as follows:

Theorem 1. *The maximum likelihood estimators for the parameters in (2) are consistent estimators of* θ_0*, i.e., they converge to the true parameter* $P_{\theta 0}$ *a.s.*

Theorem 2. *The maximum likelihood estimators of the parameters* θ_0 *for model (1.1) are asymptotically normal.*

The asymptotic variance is estimated substituting the unknown parameter θ_0 by the corresponding m.l.e., as in the following proposition, which is an immediate consequence of the *Law of Large Numbers.*

Remark 3. The results obtained for an AR(1) can be extended without difficulty to an ARMA(1,q) by noting that any linear combination of independent stable random variables distributes also stable with the corresponding change in the scale parameter. Note that a linear combination of stable laws leads to another stable law hence Theorems 1 and 2 apply in this case. Here instead of classical Law of Large Numbers and a Central Limit Theorem a convergence result for m-dependent random variables is needed.

On the other hand it is possible to write an AR(p) model as a p-dimensional AR(1), again Theorems 1 and 2 apply using a multidimensional Central Limit Theorem for m-dependent random variables. Here, in order to have stability, the roots of the polynomial characteristic associated with the autoregressive part should be outside the unit disk.

Numerical Implementation and Simulation Examples

Weron's algorithm[16] is used to generate stable numbers and then stable ARMA data. In Fig. 8.2 some simulations results for given parameters are included. We use previously calculated values of the density with different parameter values and then a bilinear interpolation to get the points needed in the optimization procedure is applied. In this way we save a lot of calculation time.

The maximization of the likelihood is implemented with the use of a quadratic sequential quasi-Newton technique. The Hill estimator is used as initial approximation.

We perform a simulation study with sample sizes 250, 500 and 1,000, different parameter sets ($\alpha \in \{1.5; 1.7; 1.9\}$; $\sigma \in \{0.02; 1\}$, $a \in \{0.3; 1\}$) and 60 repetitions

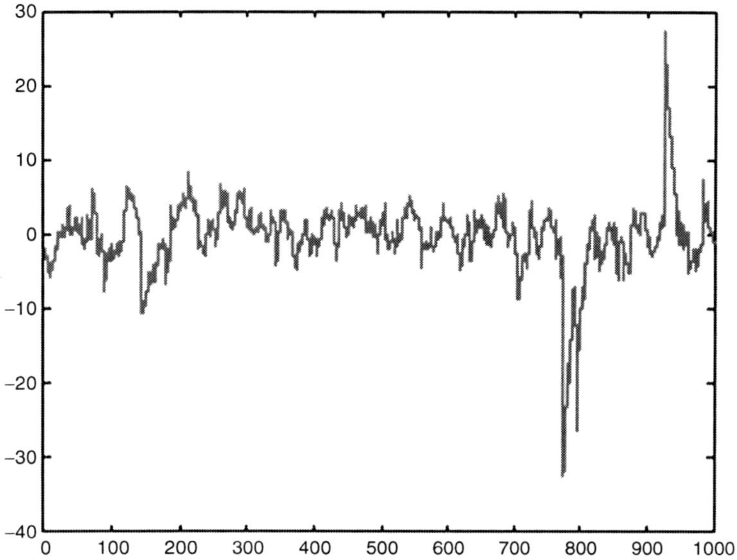

Fig. 8.2 A simulated trajectory of an AR(1) stable with parameters α = 1.5; σ = 0.6; μ = β = 0 and a = 0.9

for every trajectory. After it, we calculate the mean and the standard deviation of the estimates and we compare with the original values. The bias and the standard deviation go to zero as the sample size increases in accordance with Theorem 1.

The standard deviation is calculated for different sample sizes using an approximation of the Fisher's information matrix.

We also compute the VaR for an Autoregressive model of order one when stable and Gaussian noises are considered and we compare them with empirical simulation data from a large number of observations. The results are given in Table 1.5. They show the risk of considering Gaussian autoregressive models instead of stable ones for a VaR at 5 and 10% levels. Similar results have been obtained for the independent and identical distributed case.

GARCH Calibration and Some Numerical Problems

We consider Generalized Autoregressive Conditional Heteroscedastic models.[17] A GARCH(p,q) is defined by:

$$X_t = c_0 + \sum c_i X_{t-i} + \sigma_t \varepsilon_t \tag{3}$$

$$\sigma_t^2 = a_0 + \sum a_i X_{t-i} + \sum b_i \sigma_{t-i}^2 \tag{4}$$

where (ε_t) is an independent equally distributed sequence of random variables and the sums are taken from i = 1 to r, p and q respectively. In addition it is assumed that the noise follows a stable law. For simplicity we consider symmetric stable noises with $\beta = \mu = 0$. Also we assume $1 < \alpha \leq 2$ and $a_0 = 0$.

The existence of a stationary solution and a causal representation of the process given is a well known result. Moreover a stationary condition for a stable GARCH (p, q) process is given by:

$$\sum (a_i + b_i) < 1$$

The case of a GARCH(1,1) is considered fro simplicity. Its conditional log-likelihood is given by:

$$l_n(\theta) = -\sum \log \sigma_t + \sum \log f\varepsilon_t(X_t/\sigma_t)$$

where $f\varepsilon_t$ is the common density of the stable noises ε_t.

Consistency and asymptotic normality properties of the m.l.e. for GARCH models heavily rely on the existence of moments of order higher than one, it seems difficult to extend them to the case of stable GARCH models. An analysis based on Monte Carlo simulations is introduced in the remainder of this section.

Stable GARCH(1, 1) Models

From simulated stable GARCH (1,1) data with parameters $\alpha = 1.5$, $c_0 = 0$, $k = 0.2$, $a_1 = 0.1$, $b_1 = 0.6$ and sample sizes 250, 500, 1,000, 2,000 and 10,000 m.l.e. are obtained. The true parameters are recovered; moreover, the standard deviation of the estimators decreases when the sample size increases. The results can be seen in Fig 8.3.

A comparison between the VaR under normal and stable noises is done in Table 8.1 for parameters $c_0 = 0$, $k = 0.13$, $a_1 = 0.08$ and $b_1 = 0.57$ with four different sample sizes.

The results illustrate the danger of using a incorrect model from a risk management perspective. The parametric VaR under normal and stable laws differ considerably from the historical one generated from a stable GARCH(1,1) model.

An Empirical Fitting of Stable GARCH Models

A stable GARCH(1,1) model is fitted to daily closure exchange rates between Sterling Pound and Canadian Dollar vs. U.S. Dollar. Microsoft daily closure prices are considered as well. The period studied is 1999–2001. A Kolmorov–Smirnov

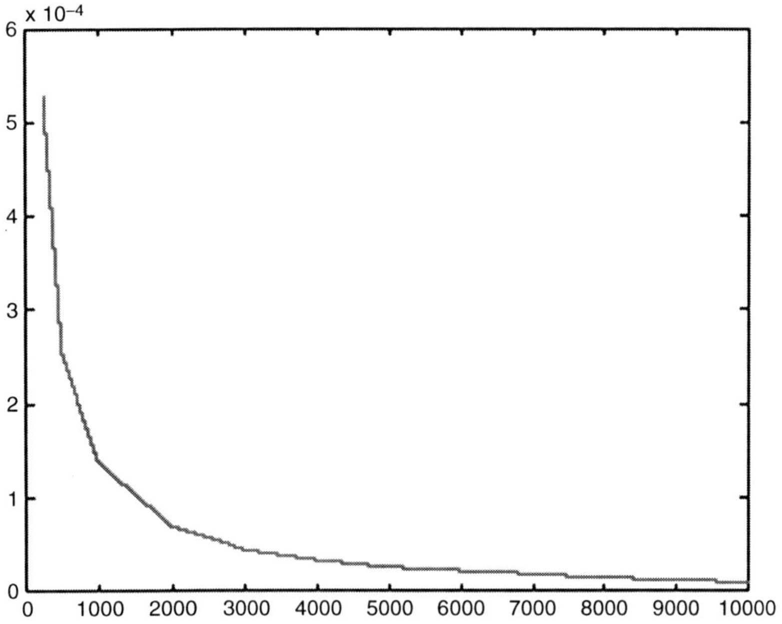

Fig. 8.3 Graph of the standard deviation taking $\alpha = 1.5$; $c_0 = 0$; $k = 0.2$; $a_1 = 0.1$ and $b_1 = 0.6$ for several sample sizes

Table 8.1 A comparison between the empirical value at risk and the parametric value at risk under normal and stable GARCH(1,1), different levels and sample size 1,000

VaR	1%	5%	10%
Empirical	15.447	4.999	2.891
Normal	41.879	20.563	13.919
Stable	14.157	4.437	2.134

test rejects the hypothesis of normality of the returns. Another test regarding the variance rejects the hypothesis of homoscedascity. For Sterling Pound and Canadian exchange rates the fitted models are respectively:

$$X_t = -0.0001 + \sigma_1 \varepsilon_t$$
$$\sigma_t^2 = 0.000002 + 0.023727 X_{t\_1}^2 + 0.898493 \sigma_{t\_1}^2$$
$$Xt = \_0.0002 + \sigma_t \varepsilon_t$$
$$\Sigma_t^2 = 0.000003 + 0.0633882 X_{t\_1}^2 + 0.904731 \sigma_{t\_1}^2$$

$$X_t = 0.00007 + \sigma_t \varepsilon_t$$
$$\sigma_t = 0.00005 + 0.16711 X^2_{t\_1} + 0.79553 \sigma^2_{t\_1}$$

Table 8.2 Value at risk is shown under a normal GARCH and a stable GARCH for daily Dow Jones index over the period from 1996–2006

VaR	1%	5%	10%
Empirical	0.0203	0.0114	0.0082
GARCH	0.0435	0.0145	0.0100
GARCH normal	0.2357	0.0177	0.0120

Another Kolmogorov–Smirnov test, applied to the residuals, shows a good fit to stable GARCH(1,1) model for the three series. In Table 8.2 the Value at Risk is shown under three different models; a normal GARCH(1,1), a stable GARCH(1,1) for daily Dow Jones index. These parametric VaRs are compared with historical data.

The VaR computed according to a stable GARCH(1,1) model is closer to the empirical one compared with the normal GARCH(1,1).

End Notes

1. Mandelbrot, B.B. (1963). The variation of certain speculative prices. *Journal of Business* 26:394419; Fama, E., and Roll, R. (1971). Parameters estimates for symmetric stable distributions, *Journal of the American Statistical Association* 66, 331–339.
2. Samorodnitsky, G., and Taqqu, M.S. (1994). Stable non Gaussian random processes: Stochastic models with infinite variance. Chapman and Hall, London.
3. Zolotarev, V.M. (1986). On representation of stable laws by integrals, *Selected Translation in Mathematical Statistics and Probability* 6, 84–88.
4. Weron, R. (1996). On the Chambers Mallows Stuck method for simulating skewed stable random variables. *Statistics and Probability Letters* 28, 165–171.
5. Alvarez, A., and Olivares, P. (2005). Methodes d'estimation pour des lois stables avec des applications en finance. *Journal de la Societe Francaise de Statistique*, 146:4.
6. Hill, B.M. (1975). A simple general approach to inference about the tail of a stable distribution, *Annals of Statistics* 3:5, 1163–1174.
7. McCulloch, J.H. (1986). Simple consistent estimators of stable distribution parameters. *Communication Statistics Simulation* 15, 1109–1136.
8. DuMouchel, W.H. (1971). Stable distributions in statistical inference. Ph.D. thesis, University of Ann Arbor, Ann Arbor, MI.
9. Hosking, J.R.M. (1990). L-moments: analysis and estimation of distributions using linear combinations of order statistics. *Journal of Royal Statistical Society B* 52, 105–124.
10. Maussel, H. (2001). Calculating quantile based risk analytics with l-estimators, *Algo Research Quarterly* 4:4, 45–62.
11. Carrillo, S., Escobar, M., Hernandez, N., Olivares, P., and Seco, L. (2007). A theoretical comparison between moments and Lmoments. Working paper.
12. DuMouchel, W.H. (1973). On asymptotical normality of the m.l.e when sampling from stable. *Annals of Statistics* 1, 948–957.
13. Carrasco, M., and Florens, J. (2000). Generalization of GMM to a continuum moment condition, *Econometric Theory* 16, 767–834.
14. Koutrovelis, I.A. (1980). Regression type estimation of the parameters of stable laws, *Journal of the American Statistical Association* 75, 918–928.
15. Bollerslev, T. (1986). Generalized autoregressive conditional heteroskedasticity, *Journal of Econometrics* 3, 307–327.
16. Weron, R. (1996). op cit.
17. Engle, R.F. (1982). Autoregressive conditional heteroskedasticity with estimates of the variance of U.K. inflation. *Econometrica* 50, 9871008.

Chapter 9
Hybrid Calibration Procedures for Term Structure Models

T. Schmidt

Introduction

Calibration is the well-established methodology to fit a model to observed option price data. A calibrated model reflects the current market view on its future evolution, typically under the risk-neutral measure. On the other side, statistical estimation on the basis of historical data estimates a model on the basis of past movements (hence under the historical or actual measure). While calibration is more used in pricing and hedging of derivatives, statistical estimation is the standard tool for risk management. Both approaches have their advantages and drawbacks. Calibration, reflecting actual market views, is able to react very quickly on changes while statistical estimation provides more stability. The hybrid calibration procedure suggested here combines both approaches and therefore might serve for increasing stability in calibration on one side and providing a tool for risk management which is able to react quickly on recent market changes. The paper considers a term-structure model with credit risk on the basis of Gaussian random fields proposed in Schmidt.[1] The risk-free model of Kennedy (1994)[2] is a special case and thus the methodologies may also be applied to risk-free term structures. We also discuss a methodology suggested in Roncoroni and Guiotto (2000).[3]

The market for credit portfolio products increased tremendously, Especially in the last years, while the market for single-name credit derivatives did not grow in that speed. However, the recent turmoil caused by the U.S. subprime mortgage crisis changed the view on credit portfolio products and it is likely that single-name credit derivatives become increasingly important because of their transparency and the fact that the risk management of single-name derivatives is of course much simpler. We start by a number of pricing results on single-name credit risky securities, such as digitals, bonds with zero recovery and under certain recovery assumptions, European options on bonds, and credit default swaptions with a knock-out feature. Thereafter, different hybrid calibration procedures are discussed and illustrated. Finally, we compute some risk measures for the proposed model.

D.L. Olson, D. Wu (eds.) *New Frontiers in Enterprise Risk Management*,

Preliminaries

This section follows Schmidt (2007).[4] We give the necessary results while giving reference to proofs. We generalize the approach by Kennedy (1994) to credit risk. On one side, the case of Gaussian random fields can be considered as a special case of the more general work in Schmidt (2006).[5] On the other side, this special case allows to compute the drift conditions directly, without the need to consider stochastic differential equations on Hilbert spaces. The considered market contains riskless bonds denoted by B(t, T) and bonds issued by a company with default risk, denoted by $\overline{\mathbf{B}}(t, T)$. (r_t) denotes the risk-free spot rate. We consider a finite time horizon T^* and a maximum time-to-maturity T^{**}.

The objective measure is denoted by P. Consider a measure Q which is equivalent to P. Our aim is to give conditions under which Q is also a martingale measure, hence the considered model is free of arbitrage. The dynamics of bonds subject to credit risk relate to two factors besides the risk-free interest rate: First, the creditworthiness of the bonds plays an important role. Creditworthiness is represented by the probability of default, respectively the default intensity. The second component is the price of the bond after default, named recovery.

It is possible to consider different types of recoveries in this framework, but for ease of exposition we consider on fractional recovery of the par value. In this approach a bond may face several so-called credit events in its life time. Each credit event refers to a reduction of the face value and hence implies a downward jump of the bond price. To this, we assume that the bond prices itself is given in terms of forward rates, i.e.,

$$\overline{B}(t,T) = \prod_{\tau_i \le t} (1 - L_{\tau_i}) \cdot \exp(-\int_t^T \overline{f}(t,u)du),$$

where the loss process L takes values in $(0,1)$ and the times at which credit events occur, $0 < \tau_1 < \tau_2, \ldots$, are the jump times of a Cox Process with intensity $(\lambda_t)_{t \ge 0}$. The intensity is assumed to be a nonnegative G-adapted process with $\int_0^{T^*} \lambda_t \, dt < \infty$ a.s., where the filtration G is given by

$$G_t := \sigma(B(s,T), \overline{X}(s,T) : 0 \le s \le t, T \in [s, s+T^{**}]) \tag{1}$$

G summarizes the general market information (except information on the default). Also the loss process L is assumed to be G-adapted. The whole information available to investors is represented by the filtration given by

$$F_t := G_t \vee \sigma(1_{\{\tau \le s\}} : 0 \le s \le t).$$

The forward rate itself is modeled via

$$\overline{f}(t,T) := \overline{\mu}(t,T) + \overline{X}(t,T), \tag{2}$$

where μ is a deterministic function and $(\overline{X}(s, t))_{s,\, t \in [0,\, \tilde{T}]}$ is a zero-mean, continuous Gaussian random field with covariance function

$$\mathrm{Cov}(\overline{X}_{s_1,t_1}, \overline{X}_{s_2,t_2}) = \overline{c}(s_1 \wedge s_2, t_1, t_2).$$

Conditions on the covariance functions which ensure the existence of X may be found in Adler (1981).[6]

Remark 1. Definition (1) reveals a basic fact for forward rates, namely, as for $\overline{f}(t, T)$, the two indices t and T are treated differently. The index t represents the calendar time, while T denotes maturity of the underlying bond. For any t, the whole forward curve is known, i.e., $\{\overline{f}(t, T) : T \in [t, t + T^{**}]\}$ are observable in the market.

In the following, we will assume that the random fields have independent increments w.r.t. current time which will ease computations later on. Note that this is not necessary and can be generalized if necessary.

A1 Assume that the market of risk-free bonds is free of arbitrage, $\overline{c}(0, t_1, t_2) = 0$ and for $0 \le s_1 < s_2 \le t \le s_1 + T^{**}$ the increments $\overline{X}(s_2, t) - \overline{X}(s_1, t)$ are independent of

$$\sigma(r_s, \overline{X}(s,t) : 0 \le s \le s_1, t \in [s, s + T^{**}]).$$

In practice, this information is only available for a discrete tenor structure $T_1, \ldots, T_n$, which is a basic motivation to consider market models. On the other hand, one can either interpolate those using splines or some parametric families,[7] or view the discrete observations as partial information of the whole, but unknown term structure. We take this last viewpoint and model the whole term structure. Later on, in the calibration process, we account for the discrete observations by an approximation argument.

The following result states the drift condition, under which the market is free of arbitrage. If Assumption (A1) holds, then Q is an equivalent martingale measure iff for all $t \in [0,T^*]$

$$\overline{f}(t,t) = r_t + \lambda_t L_t \tag{3}$$

and the drift condition

$$\overline{\mu}(t,T) = \overline{\mu}(0,T) + \int_0^T \overline{c}(t \wedge v, v, T)\,dv \tag{4}$$

holds for any $T \ge t$.

For the sake of completeness, the proof of the theorem is given in the appendix. It basically combines the results of Kennedy (1994) with the credit risky setting. To obtain the drift conditions, Kennedy (1994) makes use of the fact that the bond price is of the form $\exp(\xi)$, where ξ is a normally distributed random variable and hence expectations are computed easily.

Equation (3) yields that the credit spread consists of the product of default intensity and loss rate. Hence credit spreads themselves do not allow to disentangle default intensity and recovery. Practitioners typically fix the recovery rate to a constant and hope for the robustness of this approach.

A number of interesting special cases exist in the literature. For example, the Vasicek[8]-model is a special case. This is also the case for the intuitive four factor implementation proposed in Schmid, Zagst and Antes.[9]

Explicit Pricing Formulas

The main ingredient for efficient calibration procedures are pricing formulas which lead to a fast implementation. In this section we provide numerous pricing formulas, which are all explicit and therefore the implementation is extremely fast. Proofs are available from the author if desired.

Default Digitals

A basic derivative of an underlying which faces credit risk is the default digital put. It promises a fixed payoff, say 1, if a default occurred before maturity, and zero otherwise. We focus on the derivative where the payoff is settled at maturity.

It may be recalled that the default digital put with payoff at maturity is intrinsically related to the zero recovery bond, as

$$p^d(t,T) + B^0(t,T) = B(t,T)$$

A2 Assume that both risk-free and defaultable forward rates admit a representation via Gaussian random fields. For the defaultable forward rates this is specified in Assumption (A1) and we assume a similar structure for the risk-free bonds with $(X(s,t))_{s,t\in[0,\tilde{T}]}$ being a zero-mean, continuous Gaussian random field with covariance function $c(s_1 \wedge s_2, t_1, t_2)$ and $c(0, t_1, t_2) = 0$. Furthermore, assume that the drift-conditions as well as (3) are satisfied and the loss function (L_t) is deterministic. Besides this, we assume joint independent increments of X and $\bar{X}$.

If Assumption (A2) holds, the market is free of arbitrage. Furthermore, we deduce from (3) that

$$\lambda_t = \frac{\bar{f}(t,t) - f(t,t)}{L_t} \tag{5}$$

Instead of defining the dynamics of f and λ and then deriving $\bar{f}$, we want to propose the dynamics of f and $\bar{f}$ and investigate the consequences for λ. This reflects the fact that λ is not observable in the market, while the forward rates are. Therefore, we use (5) as a starting point for this section.

A first consequence of this approach is, that because L is deterministic, λ turns out to be a Gaussian random field. The assumption that the recovery rate is deterministic is often used in practice but has serious drawbacks. Anyway, random recovery can be easily introduced in the presented framework if it is assumed to be independent of the other processes.

For ease of notation we write $\bar{f}_u$ instead of $\bar{f}(u, u)$ and similarly μ_u, $\bar{\mu}_u$, X_u and $\bar{X}_u$ and consider $t = 0$ as the current time.

We will need a measure for correlation between risk-free and defaultable rate. To this, define

$$\xi(s,t_1,t_2) := \mathrm{Cov}(\bar{f}(s,t_1), f(s,t_2)) = \mathrm{Cov}(\bar{X}(s,t_1), X(s,t_2)) \tag{6}$$

Note that $\zeta(s, t_1, t_2)$ is not necessarily symmetric in t_1 and t_2. Furthermore, the assumption of joint independent increments immediately yields

$$\mathrm{Cov}(\bar{X}(s_1,t_1), X(s_2,t_2)) = \xi(s_1 \wedge s_2, t_1, t_2)$$

Often we will consider terms like $r_t + \lambda = r_t\left(1 - \frac{1}{4}\right) + \bar{f}_t \frac{1}{L_t}$. Therefore, set

$$l_t := (1 - \frac{1}{L_t})$$

Proposition 1. *Under (A2), the price of the zero recovery bond equals*

$$\begin{aligned}
\mathrm{B}^0(\mathrm{t},T) = 1_{\{\tau>1\}} B(\mathrm{t},T)\exp\{-\int_t^T \frac{1}{L_u}(\bar{f}(t,u) - f(t,u))du \\
- \int_t^T \int_0^t [l_u(c(v,v,u) - c(t,v,u)) + \frac{1}{\mathrm{L_u}}(\bar{c}(t,v,u) - \bar{c}(t,v,u)]dvdu \\
+ \frac{1}{2}\int_t^T \int_t^T [\mathrm{l}_u 1_v(c(u \wedge v,u,v) - c(t,v,u)) + 2\frac{1_u}{L_v}(\zeta(u \wedge v,v,u) - \zeta(t,v,u)) \\
+ \frac{1}{L_{..}^2}(\bar{c}(u \wedge v,u,v) - \bar{c}(t,v,u))]dvdu\}
\end{aligned} \tag{7}$$

Basically, the result follows by a careful computation of expectations. The price in (7) may be simplified if one drops the assumption of time-inhomogeneous recovery. Denote by $g(t, T)$ the exponential of last three lines in (7). Then

$$\begin{aligned}
B^0(t,T) &= 1_{\{\tau>t\}} B(t,T)\exp[-\int_t^T \frac{1}{L_u}(\bar{f}(t,u) - f(t,u))du]g(t,T) \\
&= 1_{\{\tau>t\}} B(t,T)^{1-\frac{1}{L}} \bar{B}(t,T)^{\frac{1}{L}} g(t,T)
\end{aligned} \tag{8}$$

Remark 2. If the price of the zero recovery bond is available, the following formula allows to calibrate the loss rate. Denoting the forward rate of the zero recovery bond by f^0, we have

$$\begin{aligned}
&\bar{f}_t = r_t + \lambda_t L_t = r_t + (f_t^0 - f_t)L_t \\
\Leftrightarrow\quad &L_t = \frac{\bar{f}_t - f_t}{f_t^0 - f_t}
\end{aligned}$$

Default Put

It is also possible to price a default put with knock-out feature. The put is knocked out if a default occurs before maturity of the contract, which means that the promised payoff is paid only if there was no default until maturity of the contract. Hence this put protects against market risk but not against the loss in case of a default.

For the conditional expectation w.r.t. F_t we simply write E_t. Denoting the price of a (knock-out) default put with maturity T on a defaultable bond with maturity T' by $P^k(t, T, T')$, the risk neutral valuation principle yields for $0 \leq T \leq T' \tilde{T}$

$$P^k(t,T,T') = E_t[\exp(-\int_t^T r_u\, du)(K - \overline{B}(T,T'))^+ 1_{\{\tau>T\}}]$$

Furthermore, denote by $B^k(t, T, T')$ a contract on the defaultable bond, which delivers the defaultable bond with maturity T' at time T if no default happened until T and zero otherwise. We will call this contract a knock-out bond. This derivative seems a bit synthetic, but if both default put and default call, both with knock-out, are traded, it can be replicated by a combination of put and call.

Proposition 2. *The price of a default put with maturity* $T \in ((0, T^*)$ *on a defaultable bond with maturity* $T' \in (T, T^*)$ *which is knocked out if default occurs before* T*, equals*

$$P^k(t,T,T') = B^0(t,T)K\Phi(-d_2) - B^k(t,T,T')\Phi(-d_1), \tag{9}$$

with deterministic terms

$$\tilde{\sigma}\ (t,T,T') := \int_T^{T'}\int_T^{T'} (\overline{c}(T,u,v) - \overline{c}(t,u,v))\, du\, dv,$$

$$\tilde{\mu}\ (t,T,T') := \int_T^{T'}\int_t^{T} \{\overline{c}(v,v,u) - \ (\tilde{\mu}(v,u,v) - \ \varsigma(t,u,v) - \overline{c}(t,u,v))lv$$

$$+\overline{c}(T,u,v)\frac{1}{L_v}\}\, dv\, du, + \ln\frac{\overline{B}(t,T)}{\overline{B}(t,T')}$$

$$d_2 := \frac{-\tilde{\mu}(t,T,T') - \ln K}{\tilde{\sigma}(t,T,T')},\ d_1 := d_2 + \tilde{\sigma}\ (t,T,T')$$

Note that the price of a put without knock-out can be obtained using similar methods. The price of the knock-out bond equals

$$\begin{aligned} B^k(t,T,T') &= B^0(t,T)e^{\frac{\tilde{\sigma}(t,T,T')}{2} - \tilde{\mu}(t,T,T')} \\ &= B^0(t,T)\frac{\overline{B}(t,T')}{\overline{B}(t,T)}g^k(t,T,T') \end{aligned} \tag{10}$$

where the explicitly known, deterministic function g^k can be calculated immediately from the above stated expressions for $\tilde{\mu}(t, T, T')$ and $\tilde{\sigma}(t, T, T')$.

Credit Spread Options

The pricing of credit spread options can be done in a more or less similar fashion. To ease the notational burden, we consider the derivatives prices at time $t = 0$. A credit spread call with strike K offers the right to buy the underlying, i.e., the defaultable bond, at maturity for a price which corresponds to a yield spread K above the yield of an equivalent risk-free bond. Precisely, for maturity T of the credit spread call and maturity T' of the underlying defaultable bond $\bar{B}$ the value of the credit spread call at T equals

$$(\bar{B}(T,T') - e^{-K(T-T')}B(T,T'))^+$$

Typically these securities are traded with a knock-out feature, s.t. the derivative has zero value after default. Hence such credit derivatives protect against spread widening risk, but not default risk.

Proposition 3. *Under assumption (A2), the price of the (knock-out) credit spread call with maturity* $T \in [0, T^*]$ *on a defaultable bond with maturity* $T' \in [T, t^*]$ *equals*

$$P_{CS}^k(0,T,T') = B^k(0,T,T')\Phi(d_1) - e^{K(T'-T)}B^0(0,T)\Phi(d_2),$$

with the abbreviations

$$\mu_1 := -\int_T^{T'} [\tilde{\mu}(0,u) - \mu(0,u) + \int_0^u (\bar{c}(v \wedge T, v, u) - c(v \wedge T, v, u))]\,dv\,du,$$

$$\sigma_1 := \int_T^{T'}\int_T^{T'} [\bar{c}(u \wedge v, u, v) - \zeta(T,u,v) - \zeta(T,v,u) + c(u \wedge v, u, v)]\,dv\,du,$$

$$\sigma_2 := \int_0^{T'}\int_0^{T'} 1_1(u,T)l_1(v,T)c(u \wedge v,u,v)\,dv\,du + \int_0^T\int_0^T \frac{\bar{c}(u \wedge v,u,v)}{L_u L_v}\,dv\,du$$

$$+2\int_0^{T'}\int_0^T \frac{1_1(u,T)}{L_v}\zeta(u \wedge v, v, u)\,dv\,du,$$

$$\rho := \int_0^{T'}\int_T^{T'} 1_1(u,T)[\zeta(u \wedge T, v, u) - c(u \wedge T, v, u)]\,dv\,du$$

$$+\int_0^T\int_T^{T'} \frac{1}{L_u}[\bar{c}(u \wedge T, u, v) - \zeta(u \wedge T, u, v)]\,dv\,du,$$

$$d_2 := \frac{\mu_1 - \ln K}{\sigma_1} + \rho\sigma_2, \qquad d_1 := d_2 + \sigma_1,$$

$$1_1(u,T) := 1_{\{u \le T\}}1_u + 1_{\{u > T\}}$$

Credit Default Swap and Swaption

In this section we consider the pricing of a credit default swaption, in particular the price of a so-called CDS call with knock-out. This is a call on the swap premium which is knocked out if a default of the underlying entity occurs before maturity.

If the swap offers the replacement of the difference to an equivalent risk-free bond on default, the swap rate is

$$\overline{S}(T) = \frac{B(T,T_n) - \overline{B}(T,T_n)}{\sum_{i=1}^{n} B^0(T,T_i)}$$

The pricing of the credit default swap mainly relies on the pricing of the zero recovery bond. Therefore, Proposition 1 immediately leads to a price of the credit default swap and we obtain the following price of the CDS call

$$\begin{aligned} & C_S^k(0,T,T') \\ &= E[\exp(-\int_0^T r_u\,du)(B(T,T_n) - \overline{B}(T,T_n) - K\sum_{i=1}^{n} B^0(T,T_i))^+ 1_{\{\tau > T\}} \\ &= E[\exp(-\int_0^T (r_u + \lambda_u)\,du)(B(T,T_n) - \exp(-\int_T^{T_n} \overline{f}(T,u)\,du) \\ &- K\sum_{i=1}^{n} \exp(-\int_T^{T_i} f^0(T,u)\,du))^+] \end{aligned} \tag{11}$$

Usually the final repayment, represented by $\overline{B}\ (T, T_n)$, dominates the coupon payments. This justifies the following assumption.

A3 For the considered maturity $T \in [0, T^{**}]$ and the tenor structure $T < T_1 < \ldots < T_n \leq \tilde{T}$; assume that the random variable

$$\exp(-\int_T^{T_n} \overline{f}(T,u)\,du) + K\sum_{i=1}^{n} \exp(-\int_T^{T_i} f^0(T,u)\,du) \tag{12}$$

can be approximated by a log-normal random variable, which we denote by $\tilde{B}\ (T, T_1,.., T_n)$.

Under Assumption (A3), the pricing of the credit default swaption is very similar to the pricing of a credit spread call, where the underlying is $\tilde{B}(T, T_1.., T_n)$.

We introduce an auxiliary product which we call the *converting bond*, $B^C(t, T, T')$. It is used as an abbreviation in the pricing formula for the swaption, and an explicit formula for its price is available. The converting bond is a derivative which pays 1 at maturity T' if no default occurred until $T < T'$. Thus, it behaves like a zero recovery bond until T and is converted into a default-free bond at T, if no default occurred so far. Denote

$$B^C(t,T,T') := E(\exp(-\int_t^T \lambda_u\,du - \int_t^{T'} r_u\,du) \mid F_t)$$

Recall that $\tilde{m}$ and $\tilde{\sigma}^2$ have been computed in Lemma A.6. The following result gives the price of call on a credit default swap which is knocked out at default.

Proposition 4. *Under assumptions (A2) and (A3) the price of a call on a credit default swap with knock-out equals*

$$S_C(0,T,T_n) = B^C(0,T,T_n)\Phi(-d_2)$$
$$- [B^k(0,T,T_n) + K\sum_{i=1}^{n} B^0(0,T_n)]\Phi(-d_1),$$

with deterministic

$$\mu := \tilde{m} + \frac{B(0,T)}{B(0,T_n)} + \int_T^{T_n}\int_0^u c(v,u,v)\,dv\,du,$$

$$\sigma_1 := \ln[\frac{\tilde{\sigma}^2}{\tilde{m}^2} + 1] + \int_T^{T_n}\int_T^{T_n} c(T,u,v)\,du\,dv - [\tilde{m} + \frac{\tilde{\sigma}^2}{2}]$$
$$+ \ln[\frac{\overline{B}(0,T_n)}{\overline{B}(0,T)}\exp(-\int_T^{T_n}\int_0^T \overline{c}(v,u,v)\,dv\,du - \int_T^{T_n}\int_T^{T_n} \zeta(T,u,v)\,dv\,du)$$
$$+K\sum_{i=1}^{n}\frac{B^0(0,T_i)}{B^0(0,T)}\exp(-\int_T^{T_i}\int_0^T c^0(v,u,v)\,dv\,du - \int_T^{T_i}\int_T^{T_n} l_T c(T,u,v)$$
$$+ \frac{\varsigma(T,u,v)}{L_T}\,dv\,du)],$$

$$\sigma_2 := \int_0^{T_n}\int_0^{T_n} l_2(u,T)l_2(v,T)c(u\wedge v,u,v)\,dv\,du + \int_0^T\int_0^T \frac{\overline{c}(u\wedge v,u,u)}{L_u L_v}\,dv\,du$$
$$+2\int_0^{T_n}\int_0^T \frac{l_2(u,T)}{L_v}\sigma(u\wedge v,v,u)\,dv\,du,$$

$$d_2 := \frac{\mu - \ln K}{\sigma_1} + \rho\sigma_2, \qquad d_1 := d_2 + \sigma_1,$$

$$l_2(u,T) := 1_{\{u\le T\}} - l_u + 1_{\{u>T\}}$$

Here ρ is defined as the following covariance:

$$\rho := \mathrm{Cov}[\ln\frac{\tilde{B}(T,T_1,\quad,T_n)}{B(T,T_n)}, -\int_0^T r_u + \lambda_u\,du - \ln B(T,T_n)]$$

If the swap is assumed to pay the "difference to par" on default, pricing formulas are obtained in a similar way.

Remark 3. It is interesting, that the above formulas immediately lead to hedging strategies for knock-out derivatives. We refer to Schmidt (2007) and Schmidt (2003) for full details.

Hybrid Calibration Procedures

The main goal of this section will be to discuss a number of hybrid calibration procedures, to begin with a procedure based on Gaussian random fields and the obtained formulas.

Hybrid Calibration Using Gaussian Random Fields

This chapter introduces a hybrid calibration procedure based on Gaussian random fields. Two different, related approaches to calibrating particularly interest rate models include Pang[10] (1998) and Roncoroni and Guitto (2000).[11] The first one applies the classical calibration methodology to Gaussian random field models of interest rates and shows that the calibration is more stable if the number of factors is not fixed a priori. The second article also proposes a hybrid approach to calibration which we discuss in detail later in Sect. 4.2.

We use historical information for an estimation of the typical shapes of the volatility surface and summarize this in a kind of parametric model which is then calibrated to the actual option prices. We describe the procedure in more detail now. We introduce the method for credit derivatives, where the ideas are similarly applied to interest rates or local volatility models for stock prices.

A primary motivation of the following approach were the results of Pang (1998), who showed that in the interest rate case the calibration of a random field model in comparison to an n-factor HJM model permits more stability over time and frequent re-calibration can be avoided. This is due to the different approaches for specifying the number of significant factors:

In n-factor models, n is pre-specified by some reasoning and then the calibration is carried out. In contrast to this, in random field models n is specified during the calibration, such that the error of the n-dimensional approximation does not exceed a certain level and so n is chosen depending on the data and the required precision.

If we want to avoid assuming a parametric covariance structure as in Kennedy (1997),[12] a relatively large data set needs to be available. We therefore assume that prices of credit default swaps and swaptions are accessible.

We assume that the risk-free market is readily calibrated and for a quick implementation we require:

1. The covariance functions satisfy

$$\bar{c}(s,t_1,t_2) = \int_0^s \bar{g}(t_1 - u, t_2 - u)\,du,$$

$$\varsigma(s,t_1,t_2) = \int_0^s g(t_1 - u, t_2 - u)\,du$$

2. Furthermore, the surfaces $\bar{g}$: $R \mapsto R$ and $\bar{g}$: $R^2 \mapsto R$ are piecewise triangular: For nodes $\{u_1,\dots, u_m\}$ any (u_i, u_i), (u_{i+1}, u_i), (u_{i+1}, u_{i+1}) or (u_i, u_i), (u_i, u_{i+1}), (u_{i+1}, u_{i+1}) define the corners of the surfaces' triangles.

The first assumption yields stationary volatility factors, while the second assumption allows for quick calibration of the covariance function. The $\{u_1,.., u_m\}$ do not necessarily coincide with the tenor structure, denoted by $\{T_1,.., T_n\}$. For example, as in Fig. 9.1 the $\{u_1,.., u_m\}$ are multiples of 3 while the tenor structure is $\{3, 5, 7, 10, 15, 20, 30\}$.

For the calibration data of some weeks or a month is appropriate and standard optimization software can be used to minimize the residual sum of squared differences

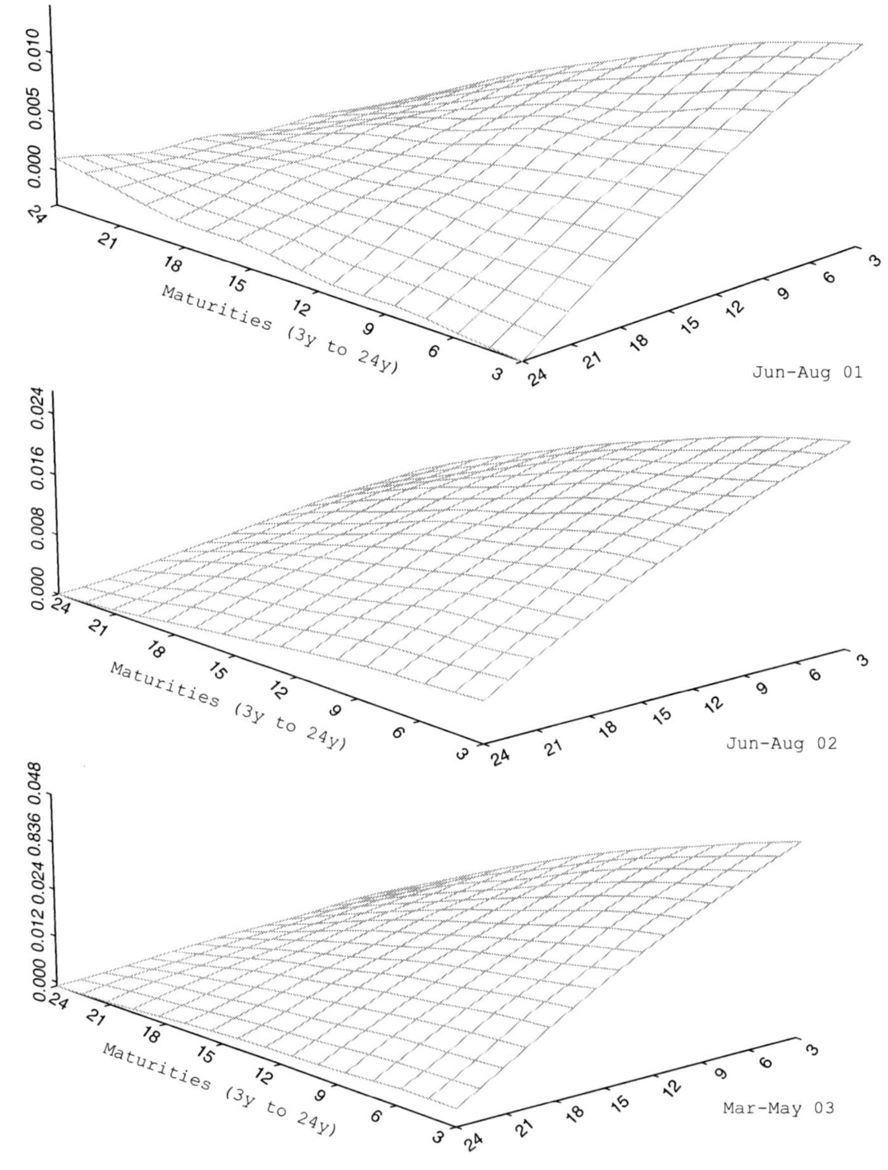

Fig. 9.1 Estimated covariance functions (the eigenvectors are given in Fig. 9.2) for greek Treasury data

between the calculated prices and market prices. In this procedure, calculating model prices is done in two steps. First, determine $\overline{c}(s, t_1, t_2)$ and $\varsigma(s, t_1, t_2)$ on the basis of $\overline{g}(u, v)$ and $g(u, v)$ for $u, v \in \{u_1,.., u_m\}$, $t_1, t_2 \in \{T_1,.., T_n\}$ and every considered data time $s \in \{s_1,.., s_p\}$. For the second step, the prices of the considered derivatives are computed using the $\bar{c}(s, t_1, t_2)$ and $\varsigma(s, t_1, t_2)$ determined in the first step.

Implementation

Consider the covariance function $\bar{c}$. Then $\bar{c}$ can be decomposed into

$$\bar{c}(\cdot,t_1,t_2) = \sum_k \lambda_k(\cdot)e_k(t_1)e_k(t_2),$$

using any orthonormal basis $\{e_k : k \in N\}$ of $L^2(\mu)$, the Hilbert space of functions $f: R \mapsto \mathrm{R}$ which are square integrable w.r.t. a suitable measure μ. We are free to choose μ, which allows putting different weights onto different maturities, as suggested in Filipović (2001).[13]

Note that in order to determine the covariance function, one has to specify both the $\{e_k : k \in N\}$ and the $\{\lambda_k : k \in N\}$. The idea is to retain the shape of the estimated covariance function by taking fixed eigenvectors and just calibrating the eigenvalues so to obtain a good fit. The eigenvectors will be obtained from a principal component analysis.

The first step is to estimate the eigenvectors using a set of historical data. Consider a small time interval, so that stationarity of the considered random fields in this time interval may be assumed. The historical data consists of observations of $\bar{f}(s, t)$ at a set of time points $T' := \{(s_i, t_j) : 1 \le i \le n_1, 1 \le j \le n_2\}$. Hall et al. (1994) propose a covariance estimator based on kernel methods in the case of real valued and stationary processes.[14] In the following, we apply their methodology to the random field case. For the points $\mathbf{a}, \mathbf{b} \in [0, T^*]\times[0,T^{**}]$ we define the covariance estimator by

$$\tilde{c}(\mathrm{a},\mathrm{b}) := \frac{\sum_{\mathbf{c}_i,\mathbf{d}_j \in T'} K(\frac{\mathbf{a}-\mathbf{c}_i}{h},\frac{\mathbf{b}-\mathbf{d}_j}{h})\cdot[X(\mathrm{c}_i)-\bar{X}][X(\mathrm{d}_j)-\bar{X}]}{\sum_{\mathbf{c}_i,\mathbf{d}_j \in T'} K(\frac{\mathbf{a}-\mathbf{c}_i}{h},\frac{\mathbf{b}-\mathbf{d}_j}{h})}$$

where K(c,d) is a symmetric kernel. Observe that the sum is over all time points in T', labeled c_i and d_j, respectively. Estimation of the covariance function $\bar{c}\,(s, t_1, t_2)$ is thus obtained by considering $a_1 = b_1 = s$.

Remark 4. An additional step may ensure positive definiteness of the estimator. The following second step is optional, but ensures that the estimator is positive definite, thus a covariance function itself. This yields increased performance for the eigenvector decomposition below. We invert the characteristic function of our estimator,

$$\phi(\lambda) := \int_{R^2} \exp(\mathrm{i}\lambda^{\top}\mathrm{t})\tilde{\rho}(\mathrm{t})\,dt \text{ for } \lambda \in R^2$$

Because the estimator is symmetric, we have

$$\phi(\lambda) = \int \cos(\lambda^{\top}\mathrm{t})\tilde{\rho}(\mathrm{t})\,dt$$

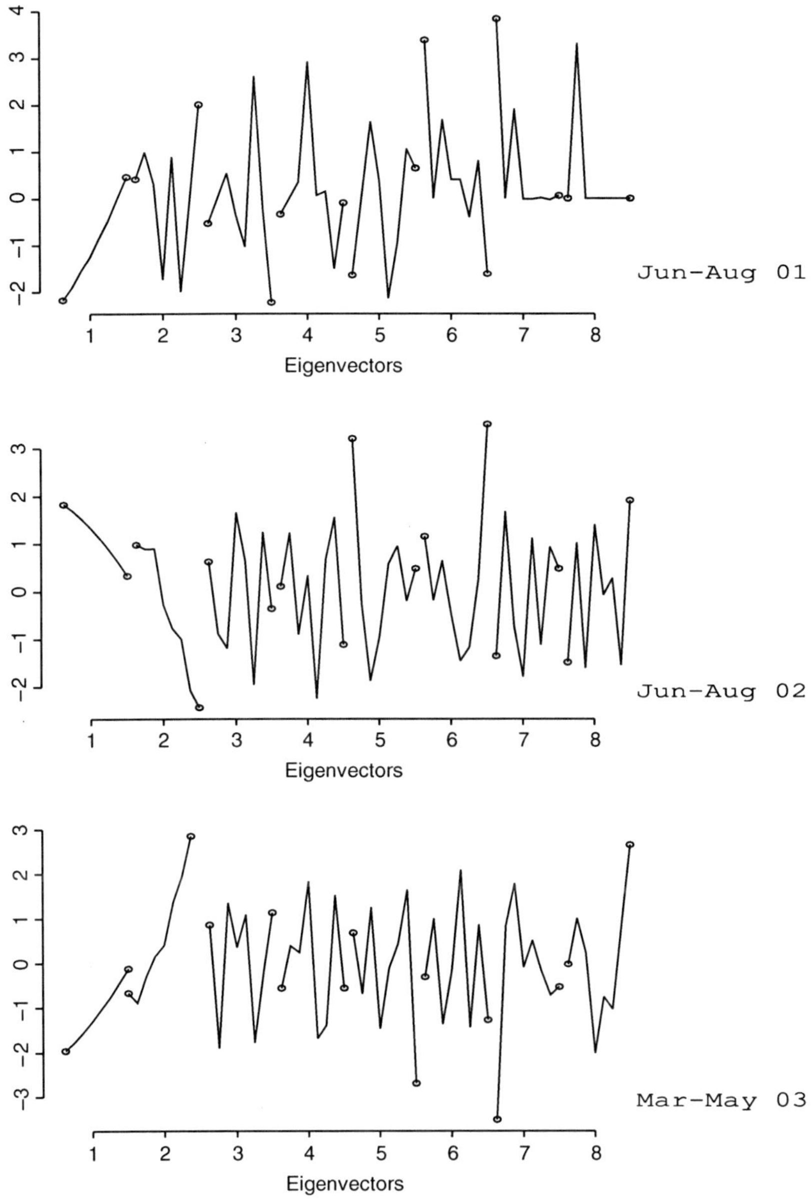

Fig. 9.2 The estimated eigenvectors according to Fig. 9.1

Following Bochner's theorem, we need $\phi(\lambda) \geq 0$ to ensure that p is a covariance function, thus we use the positive part of $\phi(\lambda)$ in the inversion of the Fourier transform and suggest the following estimator of the covariance function

$$\hat{\rho}(t) = \frac{1}{(2\pi)^2} \int \cos(\lambda^T t)[\phi(\lambda)]^+ \, d\lambda$$

Figure 9.3 shows the result of the covariance estimation on a set of U.S. Treasury data using historical data of four weeks. The implementation uses a Gaussian kernel and the covariance estimator is plotted for maturities of three months to three years. After obtaining an estimator for the covariance function, we can calculate its eigenvectors up to a required precision. The eigenvector decomposition is done by applying the Mises-Geiringer iteration procedure. Figure 9.3 also shows the calculated eigenvectors for the U.S. Treasury data. The first two eigenvectors show sig-

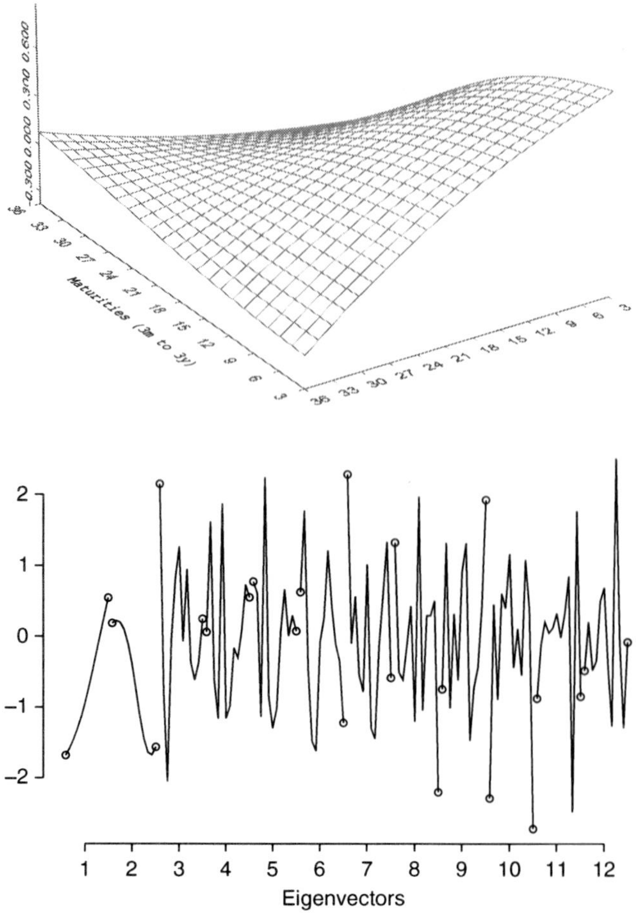

Fig. 9.3 The *upper graph* shows the estimated covariance function for U.S. Treasury data (May 2002). The estimation uses a Gaussian kernel and shows maturities of 3,6,..,36 months. The *lower graph* shows the obtained eigenvectors. The first two eigenvectors correspond to the eigenvalues 3.4224 and 0.0569, respectively, while the further are of magnitude 10^{-15}

nificant eigenvalues (3.4224 and 0.0569), while the remaining eigenvalues are of much smaller magnitude. In this example, therefore, it turns out to be sufficient to use the first two eigenvectors only.

More generally, assume that we have already determined the first N eigenfunctions. Then we use the following covariance function for the calibration:

$$\hat{\rho}(\lambda_1,\ldots,\lambda_N,t_1,t_2) := \sum_{k=1}^{N} \lambda_k e_k(t_1)e_k(t_2)$$

As before, a standard software package can be used to extract the $\lambda_1,\ldots,\lambda_N$ from observable derivatives prices by a least-squares approach. Note that in comparison to the previously presented model, a much smaller set of derivatives can be used for the calibration. The implementation of this last step using credit derivatives data is subject to future research.

Nevertheless, we already analyzed some bond data and estimated the covariance functions and the eigenvectors/-values. Take, for example, the data from Greek Treasury bonds. The estimation results may be found in Fig. 1. First, note that the variance for bonds with small maturities is higher than for bonds with large maturities. This is usually referred to as "volatility hump." Second, for the period June to August 2001 negative correlations for bonds with small versus bonds with large maturities were observed. This reflects the fact that, in this period, interest rates with short maturities compare to long-maturity ones moved into the opposite direction.

Taking a closer look at the eigenvectors reveals the components of the covariance function. The first eigenvector generates more or less the shape of the covariance functions. The already-mentioned effect that larger maturities relate to a smaller variance may be observed here as well. The second eigenvector covers the wriggly structure of the covariance function.

The Hybrid Calibration Suggested in Roncoroni and Guitto (2000)

In the paper of Roncoroni and Guitto (2000) two calibration procedures for infinite dimensional term structures of interest rates (i.e., without credit risk) has been put forward. We give a short outline.

Historical Calibration

The first proposed procedure gives a way of using historical data to estimate the dynamics of the forward rates. To reduce the number of parameters to a finite number it is assumed that the yield curve falls into a class of parametric families (e.g., polynomial or spline). Thus, a observed yield curve may be approximated well by $F(a_1,\ldots,a_n)$ for a suitable n. The parameters itself follow a diffusion in R^n,

$$da(t) = \mathrm{b}\,dt + \leq d\mathrm{w}_t.$$

The goal is to estimate the parameters of this diffusion from historical data and thereafter reduce the number of parameters by a principal component analysis for $a(t) = (a_1(t),.., a_n(t))$. To this, historical data for yield curves are used. Every observed yield curve leads (by suitably inverting F) to an observation of **a**, such that **b** and Σ are easily estimated. Finally, a principal component analysis on **a** is used to reduce the dimension of Σ to a suitably small n.

Historical-Implicit Calibration

The estimated dynamics of **a** implies certain covariance functional of $f(t, T)$, namely

$$\mathrm{Cov}(f(t,t_1); f(t,t_2)) = \sum_{k=1}^{n} \lambda_k f_k(t_2) f_k(t_2)$$

where λ_k and f_k can be derived from F and the estimated dynamics of **a**. However, derivative's prices computed from this dynamics typically do not match observed market prices. The authors therefore suggest to allow λ_k to depend on time. These functions are obtained by calibrating the now time-dependent model to prices of derivatives.

Risk Measures

This section considers the application of the considered framework to Risk Management. First, note that for calibrating and pricing the model needs to be considered under the risk-neutral measure Q while for risk management the distribution of portfolio changes under the real-world measure P are needed. Due to the Girsanov-Theorem, the transition from P to Q may change the default intensity as well as the mean of the Gaussian random fields X and $\overline{X}$. However, the covariance functions remain the same.

Under P we therefore have to estimate the default intensity as well as the drift, while the covariance functions may be recovered from the proposed calibration procedures. As the riskiness of the products is heavily influence by the covariance function, the calibrated covariance gives a useful tool which incorporates actual market data. For the estimation of the drift, well-known kernel estimates may be used. For the estimates of the default intensity one may relay one estimates published by rating agencies or use other available methods. In the following we assume that these values are at hand and we compute two risk-measures, Value-at-Risk (VaR) and Expected Shortfall (ES) for zero-coupon bond prices in the proposed model. For more information on risk-measures the reader may want to consider McNeil et al. (2005).[15]

We assume that (A1) holds and that the defaultable forward rate follows (2) under the real-world measure P. Note that (3) gives the relation of $\bar{f}$; and λ, the default intensity. We have the following result:

Proposition 5. The value at risk of a defaultable zero-recovery bond $B^0(\cdot,T)$ over a period Δ is given by

$$\mathrm{VaR}_\alpha = \exp(\mu_\lambda + \sigma_\lambda^2/2)\Phi\left(\frac{\ln(x+B^0(0,T))-\mu}{\sigma} - \rho\sigma_\lambda\right) + 1 - \exp\left(-\mu^\lambda + \frac{(\sigma^\lambda)^2}{2}\right)$$

while the expected shortfall equals

$$\frac{1}{1-\alpha}\exp\left(\mu+\mu_\lambda+\frac{\sigma_\lambda^2+\sigma^2+2\rho\sigma\sigma_\lambda}{2}\right)$$
$$\Phi\left(\frac{-\ln\mathrm{VaR}_\alpha+\mu}{\sigma}+(\rho\sigma_\lambda\sigma+\sigma^2)(\sigma_\lambda^2+\sigma^2+2\rho\sigma_\lambda\sigma)\right)$$

Proof. The proof heavily relies on the expression (7), derived in Proposition 7. Note that this formula holds under P as well as under Q, just that the dynamics of $\bar{f}$ and f as well as the default intensity differ. This gives that

$$B^0(0,T) = 1_{\{\tau>t\}}\exp(\mu+\sigma\xi),$$

where $\xi \sim N(0,1)$. From (7), we obtain that

$$\mu = \mu(T) = -\int_0^T (\mu(0,u)(1-L_u^{-1}) - \bar{\mu}(0,u)L_u^{-1})du$$
$$+\frac{1}{2}\int_0^T\int_0^T [1_u 1_v(c(u\wedge v,u,v)-c(0,u,v)) + 2\frac{l_u}{L_v}(\zeta(u\wedge v,v,u)-\zeta(0,v,u))$$
$$+\frac{1}{L_u^2}(\bar{c}(u\wedge v,u,v)-\bar{c}(0,u,v))]dv\,du\}$$

as well as

$$\sigma = \sigma(T) = \int_0^T\int_0^T \frac{\bar{c}(0,u,v) - 2(1+L_v)\zeta(0,v,u) + (1+L_u)(1+L_v)c(0,u,v)}{L_u L_v} du dv$$

By (5) the default intensity is also normally distributed. Hence,

$$\begin{aligned}P(B^0(\Delta,T) - B^0(0,T) \le x) &= P(1_{\{\tau>\Delta\}}\exp(\mu+\sigma\xi) \le x + B^0(0,T)) \\ &= E^P(\exp(-\int_0^\Delta \lambda_u du)1_{\{\exp(\mu+\sigma\xi)\le x+B^0(0,T)\}}) \\ &\quad + 1_{\{0\le x+B^0(0,T)\}}P(\tau\le\Delta)\end{aligned} \tag{13}$$

First,

$$P(\tau \le \Delta) = 1 - E^P(\exp(-\int_0^\Delta \lambda_u du)) = 1 - \exp(-\mu^\lambda + \frac{(\sigma^\lambda)^2}{2})t$$

where a small calculation gives

$$\mu^\lambda = \int_0^\Delta \frac{\bar{\mu}(u,u) - \mu(u,u)}{L_u} d_u$$

$$(\sigma^\lambda)^2 = \int_0^\Delta \int_0^\Delta \frac{\bar{c}(u \wedge v,u,v) - 2\zeta(u \wedge v,u,v) + c(u \wedge v,u,v)}{L_u L_v} dudv$$

It is well-known (cf. Schmidt (2003), App. B) that

$$E(e^{\zeta_2} 1_{\{\zeta_1 \le a\}}) = \exp(\mu_2 + \sigma_2^2/2)\Phi(\tfrac{a-\mu_1-\rho\sigma_1\sigma_2}{\sigma_1})$$

if ξ_i are $N(\mu_i, \sigma_i^2)$ and the correlation is ρ. Hence the first term in (13) equals

$$E^P(\exp(-\int_0^\Delta \lambda_u du) 1_{\{\xi \le \frac{\ln(x+B^0(0,T))-\mu}{\sigma}\}})$$
$$= \exp(\mu_\lambda + \sigma_\lambda^2/2)\Phi(\frac{\ln(x+B^0(0,T))-\mu}{\sigma} - \rho\sigma_\lambda)$$

where

$$\rho = \int_0^T \int_0^\Delta (\frac{\bar{c}(0,u,v)}{L_u L_v} + \frac{c(0,u,c)(1+L_u)}{L_u L_v}$$
$$- \frac{\zeta(0,u,v) - \zeta(0,v,u)(1+L_u)}{L_u L_v}) dv\, du$$

Let $a = \mathrm{VaR}_\alpha$. The next step is to compute ES, which is equal to

$$\frac{1}{1-\alpha} E(1_{\{\tau>t\}} \exp(\mu + \sigma\xi) 1_{\{1_{\{\tau>t\}} \exp(\mu+\sigma\xi)>a\}})$$
$$= \frac{1}{1-\alpha} E(1_{\{\tau>t\}} \exp(\mu + \sigma\xi) 1_{\{\exp(\mu+\sigma\xi)>a\}})$$
$$= \frac{1}{1-\alpha} E(\exp(-\int_0^\Delta \lambda_u du + \mu + \sigma\xi) 1_{\{\exp(\mu+\sigma\xi)>a\}})$$

provided $a > 0$, or stated otherwise α smaller than the default probability. As previously, this expression is computed easily and we obtain the stated formula.

Conclusion

We considered hybrid calibration techniques in pricing of single-name credit risky securities and risk management. After deriving necessary drift conditions and relevant pricing formulas of a number of relevant single-name credit derivatives, which were obtained in explicit form, we discussed different hybrid calibration approaches. The hybrid calibration proposed in Schmidt (2003) is particular attractive for the use in risk management for several reasons: first, it combines the advantages of estimation and classical calibration. It is also acknowledged that starting from an infinite factor approach the flexibility gained in choosing the number of factors on-the-run leads to an improved stability. Second, it can be used in a market where credit derivatives data are scarce as the combination with historical data leads to an increased stability. Finally, applications to risk management were discussed.

End Notes

1. Schmidt, T. (2003). Credit Risk Modeling with Random Fields, Ph.D. thesis, University of Giessen.
2. Kennedy, D.P. (1994). The term structure of interest rates as a Gaussian random field, *Mathematical Finance 4*, 247–258.
3. Roncoroni, A., and Guiotto, P. (2000). Theory and calibration of HJM with shape factors, *in* Mathematical Finance – Bachelier Congress 2000, Springer, Berlin Heidelberg New York, 407–426.
4. Schmidt, T. (2007). Hybrid calibration for defaultable term structures with gaussian random fields, *in* International Conference on Management Innovation, Shanghai, Vol. 1, Shanghai University of Finance and Economics and Risk China Research Center, University of Toronto.
5. Schmidt, T. (2006). An infinite factor model for credit risk, *International Journal of Theoretical and Applied Finance 9*, 43–68.
6. Adler, R.J. (1981). *The Geometry of Random Fields*, Wiley, New York.
7. Filipović, D. (2001). *Consistency Problems for Heath-Jarrow-Morton Interest Rate Models*, Vol. 1760 of *Lecture Notes in Mathematics*, Springer, Berlin Heidelberg New York.
8. Vasicek, O. (1977). An equilibrium characterization of the term structure, *Journal of Financial Economics 5*, 177–188.
9. Schmid, B., Zagst, R., and Antes, S. (2008). Pricing of credit derivatives, *submitted.*
10. Pang, K. (1998). Calibration of Gaussian Heath, Jarrow and Morton and random field interest rate term structure models, *Review of Derivatives Research 4*, 315–346.
11. Roncoroni, A., and Guiotto, P. (2000). op cit.
12. Kennedy, D.P. (1997). Characterizing Gaussian models of the term structure of interest rates, *Mathematical Finance 7*, 107–118.
13. Filipovic, D. (2001). op cit.
14. Hall, P., Fisher, N.I., and Hoffmann, B. (1994). On the nonparametric estimation of covariance functions, *Annals of Statistics* 2115–2134.
15. McNeil, A., Frey, R., and Embrechts, P. (2005), *Quantitative Risk Management: Concepts, Techniques and Tools*, Princeton University Press.

Chapter 10
The Sarbanes-Oxley Act and the Production Efficiency of Public Accounting Firms

H. Chang, H.L. Choy, W.W. Cooper, and M.-H. Lin[a]

Introduction

In response to a series of corporate and accounting frauds at high-profile companies such as Enron, WorldCom, Global Crossing, etc, President Bush signed the Sarbanes-Oxley Act (SOX) into law on July 30, 2002. The Act represents the most significant reform of the securities laws since passage of the Securities Act in 1933. One of the primary objectives of the Act is to improve the independence of auditors and the quality of audit services. For instance, the Act prohibits public accounting firms from providing certain non-audit services that can potentially compromise their independence. It also requires these audit firms to attest to their clients' assessment of the effectiveness of internal control systems in their audit reports, and sets up a new private regulatory board, the Public Company Accounting Oversight Board (PCAOB), to oversee and investigate the audits and auditors of public companies.

Over the last seven decades, the requirement that all publicly traded companies have an annual audit of financial statements by an independent CPA has probably been the single biggest contributor to public accounting firm revenues. Historically, the second largest contributor to public accounting firm revenues has been the complexity of the Internal Revenue Code. However, the sector that has provided the greatest growth in public accounting firm revenues in recent years is management advisory services (MAS) or consulting. The increased complexity of the globally competitive economy and continuing developments in the information technology intensive business environment both spurred growth in the consulting area and this enabled the "Big 5" accounting firms to post double-digit annual revenue growth rates during the mid-1990s.[1]

With the advent of a global information economy, specialized consulting services are believed to be more productive than traditional auditing or tax services in revenue generation. Banker, Chang and Natarajan observed that profitability of the CPA firms had been largely sustained in recent years by the impact that MAS had on firm productivity.[2] Since SOX (Section 201) restricts auditors from providing

[a]The Authors, are grateful to this *International Journal of Services Sciences* for permission to reproduce this article from vol. 1, no. 1 2008.

certain consulting services to their clients, such a restriction could reduce public accounting firm revenues generated from MAS services and decrease their productive efficiency because of inappropriate staff compositions and sizes. On the other hand, the Act (Section 404) requires business firm managements to assess the effectiveness of their internal control systems and it requires auditors in their audit reports to attest to management assessments. Furthermore, in response to SOX, many companies also hire public accounting firms other than their auditors to document and test their internal control systems. Thus, the mandated new attestation services for audit clients, and the internal control systems documentation and testing services for non-audit clients, can add to revenues generated from the customary accounting and audit services of public accounting firms and could possibly also increase their production efficiency.

Given these opposing effects in different provisions of SOX, the question of whether the efficiency of public accounting firms increased or decreased after the passage of SOX becomes an interesting empirical research issue. A few studies using client level data have looked at the effect of the Act on audit services and observed improvements in auditor independence[3] and an increase in audit fees charged by the Big 4 in 2002.[4] To our best knowledge, there is little empirical evidence, on how SOX affects the efficiency of public accounting firms. In this study we therefore seek to document empirically the effect of the Act, as a regulatory intervention by the Federal Government, on the productive efficiency of public accounting firms.

We employ two different techniques based on two different estimating principles. Data Envelopment Analysis (DEA), which is one of the techniques we employ, is non-parametric and oriented to frontier rather than central tendency estimates.[5] We also use the central tendency and parametric methods that are involved in OLS regressions. In this way we protect against the "methodological bias" that can occur when only one method of analysis is used.[6]

The first of these two methods is designed to evaluate productive efficiencies which we use to evaluate the performances of public accounting firms using annual operations data from 58 of the 100 largest accounting firms in the U.S. over the period 2000–2004. We then use both DEA-based and conventional test procedures to test for production efficiency differences between pre- and post-SOX periods. Our statistical test results indicate that the production efficiency of public accounting firms increased after the passage of SOX. Moreover, our results are robust even after controlling for service mix, the number of public clients, and the operating size of public accounting firms.

Background and Hypothesis Development

The nature and extent of leading public accounting firm involvements in numerous accounting scandals at high profile companies in the late 1990s and early 2000s led to reforms of public accounting through attempted improvements in the independence of auditors and the quality of audit services. Section 201 of SOX prohibits auditors from providing eight types of services to their clients: bookkeeping, financial information systems design and implementation, appraisals or valuation services, actuarial services, outsourcing internal audit services, management and human resources services, broker/dealer and investment banking services, and legal or expert services unrelated to audit services. In addition, auditors cannot offer any service that the PCAOB determines to be impermissible. For non-audit services other than those listed above, such as tax services, an approval by the audit committee is required.

These new rules and regulations are aimed at limiting certain "lucrative" services of public accounting firms that might compromise their independence. If public accounting firms are forced to give up revenues from these lucrative services for which they are already organized and staffed, their production efficiency is likely to be decreased. This possibility is further extended because prior studies report a positive relation between service fees and the joint provision of audit and non-audit services.[7] By offering joint services, an accounting firm may benefit from potential knowledge spillover across services. These synergies may then result in cost savings or revenue augmentations that increase production efficiency. Since public accounting firms can no longer provide non-audit services to their audit clients, their production efficiency is, instead, likely to be decreased.

Section 404 of SOX moves in the opposite direction. It requires auditors in their audit reports to attest to management assessments of the internal control systems. The new requirements offer opportunities for public accounting firms to generate extra revenues from both additional audit procedures and accounting services. Specifically, on the audit services side, auditors likely pass on the costs of additional audit steps to their clients with a resulting increase in audit service revenues. On the accounting services side, many firms hire other public accounting firms to document, update and test their internal control systems as required by Section 404. This provides public accounting firms an opportunity to generate revenues from additional accounting services. A recent survey conducted by Financial Executives International on 217 firms with average revenue of $5 billion or more report that firms in their sample spent an average of $4.36 million to comply with Section 404 in 2004. An average of $1.34 million was spent internally and $1.72 millions on external accounting/consulting and software fees to comply with the provisions of Section 404. The remaining $1.3 million was spent on additional audit fees for attestations of the system, with a resulting average increase of 57% over the regular financial statement audit fees.[8]

Research Hypothesis

In recent decades many public accounting firms offered MAS or consulting practices in which they employed specialists in fields as varied as information systems and human resources management. For many firms, the MAS part of the practice was the fastest growing segment. Unlike traditional auditing or tax practices, MAS services offer opportunities for specialized services and potential for higher markup of fees over costs. Non-audit services are lucrative businesses that yield higher margins than do audit fees.[9] MAS services are more efficient than A&A and TAX services in generating revenues from the same level of human resource inputs since the provision of joint audit and non-audit services creates synergies. Therefore, Section 201 of the Act, which constrains public accounting firms from offering certain consulting services to their public clients, can both take away the synergy and reduce efficiency. However, these consulting businesses remain available for serving non-audit or private clients, so the provisions of Section 201 may not lead to a substantial reduction in revenues generated from MAS services. Hence this section of the Act need not significantly reduce the production efficiency of public accounting firms.

Section 404 requires management evaluation of internal control systems and strengthens audit requirements. These provisions increase potential revenues to accounting firms from additional audit services. Some evidence indicates that firms with revenues of at least a billion dollars experience, on average, a 57% increase in their audit fees in order to comply with SOX.[10] Further, as described earlier, in response to Sect. 2.1 many publicly traded companies hire auditors other than their own to document and test their internal control systems. With large-scale implementation of Section 404, we could expect public accounting firms to improve their efficiency in the post SOX period because of increases in revenues from Section 404 compliance services. This is especially true for the initial years (e.g., 2003 and 2004) because accounting firms may have flexibility to charge a premium for accounting and auditing services related to compliance partly because PCAOB has not yet set up a standard of compliance. Therefore, we state our hypothesis in both null and alternate forms as follows:

H_0 (null): SOX has had no effect on the production efficiency of public accounting firms.

H_A (alternate): SOX has had a positive effect on the production efficiency of public accounting firms.

Research Design

Our objective in this study is to evaluate the effect of SOX on the efficiency of public accounting firms. Toward this end, we conduct our research in two stages. Stage 1 is a univariate analysis which involves two steps. In the first step, we use Data Envelopment Analysis (DEA) to estimate an efficiency score for each of our sample of public accounting firms during the period 2000–2004. We then employ both DEA-based and conventional test procedures in the second step to test for efficiency differences of these firms between the pre- and post-SOX periods. Stage 2 is a multivariate analysis in which we specify and estimate two fixed-effects regression models to assess the effect of SOX on the efficiency of public accounting firms after controlling for potential confounding effects of explicitly identified contextual variables.

DEA and Its Test Statistics

DEA is an estimation methodology that evaluates the relative efficiency of decision making units. It was introduced by Charnes, Cooper and Rhodes[11] and extended by Banker, Charnes and Cooper.[12] In less than 30 years since its inception, DEA has become an important and widespread analytical tool to estimate production functions and relative efficiency of business firms and many other types of entities. For instance, the bibliography by Emrouznejad, Parker and Tavares[13] references 3,236 publications written by 2,167 authors using DEA to deal with efficiency evaluation problems in 42 countries during the period 1978–2003.[14] In addition, several studies have documented that DEA is preferable for modeling production functions compared to traditional parametric methods.[15] In the accounting literature, DEA has been employed to estimate the productive efficiency of public accounting firms.[16]

The original DEA models, which are deterministic, specify the production set relating outputs to inputs only in terms of properties such as convexity and monotonicity and do not impose any explicit parametric structure on the production set or the distribution of efficiency of individual observations. However, statistical properties have been derived for the DEA efficiency estimators and a variety of statistical tests can be used if additional structure is specified.[17]

To see what is involved, let $Y_j = (y_1,...y_j,...y_N) \geq 0$ and $X_j = (x_{1j},...x_{ij},...x_{lj}) \geq 0$, $j = 1,....N$ be the observed output and input vectors with components used in DEA to generate an underlying "production possibility set" $S = \{(X,Y)|$ output Y can be produced from inputs X$\}$ for a sample of N public accounting firms. The inefficiency $\theta_j^* \geq 1$ of an observation $(X_j, Y_j) \in S$, is measured radially by the reciprocal of Shephard's output distance function and given by $\theta_j^*\ \theta\ \theta^*(X_j, Y_j) = \text{SUP}\ \{\theta|\ X_j, \theta Y)_j\ S\}$ as obtained from the following model,

$$
\begin{aligned}
&\theta_j^* = \max \theta \\
&\text{subject to} \\
&\qquad \sum_{k=1}^{n} y_{rk}\lambda_k \geq \theta y_r, \qquad r = 1,...,s \\
&\qquad \sum_{k=1}^{n} x_{ik}\lambda_k \leq x_{ik}, \qquad r = 1,...,s \qquad (1) \\
&\qquad \sum_{k=1}^{n} \lambda_k = 1 \\
&\qquad \theta, \lambda_k \geq 0 \quad \forall k
\end{aligned}
$$

so that θ_j^* is associated with firm $j = 1, \ldots, n$.

Here $\theta_j^* \geq 1$ is the Debreu-Farrell measure of efficiency.[18] We have $\theta_j^* = 1$ if and only if technical efficiency is achieved and $\theta_j^* > 1$ when this is not the case so that

$\theta_j^* y_r - y_r > 1$ represents the shortfall in output $r = 1, \ldots, s$ due to technical inefficiency in the performances of firm j.

To conclude this part of the discussion we introduce the following:

Definition: Technical efficiency is achieved in the performance of firm j if and only if it is not possible to improve any input or output amount without worsening some other input or output amount. *Conversely*, technical inefficiency is present if and only if it is possible to improve some input or output amount without worsening any other input or output amount.

Notice that such evaluations do not require unit price or cost information. This is unlike other types such as "allocative efficiency" where such unit prices and costs make substitutions possible so that improvement in some input or output amounts may be improved to increase the efficiency score at the expense of worsening other input or output amounts.[19]

The θ_j are consistent estimators, so we can employ the following two DEA-based test statistics that we now describe to test for the effect of SOX on the production efficiency of public accounting firms.

We turn now to the first statistical test. We start by assuming that θ_j is exponentially distributed. This is a standard way of allowing for the fact that the efficiency measure is non-negative. Then to test the null hypothesis (that SOX has no effect on the production efficiency of public accounting firms) against the alternate hypothesis (that SOX has a positive effect on the production efficiency of public accounting firms), we can employ the test statistic given by

$$T_{\exp} = \sum_{j \in N1} (\hat{\theta}_j - 1) / \sum_{j \in N2} (\hat{\theta}_j - 1) \tag{2}$$

which is evaluated by the F-distribution with (2N1, 2N2) degrees of freedom, where N1 and N2 are the number of sample public accounting firms in the periods before and after 2002 (the year in which the Act was passed), respectively.

Another statistical assumption is to use only the non-negative portion, or non-negative half of the normal distribution, instead of the exponential distribution. If the θ_j are assumed to be half-normally distributed for public accounting firms we can test the null hypothesis against the alternate hypothesis, described above, by employing the test statistic given by

$$T_{hn} = \sum_{j \in N1} (\hat{\theta}_j - 1)^2 / \sum_{j \subset N2} (\hat{\theta}_j - 1)^2 \tag{3}$$

which is evaluated by the F-distribution with (N1, N2) degrees of freedom.

In addition to the two DEA-based statistical tests described above, which are oriented toward efficiency frontier evaluations – see Cooper et al. (2006) – we also use three conventional parametric based tests, (1) the Welch two-sample test, (2) the Wilcoxon two-sample test and (3) the Kolmogorov-Sminrov two-sample tests to test for the effect of SOX on the efficiency of public accounting firms.

Regression Analysis

As was discussed above, MAS services have been found to be more efficient than traditional A&A and TAX services in generating revenues for the same level of human resource inputs. The SOX Act impacts all three types of professional services as offered by public accounting firms. Hence public accounting firms might have adjusted their service mix in response to the regulatory intervention of SOX. As a result, their efficiency could change due to changes in their service mix. Therefore, we include two service mix variables, A&A% and MAS% in our regression model to examine the effect of SOX on the production efficiency of public accounting firms. We do not include TAX% as the sum of A&A%, TAX% and MAS% equals one.

Prior research on audit effort has demonstrated that human resource inputs for clients with public ownership are significantly greater than that for clients with private ownership.[20] Publicly owned firms tend to be larger than private firms and have to comply with listing requirements of exchanges when they are listed; thus, audits of public clients are expected to require more inputs than those of private ones. Audits of publicly owned clients can also expose an auditor to the risk of class action lawsuits. This leads to higher insurance costs so a higher service fee will generally be charged for public clients. These factors could all lead to a gain in production efficiency. Thus, we include a dummy variable to control for the potential effect of public ownership of the firms being serviced.

Following Banker, Chang and Cunningham, we also include the number of branch offices of the accounting firm as a control variable.[21] Finding that the productivity of accounting firms is negatively correlated with the number of offices an accounting firm has, Banker, Chang and Cunningham argue that, as the number of offices increases, the given human resources are spread over a larger number of offices and this increases control and communication problems and related expenses.

Prior studies have documented that the Big 4 accounting firms charge a premium for their audit services.[22] The Big 4 are also likely to charge a premium for other services they provide. Clients are willing to pay the premium, in part, for Big 4 reputation. Further, the production correspondence at the scale levels achieved by Big 4 firms may be different from the production performance possibilities of non-Big 4 firms.[23] To control for potential effects of a Big 4 price premium on production efficiency, we add a dummy variable to our regression models when the Big 4 firms are included in our estimation.

Regression Models

To investigate the effect of SOX on the production efficiency of public accounting firms while controlling for the potential effects of the contextual variables, we specify and estimate the following two fixed-effects models:

$$\ln \Phi = \beta_0 + \beta_1 YEAR01 + \beta_2 YEAR03 + \beta_3 YEAR04 + \beta_4 A\&A\% + \beta_5 MAS\% + \beta_6 \ln SEC\_CLIENT + \beta_7 \ln OFFICES + \beta_8 BIG4 + \varepsilon \tag{4a}$$

and

$$\ln \varphi = \beta_0 + \beta_1 YEAR01 + \beta_2 YEAR03 + \beta_3 YEAR04 + \beta_4 A\&A\% + \beta_5 MAS\% + \beta_{24} YEAR03 * A\&A\% + \beta_{34} YEAR04 * A\&A\% + \beta_{25} YEAR03 * MAS\% + \beta_{35} YEAR04 * MAS\% + \beta_6 \ln SEC\_CLIENT + \beta_7 \ln OFFICES + \beta_8 BIG5 + \varepsilon \tag{4b}$$

where *lnφ* is the logarithm of efficiency estimated from the DEA model in (1), YEAR0t = 1 for t = 1, 3 and 4, and zero otherwise, A&A% represents the proportion of revenues generated from A&A services, MAS% denotes the proportion of revenues generated from MAS services, lnSEC_CLIENT represents the logarithm of the number of public clients while lnOFFICES denotes the logarithm of the number of branch offices, and BIG4 is a dummy variable taking on a value of one if the firm is one of the Big4 firms and zero otherwise. We take the logarithm on the estimated production efficiency to reduce heteroscedasticity.

Note that, YEAR01 is included to capture the difference in the efficiency between the two years in the pre SOX period, years 2000 and 2001. YEAR03 and YEAR04 are used to capture the efficiency difference between 2000 and the two years, 2003 and 2004, after the passage of SOX. These three dummies enable us to evaluate whether there is a significant difference in the production efficiency of public accounting firms between the pre and the post SOX periods.

Our research design on the use of the two-stage approach represented in (4a) and (4b) by first estimating production efficiencies and then seeking to correlate these efficiencies with various contextual variables is motivated by prior research. For instance, Ray regressed DEA scores on a variety of socio-economic factors to identify key performance drivers in school districts.[24] Banker, Chang and Kao employed the two-stage DEA method to evaluate the impact of IT investment on public accounting firm productivity.[25] Recently, Banker and Natarajan have provided theoretical justification for the use of the two-stage models in DEA to evaluate contextual variables affecting DEA efficiency ratios.[26]

Empirical Estimation and Results

The sample of public accounting firms that is included in this study is obtained from *Accounting Today*'s annual survey of the top 100 accounting firms in the US for the period 2000–2004. All data reported in these annual surveys are for domestic U.S. operations and exclude foreign holdings. This annual survey of the profession's largest firms has become one of the most often cited sources in the field.[27]

We confine our sample to these top 100 accounting firms because the revenue information of other accounting firms is not publicly available. As the main objective of this study is to evaluate the impact of SOX on the production efficiency of public accounting firms, we also eliminate any non-CPA firms (e.g., H&R Block, Century Business Services, American Express, etc.) from the sample. Section 201 of SOX restricts the MAS services *auditors* can provide to their clients and Section 404 requires the evaluation and attestation of *auditors* to management evaluations of the internal control system. The effect of both sections is likely to be minimal on non-CPA firms. Observations in the year 2002 are excluded from our analysis since nearly half of this year was in the pre-Act period (up until July 30, 2002) while the other half was in the post-Act period. Our data do not allow us to differentiate between these two periods in 2002. To minimize the problem of misclassification, we focus our study on the sample after excluding observations from 2002. Our final sample consists of 58 firms for which data are available for the four-year period beginning 2000 and ending 2004 (excluding 2002), providing us with a total of 232 (=58 × 4) firm-year observations for analyses.

We focus on production correspondences between total service revenues generated and human resources employed by public accounting firms. The total revenues, measured in millions of dollars of revenues, include revenues from accounting and auditing services (A&A), taxation services (TAX), and management advisory services (MAS). The three human resource input variables considered are the number of partners (PARTNERS), the number of other professionals (PROFESSIONALS) and the number of other employees (OTHERS).

Personnel costs constitute a significant fraction of total costs for public accounting firms. A recent national survey indicates that employee costs and partner compensation account for about 75% of the revenues, while capital costs are less than 7%, for accounting practices with revenues in excess of one million dollars.[28] While data on the total service revenue is obtained from the annual survey of *Accounting Today*, the number of each of the three professional staff levels was hand collected from annual reports of accounting firms that were filed with the American Institute of Certified Public Accountants (AICPA). After the enactment of the SOX, any public accounting firm that audits financial statements of public companies has to register with the Public Company Accounting Oversight Board (PCAOB). One of the requirements for such registration is the participation of the firm in the peer review program. Hence, in the post-SOX period, all auditors of public firms must have their annual reports filed with AICPA.

Descriptive Statistics on Output and Inputs

Table 10.1 provides descriptive statistics for total revenues and the three human resource variables for all four years. To facilitate comparison, the total revenues are inflation adjusted to 2,000 dollars. The high orders of the standard deviations for all of the variables suggest that the firms in the sample vary significantly in size and

Table 10.1 Descriptive statistics on outputs and inputs of public accounting firms

Variables	Mean	Std Dev	Median
Year: 2000 (No. of obs. = 58)			
REVENUES	$475.6M	$1,610.1M	$25.5M
PARTNERS	187.9	509.2	29.5
PROFESSIONALS	1,524.9	5,347.6	135
OTHERS	582.8	1,756.8	65
Year: 2001 (No. of obs. = 58)			
REVENUES	$431.9M	$1,431.5M	$28.2M
PARTNERS	194.8	514.9	32
PROFESSIONALS	1,547.7	5,193.9	136
OTHERS	539.7	1,565.5	67
Year: 2003 (No. of obs. = 58)			
REVENUE	$397.3M	$1,230.4M	$32.2M
PARTNERS	196.5	493.5	33.5
PROFESSIONALS	1,315.5	3,817.3	143.5
OTHERS	486.9	1,383.7	67.5
Year: 2004 (No. of obs. = 58)			
REVENUE	$415.3M	$1,270.6M	$38.0M
PARTNERS	194.7	477.3	34
PROFESSIONALS	1,348.9	3,802.8	160.5
OTHERS	516.8	1,496.8	68

REVENUES, Total revenues expressed in million (M) dollars deflated to 2000. PARTNERS, Number of partners. PROFESSIONALS, Number of professionals. OTHERS, Number of other employees

composition. Median values for all variables are much smaller than the means indicating large disparities between the smallest and largest firms in the sample. The mean total revenues dropped from 2000 to 2003 by about 16%, but increased in 2004 by about 5%. The mix of different types of employees (partners, professionals and others) in 2001 changed slightly from that in 2000 showing a small increase in the proportion of professionals with a corresponding decrease in the proportion of other employees. However, the mix changed again in both 2003 and 2004, showing a small increase in the proportion of partners with a corresponding decrease in the proportion of professionals.

Descriptive Statistics on Contextual Variables

Table 10.2 provides descriptive statistics on contextual variables of public accounting firms. As can be seen from Table 2, the mix of service revenue reveals a continuing increase in the share of revenue generated by A&A with a corresponding decline in the share of revenue generated by MAS after the passage of SOX. In contrast, TAX% remains quite stable across both pre- and post SOX periods. The number of branch offices increases steadily over the period from 2000 to 2004 with a slight drop in 2004.

Table 10.2 Descriptive statistics on contextual variables of public accounting firms

Variables	Mean	Std Dev	Median
Year: 2000 (No. of obs. = 58)			
A&A%	43.1	10.1	42.3
TAX%	30.6	7.8	30
MAS%	26.3	11.0	24.5
SEC_CLIENT	205.2	677.2	7
OFFICES	15.1	26.9	5
Year: 2001 (No. of obs. = 58)			
A&A%	42.1	10.9	41.5
TAX%	30.9	7.8	31
MAS%	27.0	12.1	25.5
SEC_CLIENT	208.1	688.1	8
OFFICES	15.2	26.2	4.5
Year: 2003 (No. of obs. = 58)			
A&A%	44.2	10.8	44
TAX%	31.5	7.9	32.5
MAS%	24.3	11.8	23.5
SEC_CLIENT	226.5	754.3	9.5
OFFICES	15.7	24.2	6
Year: 2004 (No. of obs. = 58)			
A&A%	44.9	10.3	44.5
TAX%	31.1	7.5	30.5
MAS%	24.0	10.6	25
SEC_CLIENT	229.7	759.0	10
OFFICES	15.6	23.7	5.5

A&A%, Proportion of accounting and auditing services (A&A) revenue. TAX%, Proportion of taxation services (TAX) revenue. MAS%, Proportion of management advisory services (MAS) revenue. SEC_CLIENT, Number of public-listed clients. OFFICES, Number of branch offices.

Table 10.3 shows the correlation matrix of the contextual variables. Since the sample is skewed, we focus our attention on the Spearman rank correlation. As expected, A&A% is negatively correlated with both TAX% and MAS%.

The number of SEC clients is positively correlated with the percentage of revenues from A&A services (a correlation of 0.1637). The number of SEC clients has a significantly negative correlation with the percentage of revenues from TAX services (a correlation of −0.1344). The number of offices is significantly positively correlated with the number of public clients. This is consistent with the assumption that public accounting firms set up offices locally in order to better serve their clients.

Empirical Results and Discussion

Estimated Production Efficiencies

In the estimation of the efficiency of public accounting firms, we treat the total revenues as the single output variable and the number of partners, the number of professionals, and the number of other employees as three input variables. Using one

Table 10.3 Correlation matrix for contextual variables and BIG4 variable

	A&A%	TAX%	MAS%	lnSEC_ CLIENT	lnOFFICES	BIG4
A&A%	1.0000	−0.1781	−0.7365	0.1637	−0.0693	0.0940
	–	(0.007)	(0.001)	(0.012)	(0.293)	(0.153)
TAX%	−0.2507	1.0000	−0.4405	−0.1344	0.0237	−0.0841
	(0.001)	–	(0.001)	(0.041)	(0.719)	(0.202)
MAS%	−0.7552	−0.4449	1.0000	−0.0880	0.0373	−0.0709
	(0.001)	(0.001)	–	(0.181)	(0.572)	(0.282)
LnSEC_ CLIENT	0.2900	−0.1821	−0.1452	1.0000	0.6592	0.4397
	(0.000)	(0.005)	(0.027)	–	(0.000)	(0.000)
lnOFFICES	−0.0080	−0.0163	0.0178	0.6654	1.0000	0.4351
	(0.923)	(0.805)	(0.787)	(0.000)	–	(0.001)
BIG4	0.1649	−0.0922	−0.0902	0.5264	0.5525	1.0000
	(0.011)	(0.162)	(0.171)	(0.000)	(0.000)	–

P-values in parentheses. Pearson correlations are below the diagonal, and Spearman correlations are above the diagonal. Variable definitions appear in Table 10.2.

output and three inputs, we estimate the production efficiency using the DEA model specified in (1). We summarize the mean estimated DEA efficiencies in Table 4. As we observe from Table 10.4, the efficiency of public accounting firms increases by about 10% from 0.626 in the pre SOX period to 0.699 in post SOX when the Big4 are excluded from the estimation. Similarly, the efficiency also increases by about 10% after the passage of SOX when the Big4 are included in the estimations.

Statistical Tests of the Difference in Production Efficiencies

As described earlier, we use two types of test procedures to test for the null hypothesis that SOX has had no impact on the production efficiency of public accounting firms. We present the statistical test results for the efficiency differences in Table 10.5. The DEA based statistical tests all lead to rejection of the null-hypothesis – viz., SOX has had no effect on production efficiencies. The test statistics are all positive which favors the alternate hypothesis of a positive effect with P values that are all significant at better than 5% except for the inclusion of the Big 4 where the P value for the exponential distribution is less than 10%. Similarly, results of the three non DEA-based statistical tests indicate that the mean difference in production efficiency between the pre and the post SOX periods is statistically significant at 1% level except for the inclusion of the Big 4 where the P value for the Welch Two-Sample test is less than 5%, indicating that the production efficiency of public accounting firms increased after the passage of SOX.

Table 10.4 Means and standard deviations of estimated production efficiencies for public accounting firms

	Relative efficiencies[a]			
	Excluding Big 4 firms		Including Big 4 firms	
Sample periods	Mean	Std. Dev.	Mean	Std. Dev.
Pre-SOX Period (2000&01)	0.626	0.146	0.518	0.158
Post-SOX Period (2003&04)	0.699	0.159	0.571	0.147

[a]Production efficiencies are estimated from the DEA model in (1)

Table 10.5 Statistical test results of equality of production efficiencies between Pre-SOX (2000&01) and Post-SOX (2003&04) periods for public accounting firms

	Excluding Big 4 firms		Including Big 4 firms	
	Test-stat.	P-values	Test-stat.	P-values
DEA-based test T_{EXP}[a]	1.29	0.006	1.19	0.093
DEA-based test T_{HN}[b]	1.52	0.015	1.41	0.032
Welch two-sample test	3.57	0.000	2.37	0.018
Wilcoxon two-sample test	3.70	0.000	3.45	0.000
Kolmogorov-Sminov two-sample test	2.04	0.001	2.03	0.001

[a]Test statistic when the inefficiency is exponentially distributed
[b]Test statistic when the inefficiency is half-normally distributed

Regression Results

The OLS regression results of the fixed-effect models presented in Table 10.6 allow us to further refine and check our findings.[b] Columns 3 and 4 report results when Big 4 firms were excluded and columns 5 and 6 report results when Big 4 firms were included. Consistent with, and extending, our previous findings, the coefficients of YEAR03 and YEAR04 (see column 3) are both positive and statistically significant for the model without any interaction terms as (4a). Furthermore, both $\text{In}\varphi_{YEAR03=}1 - \text{In}\varphi_{YEAR01=1}$ and $\text{In}\varphi_{YEAR04=}1 - \text{In}\varphi_{YEAR01=1}$ values are all positive and significant, suggesting that public accounting firms, on average, improved their production efficiency after the passage of SOX. Finally, the coefficient of lnSEC_CLIENT is significantly positive as expected.

For the model with interaction terms (4b), the impact of SOX on efficiency can be evaluated by inserting the sample means of MAS% and A&A% into the following equations:

$$\ln \varphi_{YEAR03=1} - \ln \varphi_{YEAR03=0} = \beta_2 + \beta_{24} A\&A\% + \beta_{25} MAS\% \tag{5}$$

$$\ln \varphi_{YEAR04=1} - \ln \varphi_{YEAR04=0} = \beta_3 + \beta_{34} A\&A\% + \beta_{35} MAS\% \tag{6}$$

[b]Estimation results with Tobit regressions (Tobin 1958) are similar and so are not reported.

$$\ln \varphi_{year03=1} - \ln \varphi_{year01=1} = \beta_2 + \beta_{24} A\&A\% + \beta_{25} MAS\% - \beta_1 \tag{7}$$

$$\ln \varphi_{year04=1} - \ln \varphi_{year01=1} = \beta_3 + \beta_{34} A\&A\% + \beta_{35} MAS\% - \beta_1 \tag{8}$$

The statistical test results reported in Table 10.6 (see column 4) show efficiency increases in the post SOX period at high statistical significance levels. Specifically, when Big 4 firms were excluded production efficiency increased from 2000 to 2003 and to 2004 by about 11% and 15%, respectively and also increased from 2001 to 2003 and 2004 by about 8% and 12%, respectively. The results when Big4 firms were included (see column 6) are very similar. Consequently, our hypothesis regarding the impact of SOX on the production efficiency of large public accounting firms is confirmed. That is, the production efficiency of large public accounting firms increases after the passage of SOX even after controlling for the thus identified contextual variables.

Sensitivity Checks

We conducted several additional econometric tests of our fixed-effects regression model specifications. As expected, White's[29] test did not indicate heteroskedasticity for any of the two regression models. Belsley, Kuh and Welsch's[30] diagnostics indicate collinearity between A&A% and MAS% in both models, but this may bias results against rejection of the null hypotheses. However, when (4a) and (4b) are re-estimated after dropping the A&A% or MAS% variables one at a time, our key results remain unchanged with production efficiency increasing in the post SOX period.

Finally, as still further checks on our results, we use the super-efficient model of DEA[31] to identify extreme observations. Because they are associated with possible outliers, we removed the observations for three firms and obtain results that are qualitatively similar to those discussed earlier with the full sample. We therefore conclude that our results are robust with respect to the outliers.

Conclusion

We empirically investigated the impact of SOX on the production efficiency of public accounting firms. Using operating data on the total service revenues and human resource inputs from 58 of the 100 largest accounting firms in the US, we document significant increases in production efficiency after the passage of SOX in 2002. The prohibition of certain MAS services provided by public accounting firms in the post SOX period did not have a negative effect on the production efficiency of public accounting firms. There are two possibilities for this finding. One is that the MAS services banned by the Act probably did not constitute a significant portion of MAS service revenues of CPA firms because some of them had spun off

Table 10.6 OLS regression results (T-statistics in parentheses)

		Excluding Big 4 firms (N = 216)		Including Big 4 firms (N = 232)	
		Model 4A	Model 4B	Model 4A	Model 4B
Variables	Parameters	Coefficient	Coefficient	Coefficient	Coefficient
Intercept	β_0	−0.573[a]	−0.547[b]	−0.492[a]	−0.448[b]
		(−3.91)	(−2.71)	(−3.06)	(−2.05)
YEAR01	β_1	0.032	0.031	0.023	0.022
		(0.77)	(0.73)	(0.51)	(0.49)
YEAR03	β_2	0.111[b]	−0.006	0.134[a]	0.017
		(2.67)	(−0.02)	(2.98)	(0.05)
YEAR04	β_3	0.148[a]	0.173	0.158[a]	0.101
		(3.56)	(0.52)	(3.52)	(0.28)
A&A%	β_4	−0.001	−0.001	−0.005[b]	−0.006[c]
		(−0.25)	(−0.40)	(−2.17)	(−1.84)
MAS%	β_5	0.003	0.003	0.002	0.002
		(1.49)	(1.07)	(1.06)	(0.72)
YEAR03*A&A%	β_{24}	–	0.003	–	0.003
			(0.66)		(0.53)
YEAR04*A&A%	β_{34}	–	−0.001	–	0.001
			(−0.21)		(0.11)
YEAR03*MAS%	β_{25}	–	−0.001	–	−0.001
			(−0.23)		(−0.12)
YEAR04*MAS%	β_{35}	–	0.001	–	0.001
			(0.20)		(0.23)
ln SEC_CLIENT	β_6	0.011[c]	0.012[c]	0.007	0.008
		(1.73)	(1.83)	(1.02)	(1.09)
ln OFFICES	β_7	−0.003	−0.004	−0.067[a]	−0.066[a]
		(−0.22)	(−0.26)	(−3.85)	(−3.85)
BIG4	β_8	–	–	0.708[a]	0.701[a]
				(9.05)	(8.72)
F-value		3.44	2.38	14.48	9.63
Adj. R^2		0.074	0.066	0.318	0.309
Test of production efficiency improvement					
$\ln \varphi_{YEAR03=1} - \ln \varphi_{YEAR03=0} > 0$		0.111[a]	0.110[a]	0.134[a]	0.134[a]
		(2.67)	(2.65)	(2.98)	(2.97)
$\ln \varphi_{YEAR04=1} - \ln \varphi_{YEAR04=0} > 0$		0.148[a]	0.148[a]	0.158[a]	0.159[a]
		(3.56)	(3.55)	(3.52)	(3.52)
$\ln \varphi_{YEAR03=1} - \ln \varphi_{YEAR01=1} > 0$		0.076[c]	0.079[c]	0.111[b]	0.112[b]
		(1.90)	(1.91)	(2.47)	(2.48)
$\ln \varphi_{YEAR04=1} - \ln \varphi_{YEAR01=1} > 0$		0.116[a]	0.118[a]	0.135[a]	0.137[a]
		(2.79)	(2.65)	(3.00)	(3.01)

$Ln\varphi$ = the logarithm of production efficiency estimated from the DEA in (1) using pooled data for the years 2000, 2001, 2003, and 2004; YEARt is a dummy variable that equals one if year t, t = 01, 03, or 04, and 0 otherwise; BIG4 is a dummy variable that equals one if the firm is one of the Big 4 firms, and 0 otherwise; and other variable definitions appear in Table 2.

[a]Indicates significance at 1% level

[b]Indicates significance at 5% level

[c]Indicate significance at 10% level

their consulting units well before the passage of SOX. Second is that SOX created new opportunities for public accounting firms to provide additional accounting services to their non-audit or private clients (e.g., internal control systems updates and tests). Alternatively, it is possible that these accounting firms had adjusted their human resource inputs in anticipation of the Act, thereby eliminating or ameliorating potential negative effects. Our results are also robust not only with respect to outliers but also after controlling for the service mix, the number of public clients, and the operating size of public accounting firms.

End Notes

1. *Wall Street Journal*, 7 January 1999.
2. Banker, R.D., Chang, H., and Natarajan, R. (2005). Productivity change, technical progress and relative efficiency change in the public accounting industry, *Management Science* 51, 291–304.
3. Lai, K.W. (2003). The Sarbanes-Oxley Act and auditor independence: Preliminary evidence from audit opinion and discretionary accruals. Working paper, City University of Hong Kong.
4. Asthana, S., Balsam, S., and Kim, S. (2004). The effect of Enron, Andersen, and Sarbanes Oxley on the market for audit services. Working paper, Temple University and Rutgers University.
5. Cooper, W.W., Seiford, L.M., and Tone, K. (2006). Introduction to Data Envelopment Analysis (New York: Springer Science and Business Media, Inc.).
6. Charnes, A., Cooper, W.W., and Sueyoshi, T. (1988). A goal programming/constrained regression version of the Bell system breakup, *Management Science* 34, 1–26; Evans, D., and Heckman, J. (1988) Natural monopoly and the Bell system: Response to Charnes, Cooper and Sueyoshi, *Management Science* 34, 27–38.
7. Davis, L.R., Ricchiute, D., and Trompeter, G. (1993). Audit effort, audit fees, and the provision of nonaudit services to audit clients. *The Accounting Review 68, 135–150*; Palmrose, Z. (1986). The effect of nonaudit services on the pricing of audit services: Further evidence. *Journal of Accounting Research* 24, 405–411.
8. Financial Executives International. (2005). Sarbanes-Oxley compliance costs exceed estimates. *Press Release, March 21*.
9. Levitt, A. (2000). Renewing the covenant with investors. Speech at The New York University Center for Law and Business, New York, May 10, 2000; Banker, Chang, and Natarajan. (2005). op. cit.
10. Financial Executives International. (2005). op cit.
11. Charnes, A., Cooper, W.W., and Rhodes, E. (1978). Measuring efficiency of decision-Making Units. *European Journal of Operational Research* 2, 429–444.
12. Banker, R.D., Charnes, A., Cooper, W.W. (1984). Some Models for Estimating Technical and Scale Inefficiencies in Data Envelopment Analysis. *Management Science*, 30, 1078–1092.
13. Emrouznejad, A., Parker, B., and Tavares, G. (2008). A bibliography of Data Envelopment Analysis, 1978–2003, *Socio-Economic Planning Sciences* (to appear).
14. Gattoufi, S., Oral, M., and Reisman, A. (2004). Data Envelopment Analysis Literature: A bibliography update, 1951–2001 *Socio-Economic Planning Sciences* 38, 159–229.
15. Banker, R.D., Das, S., and Datar, S. (1989). Analysis of Costs for Management Control in Hospitals, *Research in Government and Nonprofit Accounting* 5, 269–291; Mensah, Y.M., and Li, S.H. (1993). Measuring production efficiency in a not-for-profit setting: An extension. *The Accounting Review* 68, 66–68; Feroz, E., Raab, R., and Haag, S. (2001). An income efficiency

model approach to the economic consequences of OSHA Cotton Dust Regulation, *Australian Journal of Management* 26, 69–89; Abad, C., Banker, R., and Mashruwala, R. (2005). Relative efficiency as a lead indicator of profit, Working paper, Washington University in St. Louis.
16. Dopuch, N., Gupta, M., Simunic, D., and Stein, M. (2003). Production efficiency and the pricing of audit services. *Contemporary Accounting Research* 20, 79–115; Feroz, E., Kim, S., and Raab, R. (2005). Analytical procedures: A data envelopment analysis approach. *Journal of Emerging Technologies in Accounting* 2, 17–31.
17. Banker, R.D. (1993). Maximum likelihood, consistency and data envelopment analysis: A statistical foundation, *Management Science* 39, 1265–1273; Banker, R.D., and Slaughter. (1997). A field study of scale economies in software maintenance, *Management Science*, 43:12, 1709–1725; Banker, R.D., and Natarajan, R. (2004). Statistical tests based on DEA efficiency scores, in Cooper, W.W., Seiford, L.M., and Zhu, J. *Handbook on Data Envelopment Analysis* (Norwalk, CT: Kluwer); Simar, L., and Wilson, P.W. (2004) Performance of the bootstrap for DEA estimations and iterating the principle in Cooper, W.W., Seiford, L.M., and Zhu, J. (eds.). *Handbook on Data Envelopment Analysis* (Norwalk, CT: Kluwer).
18. Cooper, W.W., and Ray, S. (2008). A response to M. Stone: How not to measure the efficiency of public services (and how one might). *Journal of the Royal Statistical Society*, Series A. 171:2, 433–448.
19. Cooper, Seiford, and Tone. (2006). op cit., chapter 8.
20. Palmrose, Z. 1989. The relation of audit contract type to audit fees and hours. *The Accounting Review* 64: 488–499; Hackenbrack, K., and Knechel, W. 1997. Resource allocation decisions in audit engagements. *Contemporary Accounting Research* 14, 481–499.
21. Banker, R.D., Chang, H., and Cunningham, R. (2003). The public accounting industry production function, *Journal of Accounting and Economics* 35:2, 255–282.
22. Francis, J., 1984. The effect of audit firm size on audit prices: A study of the Australian market. *Journal of Accounting and Economics* 6, 133–151; Craswell, A., Francis, J., and Taylor, S. (1995). Auditor brand name reputations and industry specialization. *Journal of Accounting and Economics* 20: 297–322.
23. Banker, Chang, and Natarajan. (2005). op cit.
24. Ray, S. (1991). Resource-use efficiency in public schools: A study of Connecticut Data. *Management Science*, 1620–1628.
25. Banker, R.D., Chang, H., and Kao, Y. (2002). Impact of information technology on public accounting firm productivity. *Journal of Information Systems*, 209–222.
26. Banker, R.D., and Natarajan, R. (2005). Evaluating contextual variables affecting productivity using DEA. Working paper, Temple University.
27. Jerris, S., and Pearson, T. (1997). Benchmarking CPA firms for productivity and efficiency: An update, *The CPA Journal*. March, 58–62; Banker, Chang and Cunningham (2003), op cit.
28. Texas Society of Certified Public Accountants. 2005. *Management of Accounting Practice Survey*. Dallas, Texas.
29. White, H. 1980. A heteroskedasticity-consistent covariance matrix estimator and a direct test for heteroskedasticity. *Econometrica* 48, 817–838.
30. Belsley, D.A., Kuh, E., and Welsch, R.E. (1980). *Regression Diagnostics*. Wiley, New York.
31. Banker, Das, and Datar. (1989). op cit.

Chapter 11
Credit Risk Evaluation Using Neural Networks

Z. Yang, D. Wu, G. Fu, and C. Luo

Introduction

Credit risk evaluation and credit default prediction attract a natural interest from both practitioners and regulators in the financial industry. The Bank for International Settlements has been reporting a continuous increase in corporate borrowing activities.[1] In the first quarter of 2006 alone, syndicated lending for mergers and acquisitions sharply exceeded the 2005 levels. In the euro area for example, corporate demand for credit rose from 56% of international claims on all non-bank borrowers at the end of December, 2005, to 59% at the end of March, 2006. These heightened borrowing activities naturally imply increased risk related to credit default. A study by Office of the Superintendent of Bankruptcy Canada and Statistics Canada[2] reveals that while the number of Canadian firms going bankrupt has declined, the average size of losses has significantly risen. In 2005 only 0.7% businesses failed, a sharp decline from the 1992 rate of 1.54%. However, over the last quarter of the century net liabilities from business failures increased dramatically. In 1980 the losses represented 0.32% of Canada's net assets, while in 2005 they rose to 0.52%. Both trends, the acceleration in corporate borrowing and the related risks of credit defaults, command the need for a reliable and effective risk management system on part of financial institutions in order to improve their lending activities. Moreover, the new international standard on capital adequacy outlined in Basel II,[3] a regulatory requirement for financial services institutions, promotes the active involvement of banks in assessing the probability of defaults. Therefore, the accuracy of any predictive models constituting the foundation of a risk management system is clearly essential. Any significant improvement in their predictive capabilities will be worth billions of dollars and therefore deserves serious attention.

Academic theoretical models have contributed greatly to the improvement in credit risk assessment. This study, an application of Backpropagation Neural Networks (BPNN) and Probabilistic Neural Networks to form a bankruptcy prediction model, constitutes yet another attempt at enhancing the measurement of default risk. As powerful data modeling tools, neural networks are able to capture and represent complex input and output relationships. The true power and advantage of neural networks lie in their ability to represent both linear and non-linear relationships

D.L. Olson, D. Wu (eds.) *New Frontiers in Enterprise Risk Management*,

and learn these relationships directly from the data being modeled. Conversely, the traditional linear models cannot manage non-linear characteristics.

Review of Quantitative Credit Risk Prediction Techniques

Classification has an essential function in bankruptcy prediction since the criterion variable is categorical and binary, that is, bankrupt or non-bankrupt. Classification refers to a set of methods that are used to assign an object to a group based on its inherent attributes and on a training set of previously labeled objects. Binary classification, a subset of classification problem, is the task of classifying objects into one of two disjoint groups.

The binary classification problem has been extensively researched over recent decades; much work has been done in the context of the bankruptcy prediction subject. There have been numerous different approaches which have surfaced and which propose novel ways to solve the binary classification problem as related to loan default.

Atiya saw the approaches to the bankruptcy forecasting problem falling into two broad categories: empirical and structural.[4] We will adopt this classification for the purpose of surveying selected techniques that have been developed to predict credit defaults.

Empirical Approach

The empirical approach models the probability of default by learning the relationships among the object variables from the data. The following methods include statistical and intelligent techniques that have been employed for the purposes of classification.

K-Nearest Neighbor (KNN)

K-nearest neighbor is one of the simplest approaches for classifying objects. The purpose of this algorithm is to classify a new object based on attributes and training samples. The objects are represented as points defined in a feature space. An object is classified based on majority of K-nearest neighbor category, with the object being assigned the class most common amongst its k nearest neighbors. Assume that we have training data $(x_1, y_1), \ldots, (x_n, y_n)$ where x_i is the training point and y_i is the corresponding point for each $1 \leq i \leq n$. In the credit risk valuation, we can think that x_i is a financial institution and y_i is the credit rating of this financial institution. We wish to classify a new test point x. We need to calculate the dissimilarity between the test point **x** and the training points. Firstly, we find the K training points $(K_1, \ldots, K_K)$ which is closest to the test point with some given distance. The most popular distance is Euclidean distance:

$$dist(x, x_j)=|x-x_j|^2$$

Secondly, we can set the classification or label y for the test point to be the most common of the K nearest neighbors.

In spite of its simple algorithm, KNN shows a superior performance in pattern recognition and classification tasks. Ripley demonstrated that the KNN error rate was no greater than twice the Bayesian error rate.[5] However, KNN's significant limitation is the lack of any probabilistic semantics when making predictions of class membership in a consistent manner.[6]

Cluster Analysis

Cluster analysis is a set of algorithms and methods for grouping objects of similar type into respective categories, and specifically, for partitioning of a dataset into subsets (clusters) sharing common traits. Lim and Sohn adapted the clustering methods to develop a cluster-based dynamic scoring model which dynamically accommodated changes in the borrowers' characteristics at the early stages of loan.[7] For this purpose, the dataset has been fragmented into a number of clusters and the observation horizon has been fractioned in order to obtain different models based on different observation periods. The empirical tests proved that the model's misclassification rate was lower to that of the classical single rule model. However, the limited data sample used for testing does not render this model fully validated.

Discriminant Analysis (DA)

Discriminant analysis is a technique for classifying a set of observations into predefined classes based on a set of variables, named predictors. It derives a linear or quadratic combination of the features which best discriminate between the groups. Beaver was the first to adopt a multiple discriminant analysis (MDA) to bankruptcy prediction and the method has become a dominant technique in the literature for almost 20 years.[8] Let us give a specific example from Altman.[9] Altman modeled the credit score by using multiple discriminant analysis as an appropriate statistical technique for classification of the objects into one of the two groups: bankrupt and nonbankrupt firms.

$$Z = 1.2\,X_1 + 1.4\,X_2 + 3.3\,X_3 + 0.6\,X_4 + 1.0\,X_5$$

where:
X_1 – working capital/total assets,
X_2 – retained earnings/total assets,
X_3 – earnings before interest and taxes /total assets,
X_4 – market value equity/book value of total liabilities,
X_5 – sales/total assets (S/TA).
At the next stage he tested the discriminating power of the proposed model. Altman found the following cut-off points of variable Z:

1.81 or less – a high probability of bankruptcy (Interval I – no errors in bankruptcy classification);
3.00 or above – a low probability of bankruptcy (Interval II – no errors in nonbankruptcy classification);
$1.81 < Z < 2.99$ – area of uncertainty (grey area).

Several studies found DA yielding lower predictive accuracy than newer techniques; nonetheless, DA has become a standard benchmark for comparative studies. Jo, Han and Lee carried out an empirical comparison of MDA, case-based forecasting and neural networks to forecast failing companies and concluded that the neural network technique outperformed both DA and case based forecasting system.[10] In a similar study, Lennox argued that well-specified logit and probit models produced superior results to DA.[11] There have also been attempts made at integrating DA with other models in order to increase prediction performance. Jo and Han employed DA along with two AI techniques, NN and case-based forecasting to improve predictive abilities.[12] The authors established that the accuracy of the integrated model was higher than that of each stand-alone model.

Logit Analysis (LA)

Logit or logistic regression lends itself well into an analysis where outcomes fall between two discrete alternatives and that is why it has been a commonly used model for bankruptcy prediction. It provides a crisp (as opposed to fuzzy) relationship between explanatory and response variables based on the given data. We denote

$$\text{logit}(p) = \log\left(\frac{p}{1-p}\right) = \log(p) - \log(1-p)$$

where p can represents the loan default or some parameters used to measure the credit rating of some financial instructions or insurance companies.

Then we can fit the following model through the regression

$$\text{logit } (p) = f(x_1, x_2, \cdots, x_n)$$

where x_i is independent variables including the financial institution's credit history record, leverage, etc. For example, $f(x_1) = ax_1 + b$ is a simple case to model the credit scoring. In fact, in response to the limitations of MDA, Ohlson used the logit model to forecast the loan default.[13] The accuracy rate that he obtained reached the level of 96.1 and 95.5% for the first and the second year respectively. Jones and Hensher developed a mixed logit model for failure prediction and compared its performance against multinomial logit models.[14] The study indicated that mixed logit demonstrated significantly better predictive ability than multinomial logit models. Tang and Chi performed a comparative analysis of logit and fuzzy logic models using receiver operating characteristic curve analysis and concluded that in spite of the fact that fuzzy logic proved a superior predictor in terms of overall accuracy and in classifying bankrupt objects, logit yielded better results in cases where a higher accuracy in classifying non-bankrupt firms was required.[15] Currently, logit is being used in combination with other models as hybrid techniques. One such application was proposed by Tseng and Lin in the form of a quadratic interval logistic regression model based on quadratic programming.[16] The goal was to have a quadratic interval logit model support the logit model to discriminate between groups in cases of a limited number of firms for default prediction. The classification accuracy achieved was 78%. More recently, Hua et al. used logistic regression analysis to enhance Support Vector Machine (SVM) performance, and specifically, to decrease its empirical risk of misclassification.[17] The model, Integrated Binary Discriminant Rule (IBDR), reduced the misclassification risk of SVM outputs by interpreting and modifying the outputs of the SVM classifiers according to the outcomes of logistic regression analysis. The experiments showed that IBDR outperformed SVM in predictive capabilities.

Bayesian Methods

Posch et al. propose a Bayesian methodology that enables banks to improve their credit scoring models by imposing prior information.[18]

As prior information, we use coefficients from credit scoring models estimated on other data sets. Through simulations, we explore the default prediction power of three Bayesian estimators in three different scenarios and find that they perform better than standard maximum likelihood estimates.

Artificial Neural Networks (ANN)

An artificial neural network is an interconnected group of artificial neurons using a mathematical or computational model for information processing based on a connectionist approach to computation.

This paper proposes two neural network approaches, BPNN and PNN, to identify credit risk. The ANN models will be discussed in detail in the next section.

Structural Approach

The structural approach refers to modeling the driving forces of interest rates and firm characteristics and subsequently deriving the probability of failure. Several methods have emerged aiming to assess the likelihood of default; these will be briefly reviewed below.

Credit Migration Approach

The CreditMetrics framework developed by J.P. Morgan uses Monte Carlo simulation to create a portfolio loss distribution at the time horizon and is based on modeling changes in the credit quality ratings.[19] Each obligor is assigned a credit rating, and a transition matrix based on the "rating migrations" determines the probabilities that the obligor's credit rating will be upgraded or downgraded, or that the obligation defaults. The portfolio value is calculated by randomly simulating the credit quality of each obligor. The credit instruments are then repriced under each simulated outcome, and the portfolio value is simply the aggregation of these prices. Using the diversification benefits of a portfolio framework, the aggregate risk of stand-alone transactions is reduced. Correlated credit movements of obligors (such as several downgrades occurring simultaneously) are addressed, and any borrower in the portfolio will result in increased capital requirements.

CreditPortfolioView was developed by Tom Wilson, formerly of McKinsey, as a credit portfolio model by taking into account the current macroeconomic environment.[20] This method uses default probabilities conditional on the current state of the economy, rather than using historical default rate averages calculated from past data. The portfolio loss distribution is conditioned by the current state of the economy for each country and industry segment.

Option Pricing Approach

One of the earlier and popular models is the asset based approach originally proposed by Merton.[21]

KMV views a firm's equity as an option on the firm (held by the shareholders) to either repay the debt of the firm when due, or abandon the firm without paying the obligations. The Merton model bases on two assumptions. The first is that the total value of a firm is assumed to follow geometric Brownian motion,

$$\frac{dV}{V} = \mu \cdot dt + \sigma dW$$

where V is the total value of the firm, $\propto$ is the expected continuously compounded return on V, σ is the volatility of firm value and dW is a standard Weiner process.

The second critical assumption of the Merton model is that the firm has issued just one discount bond maturing in T periods.

Under these assumptions, the equity of the firm is a call option on the underlying value of the firm with a strike price equal to the face value of the firm's debt and a time-to-maturity of T. Then the KMV-Merton model will give very accurate default forecasts.

The probability of default is derived by modeling the market value of the firm as a geometric Brownian motion. The superiority of this model lies in its reliance on the equity market as an indicator, since it can be argued that the market capitalization of the firm (together with the firm's liabilities) reflect the solvency of the firm.

Reduced Form Model (Default Intensity Model)

Another approach, by Jarrow and Turnbull, introduced the basic structure of a constant default intensity model.[22] It models default as a point process, where the time-varying hazard function for each credit class is estimated from the credit spreads.

Consider a frictionless economy with a trading horizon $[0, \tau]$. Let v_1 (t, T) denote the time t value of the XYZ zero-coupon bond promising a dollar at time $T \geq t$. After we model the process of v_1 (t, T), we can price the derivatives underlying the dynamic process. Versus, we can also calibrate the parameter of the process v_1 (t, T) if we can observe the value of one derivative underlying the process v_1 (t, T). Jarrow and Turnbull's model assume that this discrete-time binomial process was selected to approximate a continuous-time Poisson bankruptcy process v_1 (t, T). They assume that the process will default with pesudoprobability $\lambda\mu_i$ at time t_i and pesudoprobabiliy $1 - \lambda\mu_i$ while default does not occur.

Hull and While reduced form models focus on the risk-neutral hazard rate, $h(t)$.[23] This is defined so that $h(t)dt$ is the probability of default between times t and $t + dt$ as seen at time t assuming no earlier defaults. These models can incorporate correlations between defaults by allowing hazard rates to be stochastic and correlated with macroeconomic variables.

Hull and White developed a model to value credit default swaps when the payoff is contingent on default by a single reference entity and there is no counterparty default risk. This model uses a hazard rate $h(t)$ for the default probability to incorporate a default density concept, which is the unconditional cumulative default probability within one period regardless of other periods. The model assumes an expected recovery rate and generates default densities recursively based on a set of zero-coupon corporate bond prices and a set of zero-coupon treasury bond prices. Then the premium of a credit default swap contract is calculated using the default density term-structure. The two sets of zero-coupon bond prices can be bootstrapped from corporate coupon bond prices and treasury coupon bond prices.

The Actuarial Approach

The CreditRisk+ product, developed by Credit Suisse Financial Products, is based on a portfolio approach to modeling credit default risk that takes into account information relating to size and maturity of an exposure and the credit quality.[24] Unlike the Merton-based approach used by Portfolio Manager and CreditMetrics, the CreditRisk+ methodology is based on mathematical models used in the insurance industry. Instead of absolute levels of default risk – such as 0.25% for a triple B rated issuer – CreditRisk+ models default rates as continuous random variables. Observed default rates for credit ratings vary over time, and the uncertainty in these rates is captured by the default rate volatility estimates (standard deviations). Default correlation is generally caused by external factors such as regional economic strength or industry weakness. CSFP argues that default correlations are difficult to observe and are unstable over time. Instead of trying to model these correlations directly, CreditRisk+ uses the default rate volatilities to capture the effect of default correlations and produce a long tail in the portfolio loss distribution. CreditRisk+ can handle thousands of exposures and uses a portfolio approach which reduces risk for diversification. Exposures can be allocated to industrial or geographical sectors and different time horizons of exposure can be incorporated. The minimal data requirements make the model easy to implement, and the analytical calculation of the portfolio loss distribution is very fast.

The above sampling of research consider only a single default time. Schönbucher and Schubert proposed a feasible model based on the reduced form approach, for the multivariate distribution of default times.[25] The basis of the analysis of multivariate dependence with copula functions is the following the theorem of Sklar.[26] Let X_1, ..., X_N be random variables with marginal distribution functions F_1, ..., F_N and joint distribution function F. Then there exists an N dimensional copula C such that for all $x \in R^N$,

$$F(x) = C(F_1(x_1), \cdots, F_n(x_n)).$$

If F_1, ..., F_N are continuous, then C is unique.

Then Schönbucher and Schubert proposed a model following the dependent-defaults model is built up in two steps: First we specify the stochastic model for individual defaults, and in a second step we introduce default dependency. In this section we describe the stochastic model for the defaults of the individual obligors.

Hull and White documented the behavior of stylized copula based models, e.g., with equal pair-wise correlations.[27] Copula function allows for incorporating the body of knowledge of modeling univariate processes into a multivariate framework. The Normal and Student copulas commonly used in the literature and by practitioners do not produce very different estimates of default risk prices.[28]

Neural Network Basics

Neural networks provide a new way for feature extraction (using hidden layers) and classification (e.g., multilayer perceptrons). In addition, existing feature extraction and classification algorithms can also be mapped in neural network architectures for efficient, implementation in terms of hardware. In this section, we discuss two neural network methods applied to credit risk evaluation in our research.

Backpropogation Neural Network (BPNN)

BPNN is the most widely used neural network technique for classification and prediction.[29] Figure 11.1 provides the structure of the backpropagation neural network.

With backpropagation, the related input data are repeatedly presented to the neural network. For each iteration the output of the neural network is compared to the desired output and an error is calculated. This error is then backpropagated to the neural network and used to adjust the weights so that the error decreases with each iteration and the neural model gets progressively closer to producing the desired output. This process is known as "training".

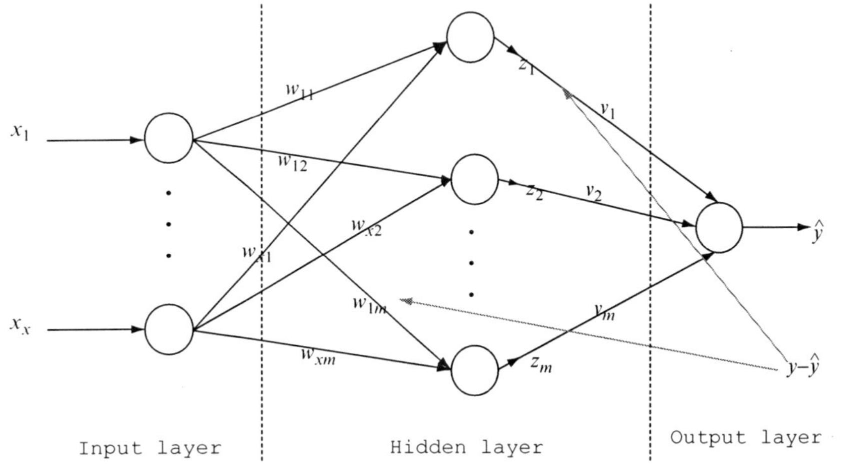

Fig. 11.1 Backpropagation neural networks

Probabilistic Neural Network

PNNs were first developed as classifiers by Sprecht D. F. for classification problems.[30] Their design is straightforward and does not depend on training. A PNN is guaranteed to converge to a Bayesian classifier providing there is enough training data. The implementation of a PNN attempts to model the actual probability distributions of classes with combinations of Gaussians, allowing the computation of the posterior probability associated with each exemplar classification. PNN architecture is illustrated in Fig. 11.2.

Input Layer Pattern Layer Summation Layer Output Layer

This PNN network consists of four layers: input layer, pattern layer, summation layer, and output layer. The neurons in the input layer distribute the inputs to the pattern units. The pattern layer usually uses a function such as $g(z_i) = \exp(\frac{z_i - 1}{\sigma^2})$.

Here, Z_i is the dot matrix of input vector and weight vector. The scale parameter σ^2 defines the width of the area of influence and should decrease as the sample size increases. When an input is presented, the pattern layer computes distances from the input vector to the training input vectors, and produces a vector whose elements indicate how close the input is to a training input. The summation layer has one neuron for each class. Each summation neuron, which is dedicated to a single class, sums the pattern layer neurons corresponding to numbers of that summation neuron's class. The activation of summation neuron n that is attained is the estimated density function of population n. The output neuron is a threshold discriminator that determines which of its inputs from the summation units is the maximum.

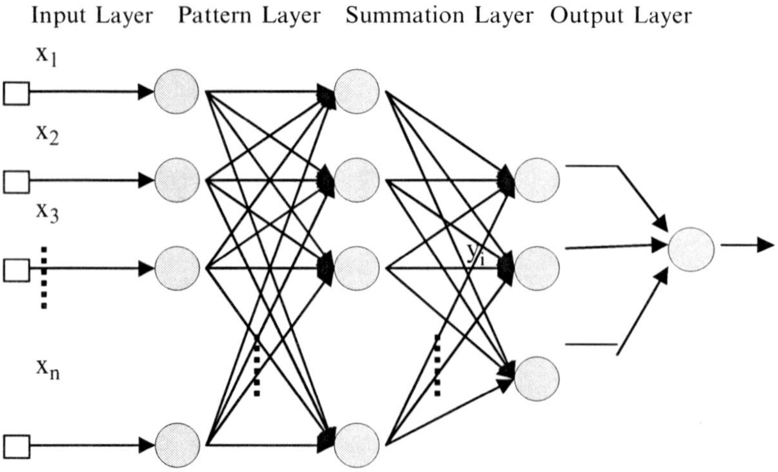

Fig. 11.2 The PNN architecture

Discussion of Models and Results

When the neural networks are trained, three problems should be taken into consideration. First, it is very difficult to select the learning rate for a nonlinear network. If the learning rate is too large, it leads to unstable learning. Conversely, if the learning rate is too small, it results in exceedingly long training iterations. Secondly, settling in a local minimum may be beneficial or detrimental depending on how close the local minimum is to the global minimum and how small an error is required. In either case, backpropagation may not always find the correct weights for the optimum solution. One may reinitialize the network several times to guarantee the optimal solution. Finally, the network is sensitive to the number of neurons in its hidden layers. Too few neurons can lead to underfitting: too many can cause overfitting. Although all training points are well fit, the fitting curve takes wild oscillations between these points.[31]

In order to solve these problems, we preprocess the data before training. The normalization function used to bound the data values by −1 and +1 is as follows:

$$Y = (y_{ij})_{m \times n} = \frac{x_{ij} - x_{ij_{\min}}}{x_{ij_{\max}} - x_{ij_{\min}}},$$

where X = (x_{ij}) is the input matrix, Y is the normalized matrix and $X_{ij\max}$, $X_{ij\min}$ are the associated maximum and minimum elements, respectively. The weights are initialized with random decimal fractions ranging from −1 to 1. In addition, there are about twelve training algorithms for BPNN. After preliminary analyses and trials, we chose the fastest training algorithm, the Levenberg–Marquardt algorithm, which can be considered as a trust-region modification of the Gauss–Newton algorithm. For small and medium size networks, Levenberg–Marquardt training is normally used if enough memory is available. This training algorithm can train any network as long as its weight, net input, and transfer functions have derivative functions. Backpropagation is used to calculate the Jacobian training performance matrix regarding the weight and bias variables.[32]

A PNN may suffer from the major problem of long operating speed because it takes more computation than other networks to do its function classification. Therefore, the operating speed becomes much slower as the sample size increases. Heuristics and optimizations such as the learning subspace method (LSM) are required to effectively prune the sample down to a more manageable size.[33]

To preprocess the data, we transform the one-dimensional input data into multi-dimensional vectors. After training the network, the prediction results of multi-dimensional vectors are retransformed to one-dimensional output data.

Computational Results

We apply the proposed methodologies to one example discussed in the literature. The data of this example are referred to in Paradi et al.,[34] which include two groups of data. One is the 1995 data for the both the companies that were to go bankrupt during 1996 and the healthy companies. The other group is the 1996 data for the 1997 bankruptcies. All the companies were from the manufacturing sector. Each company is described by ten attributes, which includes total assets (TA), working capital (WC), earnings before income, tax, depreciation and amortization (EBITDA), retained earnings (RE), shareholders equity (EQ), total current liabilities (CL), interest expense (IN), cash flow from operations (CF), stability of earnings (SE) and total liabilities (TL). The 1995 data include 17 failed companies and 160 healthy companies and the 1996 data represents 11 failed companies and 115 healthy companies. The only criterion for the healthy companies was that they did not go bankrupt before 1998. We use the 1995 data for training and the 1996 data for prediction.

BPNN Results

In order to yield the running robustness of the neural networks, two network targets are set, either of which demotes two kinds of credit conditions. In details, we let two numbers (3 and 5 or 3 and 7) represent two kinds of credit conditions (3 for bankruptcy and 5 or 7 for non-bankruptcy). The cutoff points for target setting are 4 and 5, respectively. The performance goal for the former condition is 0.001 and the latter 0.0005. It is believed that the "3"–"5" model can be completed faster than the "3"–"7" model since the diagnostic interval of the former is smaller than that of the latter, though the precision settings differ. This is verified by our results.

After the input and output patterns have been determined, some network parameters need to be carefully chosen in order to yield a good network structure. Through our experiments and experience, a one-hidden layer structure is selected. Five elements for the hidden layer are fed to the BPNNs, as well as sigmoid and, pureline functions for each of the layers.

The program has been written in C and Matlab using the neural network add-in. Next, the network training module is executed and the weight matrices determining the net structure are obtained. For the "3"–"5" demotion condition, the first-layer, second-layer weight matrix and biases of BPNN are W_1, W_2 and B:

$$W_1 = \begin{pmatrix} -2.6344 & -1.3959 & 0.25116 & 3.272 & -0.58597 & 1.5755 & 3.0648 & 1.768 & -0.8152 & 2.345 & -0.22156 & -1.5065 \\ 29.051 & 26.854 & -13.799 & 147.99 & 98.104 & -188.57 & -190.17 & 103.01 & 103.01 & -207.1 & 249.41 & 96.713 \\ -61.064 & -2.8324 & -44.785 & 79.319 & 5.1587 & -9.3826 & -41.908 & 51.863 & 51.863 & -30.01 & -45.562 & 19.656 \\ 34.467 & -224.73 & -141.25 & -53.298 & -50.128 & 21.932 & 202.3 & 75.456 & -70.225 & -0.8794 & -135.55 & -81.819 \\ -61.696 & -143.95 & -93.858 & -56.299 & -70.647 & 96.577 & 99.543 & 64.092 & -37.558 & -36.495 & -143.98 & -59.681 \end{pmatrix}$$

Figures 11.3 and 11.4 illustrate the training process of BPNN model.
In order to test the performance of the trained network, we implement the simulation of the network response to inputs of the training sample. The results compiled in Table 11.1 explain the accomplishment of training for BPNN networks.

After the training data have been successfully classified, we proceeded to developing the prediction models. The examination sample includes the 1996 data for 126 companies. Our model, using 5 as the cut-off point, successfully identified all the healthy companies and misclassified five bankrupt companies. Table 11.2 illustrates the prediction results for the bankrupt companies.

PNN Results

Our probabilistic neural network (PNN) creates a two-layer network. The first layer has radial basis transfer function neurons, and calculates its weighted inputs using the Euclidean distance weight function, and its net input using the product net input function. The second layer has competitive transfer function neurons, and calculates its weighted input using the dot product weight function and its net inputs using the sum net input function. Only the first layer has biases and the biases are all set to 0.8326/spread. The second layer weights are set to the target.[35] 177 companies are assigned in the pattern layer and two units in the class layer. This configuration represents 177 companies applied to each training session and a total of two classes allowed for two kinds of credit conditions. The network targets are the same as the targets for BPNN described in Sect. 4.1. For the training data, PNN identifies all the healthy companies and misclassifies one bankrupt company. Table 11.3 shows the details of the classification. Next, we applied our prediction PNN model to the 1996 data. We found that the model misclassified five bankrupt companies and four healthy companies as shown in Tables 11.4 and 11.5. In relative terms, the model produced 54.55% bankruptcy and 96.52% non-bankruptcy prediction accuracies. Classification and prediction accuracies of two networks are shown in Table 11.6.

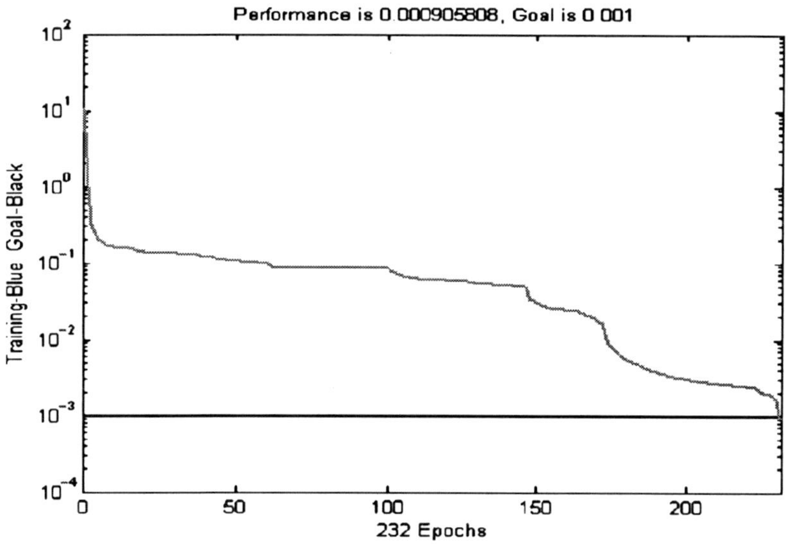

Fig. 11.3 Illustration of training process by BPNN model with two groups denoted by Number "3" and "5"

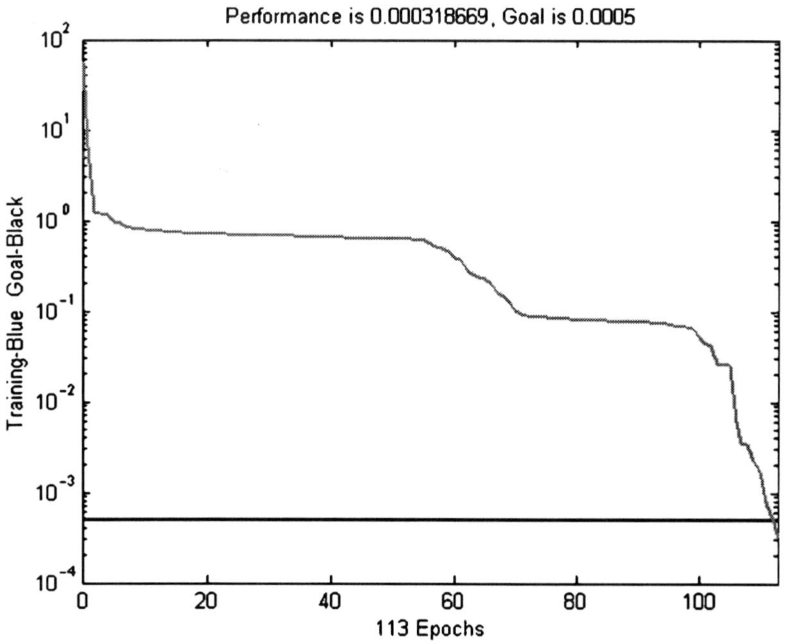

Fig. 11.4 Illustration of training process by BPNN model with two groups denoted by Number "3" and "7"

Table 11.1 (1995 data). Bankruptcy classification results using BPNN

Company ID	Pre-Specified	BPNN with cut-off "4"	BPNN with cut-off "5"	Company ID	Pre-specified	BPNN with cut-off "4"	BPNN with cut-off "5"
1	3	2.98	3.00	10	3	2.98	2.96
2	3	2.98	3.01	11	3	3.01	3.00
3	3	2.98	3.00	12	3	2.98	3.01
4	3	2.98	3.00	13	3	2.99	3.01
5	3	2.98	3.00	14	3	3.14	3.13
6	3	3.02	3.02	15	3	3.04	3.02
7	3	3.07	3.01	16	3	2.98	2.96
8	3	3.03	3.03	17	3	3.00	3.03
9	3	2.98	2.96				

Table 11.2 (1996 data). Bankruptcy prediction results using BPNN

Company ID	Pre-specified	BPNN with cut-off "4"	BPNN with cut-off "5"	Company ID	Pre-specified	BPNN with cut-off "4"	BPNN with cut-off "5"
1	3	2.9819	2.9995	7	3	2.9819	3
2	3	5.0004	6.9999	8	3	5.0004	6.9999
3	3	6.9796	6.9999	9	3	5.0004	2.9459
4	3	2.9819	3	10	3	5.0004	6.9999
5	3	3.0203	3.0120	11	3	5.0004	6.9999
6	3	2.9819	2.9613				

Table 11.3 (1995 data). Bankruptcy classification results using PNN

Company ID	Pre-specified	PNN with cut-off "4"	PNN with cut-off "5"	Company ID	Pre-specified	PNN with cut-off "4"	PNN with cut-off "5"
1	3	3	3	10	3	3	3
2	3	3	3	11	3	3	3
3	3	3	3	12	3	3	3
4	3	3	3	13	3	3	3
5	3	3	3	14	3	5	7
6	3	3	3	15	3	3	3
7	3	3	3	16	3	3	3
8	3	3	3	17	3	3	3
9	3	3	3				

Table 11.4 (1996 data). Bankruptcy prediction results using PNN

Company ID	Pre-specified	PNN with cut-off "4"	PNN with cut-off "5"	Company ID	Pre-specified	PNN with cut-off "4"	PNN with cut-off "5"
1	3	1	1	7	3	1	1
2	3	5	7	8	3	5	7
3	3	5	7	9	3	3	3
4	3	1	1	10	3	5	7
5	3	1	1	11	3	5	7
6	3	1	1				

Table 11.5 (1996 data). Non-bankruptcy prediction misclassification results

Company ID	Pre-specified	PNN with cut-off "4"	Pre-specified	PNN with cut-off "5"
29	7	1	5	1
32	7	1	5	1
38	7	1	5	1
124	7	3	5	3

Table 11.6 Classification accuracies and prediction accuracies by NN models

		Bankruptcy classification		Non-Bankruptcy classification	
		Optimal cut-off 4 (%)	Optimal cut-off 5 (%)	Optimal cut-off 4 (%)	Optimal cut-off 5 (%)
BPNN model	Classification (1995 data)	100	100	100	100
	Prediction (1996 data)	45.45	54.55	100	100
PNN model	Classification (1995 data)	94.12	94.12	100	100
	Prediction (1996 data)	54.55	54.55	96.52	96.52

Comparisons with Other Studies

Paradi et al. combined layered worst practice and normal DEA models and obtained results of 100% out-of-sample classification accuracy for the bankrupt companies and 67% for the healthy companies.[36] Their method constitutes an excellent predictor of company bankruptcy. In contrast, our study produces impressive non-bankruptcy classification accuracies. Specifically, BPNN approach identifies all healthy companies and provides 100% non-bankruptcy classification accuracies. PNN only misidentifies four healthy companies, which gives 96.52% non-bankruptcy classification accuracies. Therefore, if we combine the DEA approach and the neural network approach, the new model will likely result in exciting prediction accuracies, which would translate into substantial savings for financial institutions and consequently warrants serious attention.

Conclusions and Discussion

This chapter reviews selected credit risk detection techniques and then evaluates the credit risk using two neural network models. Both models yield an impressive 100% bankruptcy and 100% non-bankruptcy classification accuracy in simulating the training data set. BPNN provides 54.55% bankruptcy and 100% non-bankruptcy prediction rates. PNN provides 54.55% bankruptcy and 96.52% non-bankruptcy prediction rates. Such high non-bankruptcy prediction results bring direct and tremendous benefits to a number of areas of finance, namely credit approval, loan securitization and loan portfolio management. It is noteworthy that the PNN model does not suffer the dilemma of randomness, which is the main hurdle for neural network application.

End Notes

1 http://www.bis.org/publ/qtrpdf/r_qt0609b.pdf. (2006). Highlights of international banking and financial market activity, BIS Quarterly Review, part 2, September.
2. http://www.statcan.ca/Daily/English/061012/d061012c.htm.
3. http://www.bis.org/publ/bcbs107.htm.
4. Atiya, A.F. (2001). Bankruptcy prediction for credit risk using neural networks: A survey and new results, *IEEE Transactions on Neural Networks* 12:4, 929–935.
5. Ripley, B.D. (1996). Pattern Recognition and Neural Networks, Cambridge University Press, Cambridge, 1996.
6. Manocha, S., and Girolami, M.A. (2007). An empirical analysis of the probabilistic K-nearest neighbour classifier, *Pattern Recognition Letters* 28:13, 1818–1824.
7. Lim, M.K., Sohn, A., and So Y. (2007). Cluster-based dynamic scoring model, *Expert Systems with Applications* 32:2, 427–431.
8. Beaver, W. (1967). Financial ratios predictors of failure. Empirical research in accounting: Selected studies 1966, *Journal of Accounting Research*, 4, 71–111.
9. Altman, E.I. (1988). The Prediction of Corporate Bankruptcy (A Discriminant Analysis), Garland, New York.
10. Jo, H., Han, I., Lee, H. (1997). Bankruptcy prediction using case-based reasoning, neural networks, and discriminant analysis, *Expert Systems with Applications*, 13:2, 97–108.
11. Lennox, C. (1999). Identifying failing companies: A re-evaluation of the logit, probit and DA approaches, *Journal of Economics and Business*, 51:4, 347–364.
12. Jo, H., Han, I. (1996). Integration of case-based forecasting, neural network, and discriminant analysis for bankruptcy prediction, *Expert Systems with Applications*, 11:4, 415–422.
13. Ohlson, J.A. (1980). Financial ratios and the probabilistic prediction of bankruptcy, *Journal of Accounting Research*, 109–131.
14. Jones, S., Hensher, D.A. (2004). Predicting firm financial distress: A mixed logit model, *Accounting Review*, 79:4, 1011–1038.
15. Tang, T.-C., and Chi, L.-C. (2005). Predicting multilateral trade credit risks: Comparisons of Logit and Fuzzy Logic models using ROC curve analysis, *Expert Systems with Applications* 28:3, 547–556.
16. Tseng, F.-M., and Lin, L. (2005). A quadratic interval logit model for forecasting bankruptcy, *Omega*, 33:1, 85–91.
17. Hua, Z., Wang, Y., Xu, X., Zhang, B., and Liang, L. (2007). Predicting corporate financial distress based on integration of support vector machine and logistic regression, *Expert Systems with Applications* 33:2, 434–440.
18. Posch, P.N., Löffler, G., Schöne, Ch. (2005). Bayesian Methods for Improving Credit Scoring Models. Working paper.
19.http://www.financewise.com/public/edit/riskm/credit/cre-models.htm; http://www.creditriskresource.com/papers/paper_125.pdf.
20. Wilson, T. (1987). Portfolio credit risk, I, *Risk*, 10:9, Sept.; Wilson T. (1987) Portfolio credit risk, II, *Risk*, 10:10, Oct.
21. Merton, R. (1974). On the pricing of corporate debt: The risk structure of interest rates, *Journal of Finance* 29, 449–470.

22. Jarrow, R., and Turnbull, S. (1995). The pricing and hedging of options on financial securities subject to credit risk, *Journal of Finance*, 50, 53–85.
23. Hull, J., and White, A. (2000). Valuing credit default swaps I: No counterparty default risk, *Journal of Derivatives*, 8:1, 29–40.
24. http://www.csfb.com/institutional/research/assets/creditrisk.pdf; http://www.bica.com.ar/Archivos_MRM/CreditRisk+byFFT_versionJuly2004.pdf.
25. Schönbucher, P.J., and Schubert, D., Copula-dependent default risk in intensity models. Technical report, Department of Statistics, Bonn University.
26. Sklar, A. (1959). Fonctions de répartition à *n* dimensions et leurs marges, *Publications de l'Institut de Statistique de L'Université de Paris* 8, 229–231.
27. Hull, J., and White, A. (2004). Valuation of a CDO and nth to default CDS without Monte Carlo simulation, *Journal of Derivatives*, 12:2, 8–23.
28. Nelsen, R.B. (1999). An introduction to copulas, 139 *of Lectures Notes in Statistics*. Springer, Berlin Heidelberg New York; Li, D.X. (2000). On default correlation: A copula function approach. *Journal of Fixed Income* 9, 43–54, 2000.
29. Hecht Nielsen, R. (1990). Neural computing, Addison Wesley, 124–133.
30. Specht, D.F. (1988). Probabilistic neural networks for classification, mapping, or associative memory, IEEE International Conference on Neural Networks, San Dieg, CA, USA, 1525–532.
31. Lai, K.K., Yu, L., and Wang, S. (2006). Neural network metalearning for credit scoring, Lecture Notes in Computer Science 4113 LNCS – I 403; Xiong, Z.B., Li, R.J. (2005). Credit risk evaluation with fuzzy neural networks on listed corporations of China, Proceedings of the 2005 IEEE International Workshop on VLSI Design and Video Technology, 479–484.
32. Chen, H.-H., Manry, M.T., and Chandrasekaran, H. (1999). A neural network training algorithm utilizing multiple sets of linear equations, *Neurocomputing*, 25, 55–72; Liang, L., and Wu, D. (2005). An application of pattern recognition on scoring Chinese corporations financial conditions based on backpropagation neural network. *Computers and Operations Research* 32, 1115–1129.
33. Kohen, T. (1989). Self-organization and associative memory. Springer, Berlin Heidelberg New York; Yu, L.Y., Li, H.L., and Duan, Z.G. (2002). A neural network model in credit risk assessment based on new risk measurement criterion, *Proceedings of the Joint Conference on Information Sciences* 6, 1102–1105.
34. Paradi, J.C., Asmild, M., and Simak, P.C. (2004). Using DEA and worst practice DEA in credit risk evaluation, *Journal of Productivity Analysis* 21, 153–166.
35. Wasserman, P.D. (1993). Advanced Methods in Neural Computing, Van Nostrand Reinhold, New York.
36. Paredi, A., and Simak. (2004). op cit.

Chapter 12
Applying the Real Option Approach to Vendor Selection in IT Outsourcing

Q. Cao and K. Leggio

Information Technology Outsourcing

Information technology (IT) outsourcing is one of the major issues facing organizations in today's rapidly changing business environment. Due to its very nature of uncertainty, it is critical for companies to manage and mitigate the high risks associated with IT outsourcing practices including the task of vendor selection. In this study, we explore the two-stage vendor selection approach in IT outsourcing using real options analysis. In the first stage, the client engages a vendor for a pilot project and observes the outcome. Using this observation, the client decides either to continue the project to the second stage based upon pre-specified terms or to terminate the project. A case example of outsourcing the development of supply chain management information systems for a logistics firm is also presented in the paper. Our findings suggest that real options analysis is a viable project valuation technique for IT outsourcing.

What began as a means of having routine processes completed by those external to the firm has exploded into an industry that is on the frontier of product design and innovation. We are speaking, of course, of outsourcing, the reason for many corporate restructurings thus far in the twenty-first century. There does not appear to be abatement in this trend. Outsourcing offers firms the ability, in the face of limited resources, to attract specialized talent to rapidly solve a business issue. And, by outsourcing to several firms simultaneously, corporations are able to mitigate the risk of exposure to project failure by in-sourcing or single outsourcing.[1]

Outsourcing offers a firm flexibility.[2] By purchasing specialized knowledge through outsourcing agreements, firms no longer have to deploy internal resources to solve an array of problems. As circumstances change, firms that outsource have the ability to adjust and pursue different opportunities rapidly. In essence, outsourcing is a real option the firm acquires and exercises as warranted.

Information technology is in the forefront of the outsourcing phenomenon. For instance, Lacity and Willcocks report that IT outsourcing contracts alone were expected to reach US$ 156 billion by 2004.[3] It is also estimated that more than 50% of companies in the United States outsourced their IT functions in 2006.[4]

Real options is an alternative valuation method for capturing managerial flexibility that is inherent in IT projects.[5] In this study, we explore the multi-stage vendor selection issue in information technology outsourcing using real options

D.L. Olson, D. Wu (eds.) *New Frontiers in Enterprise Risk Management*,

analysis. We use the example of outsourcing the development of supply chain management information systems for a logistics firm. We find real options to be a viable project valuation technique for IT outsourcing.

Review of Literature

Information Technology Outsourcing

The past decade has seen an explosion in information technology (IT) outsourcing for building basic computer applications, systems maintenance and support, routine process automation, and even strategic systems.[6] Estimates suggest that this trend was likely to continue with projections of IT outsourcing contracts reaching $160 billion in 2005, up from $101 billion in 2000.[7]

In transferring IT activities to outside suppliers, firms expect to reap various benefits, from cost savings to increased flexibility, and from improved quality of services to better access to state-of-the-art technology.[8] However, various undesirable results have also been associated with IT outsourcing including: service degradation,[9] the absence of cost reduction,[10] and disagreement between the parties.[11] In light of the high IT outsourcing failure rate, several researchers have argued for adopting a risk management approach to studying and managing IT outsourcing based on transaction cost theory.[12] However, they neglect the vendor selection issue in managing the IT outsourcing risk.

Vendor Selection

Because IT is an intangible product that can be heavily customized for each company, it might be very difficult to accurately assess vendor quality during the bidding process. Moreover, even for situations where many aspects of performance can be measured, not all aspects of IT project outcome may be measurable to a degree where an outside party (vendor) can certify compliance.[13] As such, the vendor selection problem with non-verifiable outcomes is an important issue in practice and has attracted attention in the IT outsourcing literature.[14]

We use a two-stage vendor selection process in IT outsourcing. In the first stage, the client engages vendors for pilot projects and observes the outcome, while in the second stage, the client can offer a contract only to high-quality vendor(s). There are several characteristics of IT projects that make pilot projects particularly attractive.[15] IT projects are unique in that they involve both heterogeneity in vendor quality and nonverifiable outcomes.

A number of factors aggravate the vendor selection difficulties for IT projects. First, the unprecedented rate of technological change in IT makes it difficult at the outset to lock project specifications into an enforceable contract that can be externally monitored or verified. Second, project management of software development initiatives is much less predictable than project management for other engineering activities. Finally, the IT industry has a high degree of heterogeneity. Our two-stage vendor selection model is viable in IT outsourcing practices. First, IT contracts are increasingly structured as multistage agreements.[16] Second, it might be that the early stages represent pilot projects to help resolve uncertainty in vendor quality. Pilot projects are regularly used in IT contracting for technology exploration and technical risk reduction,[17] as they enable both clients and vendors to learn more about the needs of a project.

Real Options

Firms consider the risk of new investments prior to undertaking a new project. The firm accounts for risk through the capital budgeting function. In capital budgeting decision-making, the goal is to identify those investment opportunities whose net value to the firm is positive. Discounted cash flow (DCF) analysis is the traditional capital budgeting decision model used.[18] It involves discounting the expected, time dependent cash flows for the time value of money and for risk via the calculation of a net present value (NPV).

$$NPV = -IO + \sum_{t=1}^{n} \frac{CF_t}{(1+r)^t} \tag{1}$$

where *IO* equals the initial cash outlay for the project, *CF* is the cash flow, and *r* is the discount rate.

The NPV represents the expected change in the value of the firm which will occur if the project is accepted. The decision rule is straightforward: accept all positive NPV projects and reject all negative NPV projects. A firm is indifferent to a zero NPV project as no change in current wealth is expected.

Today, most academic researchers, financial practitioners, corporate managers, and strategists realize that, when market conditions are highly uncertain, expenditures are at least partially "irreversible," and decision flexibility is present, the static, traditional DCF methodology alone fails to provide an adequate decision-making framework.[19] It has been suggested that current corporate investment practices have been characterized as myopic due, in large part, to their reliance on the traditional stand-alone DCF analysis.[20] An alternative project valuation method is real options analysis (ROA).

Real options are a type of option where the underlying asset is a real asset, not a financial asset.[21] In general, real options exist when management has the opportunity, but not the requirement, to alter the existing strategic or the current operating investment strategy. Real option analysis allows firms to more accurately evaluate projects by explicitly valuing managerial flexibility.[22] Managerial flexibility is valuable since it allows managers to continually gather information concerning uncertain project and market outcomes, and change the firm's course of action based on this information. Real option analysis is a dynamic means of adjusting corporate strategies with innovative product offerings.[23] The most general or all inclusive real option is the option to invest.[24]

The analogy is to a financial call option: the firm has the right, but not the obligation, now or for some period of time to undertake the investment opportunity by paying an upfront fee. As with financial options, the option to invest is valuable due to the uncertainty relating to the underlying asset's future value where, in this case, the underlying asset is the investment opportunity. The investment rule is to invest when the present value of the benefits of the investment opportunity is greater than the present value of the direct cost of the investment opportunity *plus* the value of keeping the option to invest "alive":

$$\text{PV(Benefits)} > \text{PV(Cost)} + \text{Value of the Option to Invest} \quad (2)$$

Outsourcing can be thought of as staged investment. A telecommunications firm chooses to fund two research labs to develop a new cell phone technology. The firm funds the research for a period of time. At the end of that time, both outsourcing firms present the results of their research to date. The funding firm then decides whether to continue funding one, both or neither research labs. Suppose, at the first assessment stage, the telecommunications firm chooses to continue funding both research labs. As the research leads to the development of new technology, and the products work their way through the stages of development, the telecommunications company continues to assess whether to continue funding the research of the two firms.

ROA can lead to a change in decision-making. The traditional DCF analysis wants all point estimates to be as known and certain as possible, and in DCF models, an increase in risk is accounted for by increasing the discount rate, resulting in lower valuations. Thus, under traditional DCF reasoning, risk hurts. In comparison, option value is most often a positive function of the volatility of the underlying asset, as, generally, an increase in volatility leads to an increase in the range of possible future values for the underlying asset. As this line of reasoning quickly suggests, aggressive firms will seek projects with higher volatility because active management of those projects can create value for the firm. Under real options thinking, as long as management can control the downside risk of a project, firms should seek risk, at least to some degree. ROA also shows that sometimes negative NPV projects should be undertaken, given the upside potential embedded in the project.[25]

The question we are concerned with is: how can the real options framework be used to improve the analyses of IT outsourcing? The answer is that ROA can systematically organize the analysis and identify the uncertainties. ROA is, in essence, the quantification of the strategic premium – the gap between the economic value and the actual value of a firm as determined by the marketplace. It allows managers to formulate and implement strategic plans in high-commitment, high-uncertainty environments such as those found in IT projects.[26] The technique is often used at the firm level; however, more frequently what is needed is a project-level perspective.

Real Options Applications in IT

The literature contains several real options applications in IT investment research. For instance, using real options analysis, Taudes explores methods for evaluating sequential exchange options in order to obtain estimates for the value of software growth options.[27] Schwartz and Zozaya-Gorostiza develop two models for the valuation of IT investment projects using the real options approach.[28] The models account for uncertainty both in the costs and benefits associated with the investment opportunity. More recently, Fichman claims that the decision processes surrounding investments in innovative IT platforms are complicated by uncertainty about expected payoffs and irreversibilities in the costs of implementation.[29] As such he argues when uncertainty and irreversibility are high, concepts from real options should be used to properly structure the evaluation and management of investment opportunities, and thereby capture the value of managerial flexibility.

However, to our knowledge, there is no real options analysis used in IT outsourcing research or vendor selection research, let alone the two-stage vendor selection process. In this research, we apply real options analysis in two-stage IT vendor selection to reduce IT outsourcing failure.

Data and Methodology

Chic Logistics Incorporated (CLI) is a $40 million Shanghai-based transportation company with funding from American Venture Capitals. Johnson Shen, CEO and the founder of the company, states "China's economy is growing in such a rapid pace that traditional transportation and warehousing systems have been unable to meet the increasingly sophisticated demands of the market. A modern approach to logistics management provides our customers with higher efficiency, more diversification of services, and above all, better technology." In 2004, CLI determined to make the transformation by adopting a supply chain management information system (SCMS). Due to limited in-house IT capabilities, CLI decided to outsource the SCMS project based on the rationale that purchasing IT components/services from external vendors would allow them to enjoy the benefits of specialization and lower costs. CLI faced two dilemmas of IT outsourcing. First, there are too many SCMS vendors to choose from in China. Initially, they found 13 qualified SCMS vendors in China and later they reduced the selection of vendors to two finalists (SSA Global and EXE Technologies) using a Delphi Method (a subjective selection approach). However, CLI still needs to figure out an analytical screening approach in choosing the final vendor.

Second, by its very nature, IT projects such as SCMS are intangible products and as such it is difficult to identify vendor capabilities and assess vendor performance objectively. CLI decided to employ a two-stage outsourcing approach. In the first stage, namely, the prototype stage, CLI will invest in both SSA Global and EXE Technologies. The cost to invest in SSA is $2.905 million, whereas the cost to invest in EXE is $2.960 million. In the prototype stage, CLI engages each company for a pilot project and observes the outcome. Based on the outcome of the pilot projects, CLI decides whether to continue the project with one of these two companies to the second stage or to terminate the project.

Real option analysis (ROA) is chosen by CLI as the methodology for the vendor selection process. Using ROA, CLI is able to decide not only which vendor to select but also determine what is the optimal level of investment at each stage. We will provide a step-by-step demonstration of how CLI successfully utilizes the ROA framework to render a viable decision in its vendor selection process.

Real Option Methodology

The generally accepted methodology for valuing a financial call option is the Black–Scholes formula.[30] The difficulty with using this closed-form solution for valuing real options is it is difficult to explain, is applicable in very specific situations, and limits the modeler's flexibility. On the other hand, the binomial lattice model, when used to price the movement in the asset value through time, is highly flexible. It is important to note the results are similar for the closed form Black–Scholes model and the binomial lattice approach. The more steps added to the binomial model, the better the approximation.

The binomial asset pricing model is based on a replicating portfolio that combines borrowing with ownership of the underlying asset to create a cash flow stream equivalent to that of the option. The model is created period by period with the asset value moving to one of two possible probabilistic outcomes each period. The asset has an initial value and within the first time period, either moves up to *Su* or down to *Sd*. In the second time period, the asset value can be any of the following: Su^2, *Sud*, Sd^2. The shorter the time interval, the smoother the distribution of outcomes will be.[a]

The inputs for the binomial lattice model are equivalent to the inputs for the Black–Scholes model; namely, we need the present value of the underlying asset (S), the cost of exercising the option (X), the volatility of the cash flows (σ), the time until expiration (T), the risk free interest rate (r_f), and the dividend payout percentage (b). We use these inputs to calculate the up (u) and down (d) factors and the risk neutral probabilities (p).

$$u = e^{\sigma\sqrt{\delta t}} \tag{3}$$

$$d = e^{-\sigma\sqrt{\delta t}} = \frac{1}{u} \tag{4}$$

$$p = \frac{e^{(r_f - b)(\delta t)} - d}{u - d} \tag{5}$$

[a] For a thorough explanation of binomial lattice models, see Mun (2002).

where δt is the change in time and p reflects the probably outcomes that determine the risk free rate of return.

Initial research indicate the volatility of SSA's cash flows are 15% annually, and the time period represented in the binomial lattice model is 1.0 period per cellmovement (In SSA's case, therefore, $u = e^{\sigma\sqrt{\delta t}} = e^{0.15\sqrt{1}} = 1.1618$ and $d = \frac{1}{u} = \frac{1}{1.1618} = 0.8607$). Given a risk free rate of 7% and no dividends

$$p = \frac{e^{(.07-0)(1)} - 0.8607}{1.1618 - 0.8607} = 0.7034.$$[b]

The binomial lattice option model appears as in Fig. 12.1:

Results

By outsourcing SCMS, CLI expects to increase its asset value by $3.764 million regardless of which company it chooses to use for outsourcing. The underlying asset value for CLI if it chooses to outsource to SSA or EXE is as follows (Figs. 12.1–12.5):

					$S_o u^5$
				$S_o u^4$	
			$S_o u^3$		$S_o u^4 d$
		$S_o u^2$		$S_o u^3 d$	
	$S_o u$		$S_o u^2 d$		$S_o u^3 d^2$
S_o		$S_o u d$		$S_o u^2 d^2$	
	$S_o d$		$S_o d^2$		$S_o u^2 d^3$
		$S_o d^2$		$S_o d^3 u$	
			$S_o d^3$		$S_o d^4 u$
				$S_o d^4$	
					$S_o d^5$

Fig. 12.1 Binomial lattice option model

[b] EXE has a volatility of 34%. As a result, for EXE, u = 1.4049; d = 0.7118 and p = .0.5204.

					7968.39
				6858.46	
			5903.13		5903.13
		5080.87		5080.87	
	4373.14		4373.14		4373.14
3764.00		3764.00		3764.00	
	3239.70		3239.70		3239.70
		2788.44		2788.44	
			2400.03		2400.03
				2065.73	
					1777.99

Fig. 12.2 Underlying asset lattice for CLI and SSA (000s)

					20603.94
				14665.27	
			10438.31		10438.31
		7429.68		7429.68	
	5288.22		5288.22		5288.22
3764.00		3764.00		3764.00	
	2679.10		2679.10		2679.10
		1906.91		1906.91	
			1357.28		1357.28
				966.07	
					687.62

Fig. 12.3 Underlying asset value for CLI and EXE (000s)

					5063.39
				4149.85	
			3377.64		2998.13
		2726.12		2372.26	
	2180.55		1847.66		1468.14
1728.40		1419.94		1055.40	
	1078.78		752.85		334.70
		533.54		219.50	
			143.95		0.00
				0.00	
					0.00

Fig. 12.4 Intermediate stage option for EXE

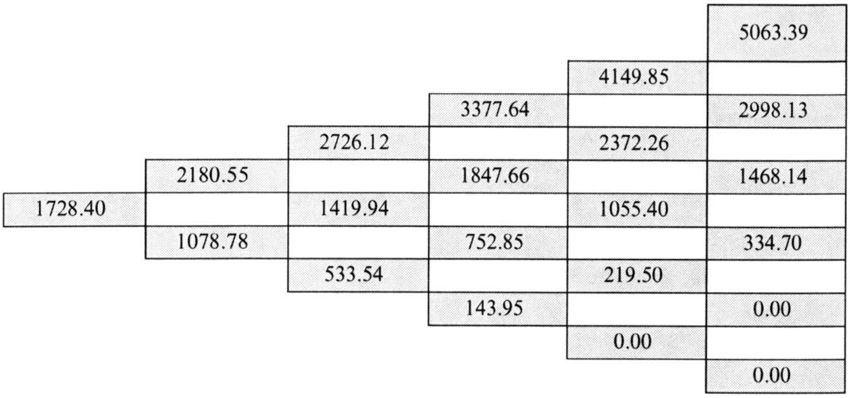

Fig. 12.5 Intermediate stage option for SSA

The binomial tree indicates the IT project value will vary from \$7.968 million to \$1.77 million at the end of time period five for SSA outsourcing; for EXE, the project value will vary between \$20.603 million and \$687 thousand.

Next CLI calculates the equity value for the second option. This is done because the value of the compound option is dependent upon the value of the second option. At each node, CLI assesses the project cash flow and compares it to zero. CLI's goal is to its returns at each node. The formula is as follows:

$$\text{Max}(\text{Benefits} - \text{Costs}, [(p)up + (1-p)down]e^{-r_f \delta t}) \quad (6)$$

With this formula in mind, the value of the second, or intermediate stage option for EXE and SSA are as follows:

For instance, in Fig. 12.5, the node 4,149. 85 is calculated by looking at the value of that same node in the underlying asset in Fig. 12.2, 6,858.46, and subtracting the cost of outsourcing, 2,905. We compare this value to the probability of an up event, 0.7034% times the up node value of 5,063.39 plus (1 – probability of an up event) times the lower node (1-0.7034)*2,998.13 and we discount this sum back one period at the risk neutral rate. The implementation of the formula is as follows:

MAX (6,858.46-2,905, (0.7034(5,063.39) + 0.2966(2,998.13)e^(-0.07(1)) = 4,149.85.

After working our way through the intermediate option value, we move to the option value for the first stage option. The First Phase Option value is dependent upon the Intermediate Stage Option value. For instance, in Fig. 12.6, 3,277.64 is calculated as follows: MAX(Intermediate Stage Option Value – Option Cost, [p(previous up node value)+(1-p)(previous down node value)e^-r(dt). = MAX(3,377.64-2,905, [(0.7034(4,149.85)+(1-0.7034)(2,372.62)e^-0.07(1) = 3,277.64.

Clearly, CLI should outsource (see Figs. 12.6 and 12.7). Both projects create value for the firm which far exceeds the development costs. The results show the

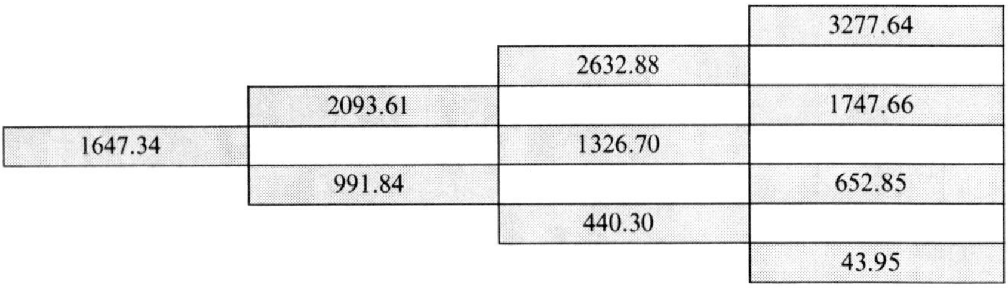

Fig. 12.6 First stage option for SSA

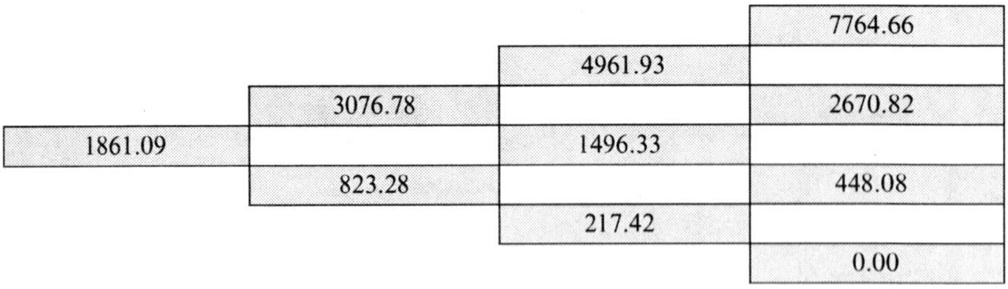

Fig.12.7 First stage option for EXE

value of outsourcing to EXE is $1,861.09 whereas the value of outsourcing to SSA is $1,647.34. CLI should choose to outsource to EXE despite the fact that the cost of outsourcing to EXE is greater for CLI. The additional volatility of EXE causes the potential upside value of partnering with EXE to be greater for CLI.

For this particular project, we have inconsistent results: the NPV analysis shows SSA is the preferred project. However, only ROA allows a firm to capture the value of upside potential within a project and use this value to help quantify a decision for the firm. Real option analysis adds real value to decision analysis when the outcome is not clear-cut. With a vendor selection problem, it is common to find a case such as this where we get conflicting investment decisions. When the volatility of the cash flows for the two vendors is different, we typically see real option and NPV decisions that conflict. For projects with growth opportunities, NPV and real option analysis frequently lead to conflicting conclusions. For projects with growth options, the decision criterion should be to accept the project with the greatest real option value.

Conclusions and Future Study

We propose a two-stage vendor selection approach in IT outsourcing using real options analysis. The conclusions from this study are much broader and have wider application. Without real options, traditional capital budgeting techniques such as net present value analysis cannot capture the potential upside potential of projects. Outsourcing information technology is an important opportunity for research firms to consider. The opportunity must be valued properly. Given the shortcomings of traditional methodologies to account for expansion options embedded in many IT projects, firms may fail to pursue outsourcing ventures due to faulty valuation techniques. It is only by using the real option methodology that we are able to accurately assess the impact of pursuing outsourcing such as the case of CLI's potential partnership with either SSA or EXE. Real options analysis is a technique that needs to be used to value projects with growth opportunities. Our paper contributes to the outsourcing literature by providing a two-stage vendor selection framework employing real options analysis. Our paper also extends the real options analysis applications to IT outsourcing risk management arena, which has never been done before, to the best of our knowledge.

It will be interesting to explore outsourcing issue beyond vendor selection stage (i.e., implementation stage) using real options analysis. It will also be interesting to examine whether the budget constraint of the outsourcing project plays a major role in vendor selection process. Finally, multiple-project comparisons will be a more viable approach to empirically test the proposed research framework. We leave these issues to be addressed by future research.

End Notes

1. DiRomualdo, A., and Gurbaxani, V. (1998). Strategic intent for IT outsourcing, *Sloan Management Review*, 39:4, 67–80.
2. Lee, J.N., and Kim, Y.G. (1999). Effect of partnership quality on IS outsourcing success: Conceptual framework and empirical validation, *Journal of Management Information Systems*, 15:4, 29–62.
3. Lacity, M.C., and Willcocks, L.P. (1998). An empirical investigation of information technology sourcing practices: Lessons from experience, *MIS Quarterly*, 22:3, 363–408.
4. Brooks, J. (1987). No silver bullet: Essence and accidents in software engineering, *IEEE Computer*, 20, 10–19.
5. Herath, H.S.B., and Bremser, W.G. (2005). Real option valuation of research and development investments: Implications for performance measurement, *Managerial Auditing Journal*, 20:1, 55–73.
6. King, W.R. (2004). Outsourcing and the future of IT, *Information Systems Management*, 21:4, 83–84.
7. Fichman, R.G. (2004). Real options and IT platform adoption: Implications for theory and practice, *Information Systems Research*, 15:2, 132–154.
8. Pinches, G. (1982). Myopia, capital budgeting and decision-making, *Financial Management*, 11:3, 6–20.
9. Moad, J. (1989). Contracting with integrators, using outside information system integrators on an information systems project, *Datamation*, 35:10, 18.
10. Raynor, M.E., and Leroux, X. (2004). Strategic Flexibility in R&D, *Research Technology Management*, 47:3, 27–33.
11. Earl, M.J. (1996). The risks of outsourcing IT, *Sloan Management Review*, 37:3, 26–32.
12. Lacity, M.C., and Hirschheim, R. (1993). Information Systems Outsourcing, Myths, Metaphors, and Realities. Chichester, England: Wiley.

13. Grover, V., Cheon, M.J., and Teng, J.T.C. (1996). The effect of service quality and partnership on the outsourcing of information systems functions, *Journal of Management Information Systems*, 12:4, 89–116.
14. Violino, J.B., and Caldwell, B. (1998). Analyzing the integrators-Systems integration and outsourcing is a $300 billion business, but are customers really getting their money's worth? Here's what IT managers really think about their hired guns, *Informationweek*, 709, 45–113; Porter, M. (1992). Capital Disadvantage: America's Failing Capital Investment System, *Harvard Business Review*. Boston, Sep/Oct; Willcocks L., Lacity M., and Kern T. (1999). Risk mitigation in IT outsourcing strategy revisited: longitudinal case research at LISA, *Journal of Strategic Information Systems*, 8, 285–314.
15. Vijayan, J. (2002). The outsourcing boom, *Computerworld*, 36:12, 42–43.
16. Kern, T., Willcocks, L., and van Heck, E. (2002). The winner's curse in IT outsourcing: strategies for avoiding relational trauma, *California Management Review*, 44:2, 47–69.
17. Mun, J. (2002). Real Options Analysis: Tools and Techniques for Valuing Strategic Investments and Decisions, New Jersey: Wiley.
18. Copeland, T., and Antikarov, V. (2001). Real Options – A Practitioner's Guide, New York, Texere LLC.
19. Lacity and Hirschheim. (1993). op. cit.
20. Dixit, A., and Pindyck, R. (1994). Investment Under Uncertainty: Keeping One's Options Open, *Journal of Economic Literature,* 32:4, 1816–1831.
21. McFarlan, F.W., and Nolan, R.L. (1995). How to manage an IT outsourcing alliance, *Sloan Management Review*, 36:2, 9–23.
22. Amram, M., and Kulatilaka, N. (1999). *Real Options: Managing Strategic Investment in an Uncertain World.* Boston: Harvard Business School Press; Newton, D.P., Paxson, D.A., and Widdicks, M. (2004). Real R&D Options 1, *International Journal of Management Reviews,* 5:2, 113.
23. Lewis, N., Enke, D., and Spurlock, D. (2004). Valuation for the strategic management of research and development Projects: The deferral option, *Engineering Management Journal,* 16:4, 36–49.
24. Scheier, R.L. (1996). Outsourcing's fine print, *Computerworld*, 30:3, 70.
25. Lacity and Willcocks. (1998). op. cit.
26. Alessandri, T., Ford, D., Lander, D., Leggio, K., and Taylor, M. (2004). Managing Risk and Uncertainty in Complex Capital Projects, *Quarterly Review of Economics and Finance*, 44:4, 751–767.
27. Taudes, A. (1998). Software growth options, *Journal of Management Information Systems* 15:1, 165–185.
28. Schwartz, E.S., and Zozaya-Gorostiza, C. (2003). Investment under uncertainty in information technology: Acquisition and development projects, *Management Science*, 49:1, 57–70.
29. Fichman. (2004). op. cit.
30. Black, F., and Merton Scholes, M. (1973). The pricing of options and corporate liabilities, *Journal of Political Economy,* 81, 637–659.

Part IV
Applications of ERM in China

Chapter 13
Assessment of Banking Operational Risk

C. Zhang, W. Zhu, S. Yang, and J. French

Oprisk and Measurement Research

The main risks in banking management are credit risk, market risk and operational risk (Oprisk). The British Bankers' Association (BBA) and Coopers and Lybrand conducted a survey in BBA's 45 members in 1997 and the report showed that more than 67% of banks considered the oprisks were of more concernment than market risk and credit risk. 24% of banks had suffered more than 100 million pound losses during the three years prior to the survey.[1] The worldwide survey on oprisks by the Basel Committee (2002) showed that respondent banks had reported 47,029 oprisk cases with losses of over 1 million EURs, with each bank experiencing 528 oprisk cases on average.[2] Over the past decade, financial institutions have suffered several large operational loss events leading to banking failures. Memorable examples include the Barings' bankruptcy in 1995, the $691 million trading loss at Allfirst Financial. Obviously, oprisk is a very serious problem in the banking system at present. These events have led regulators and the banking industry to recognize the importance of oprisk in shaping the risk profiles of financial institutions.

Unlike credit risks and market risks, oprisks have no agreed upon a universal definition. There are three viewpoints for oprisks' definition:[3] a generalized concept regards all kinds of risk except for market risk and credit risk as oprisk; a narrowed concept regards only the risks related with the operational departments in financial institutions as oprisks. Obviously, the generalized concept makes it difficult for managers to measure oprisk accurately, and narrowed concept cannot cover all the oprisks that cause banks to suffer from unexpected loss. Therefore, we prefer the third definition – the concept between generalized and narrowed. This concept firstly divided the events of banks into two types, controllable and non-controllable, and then regards the risks from controllable events as oprisks. The definitions from the Basel Committee and BBA are most representative ones belong to the third conception. In the New Capital Accord II, the Basel has incorporated into its proposed capital framework an explicit capital requirement for oprisk, defined as the risk of loss resulting from inadequate or failed internal processes, people and systems or from external events.[4] BBA indicated in their famous 1997 survey that it is difficult to control oprisk base on coherent basis if there is not a proper frame of

D.L. Olson, D. Wu (eds.) *New Frontiers in Enterprise Risk Management*,

risk management for a bank. BBA, according to their own banking practice, directly defined oprisk as "the risk of direct or indirect loss caused by the imperfections or errors of internal procedures, personnel and systems or external events."[5]

The Basel proposed three distinct options for the calculation of the capital charge for oprisk. The use of these approaches of increasing risk sensitivity is determined according to the risk management systems of the banks. The Basel was intended to improve risk management by allowing the use of different methods to measure credit risk and oprisk, and allowing banks and supervisors select one or more methods most in accord with their banking operation and financial markets status. For all types of risks, the Basel encourages banks to use their own method for assessing their risk exposure. Indeed, the absence of reliable and large enough internal operational loss databases in many banks has hindered their progress in modeling their operational losses. The three approaches for oprisk measuring (see Table 13.1) proposed by Basel Accord II are Basic Indicator Approach (BIA), Standardized Approach (SA) and Advanced Measure ment Approach (AMA).[6] In AMA the oprisk capital requirement can be described as $\sum_i \sum_j \gamma(i,j) \times EI(i,j) \times PE(i,j) \times LGE(i,j)$, i means operation type, j means risk type, $\gamma(i, j)$ is the operator to convert expected loss EL into capital requirement; parameter γ is enacted by supervision department according to the operation loss data for the whole banking industry; $EI(i, j)$ means oprisk exposure of (i, j); $PE(i, j)$ means occurring probability of loss events on (i, j); $LGE(i, j)$ means the loss degree when the events occur on (i, j). Those three parameters – $EI(i, j)$, $PE(i, j)$, *and* $LGE(i, j)$ are estimated by banks internally. However parameter γ reflected the risk distribution of whole banking industry mainly, but not always, associated with the

Table 13.1 Overview of oprisk approaches[9]

<table>
<tr><td rowspan="2">Names</td><td colspan="2">Top-down approach: Allocate a certain proportion of current capital to oprisks</td><td colspan="3">Bottom-up approach: Estimate oprisks based on actual internal loss data</td></tr>
<tr><td>Basic indicator approach</td><td>Standardized approach</td><td>Internal measurement approach</td><td>Loss distribution approach</td><td>Modeling approach</td></tr>
<tr><td rowspan="2">Business lines and risk type</td><td>Single business line</td><td>Multiple business lines</td><td colspan="3">Multiple business lines and event types</td></tr>
<tr><td></td><td colspan="2">Standardized by supervisors</td><td colspan="2">Bank discretion</td></tr>
<tr><td>Structure</td><td colspan="3">Σ{Coefficient × Indicators}</td><td colspan="2" rowspan="3">Estimate operational VaR based on frequency and severity distributions</td></tr>
<tr><td rowspan="2">Parameters</td><td>Exposure indicator (EI)</td><td colspan="2">Multiple EIs by business line PE, LGE, and RPI</td></tr>
<tr><td colspan="3">Standardized by supervisors</td></tr>
</table>

risk distribution of special institution and special operation. Meanwhile AMA has some obstacles in practice, such as most banks lack of the internal historical data needed to estimate oprisk, the external data are not matching with the potential loss of the bank, etc. The Loss Distribution Approach (LDA) based on the hypothesis of oprisk occurring probability and aftereffect severity. LDA estimates the special experiential probability distributions of the two factors by some techniques, such as Monte Carlo Simulation. While LDA only be implemented in a few big banks because of the lack of comparable internal data from different banks to be able to estimate the various distributions hypothesizes.[7] Oprisk-VaR models in financial institutions have been proposed.[8] Oprisk-VaR regards various internal controlling methods in correlative operation flows as reference points, and then estimates the maximal loss (*ML*) of every reference point when they lose control of system and probability (*P*) of control lose. So the VaR of this point is $MD \times P$. There is a huge difficulty in VaR practice of using historical simulation because of the lack of the historical data causing oprisk. Simultaneity, the oprisk events have a lower probability and a huge loss.

There are many disputes between supervisors and bankers about the definition, measuring and controlling of oprisk because of lacking practical experience in banks. Basel Accord II has not provided risk sensitivity tools for banks to measure and manage oprisk exposure. Owing to the difficulties in obtaining rating data, oprisk has been controlled by operation handbooks or risk listings for a long time.

The potential losses from oprisk, market and credit risk are different. The probabilities of credit and market risk follow the normal distribution, and can be described and quantified by the probability distribution. Therefore banks can take effective risk measurement using their historical data. Unexpected oprisk has a lower frequency, but more serious consequences. Other research focused on measurement elements and management framework,[10] and introducing fuzzy mathematics and dynamic model into this field.[11]

Oprisk Management Frame

The economic advantages of more advanced methods are more obvious for the larger banks. As to the complex methods a number of requirements must be fulfilled. The banks must be able to quantify their risk according to the basic principles in Basel II. In addition, a number of routine requirements must be fulfilled. First of all, the Banks need to set a strong frame to provide the technical and decision making for oprisk management. We confirmed the frame consisted of three aspects: oprisk stratagem established by the bank's directorate; policies implemented by the independent oprisk management department in bank; and risk supervising process (see Fig. 13.1).

The unpredictable oprisk in the time series made statistical methods unreliable. Additionally, considering our current commercial banks' incomplete internal factors and our immature capital market, etc., these conditions cannot satisfy the hypothesis of oprisk model in mature markets.

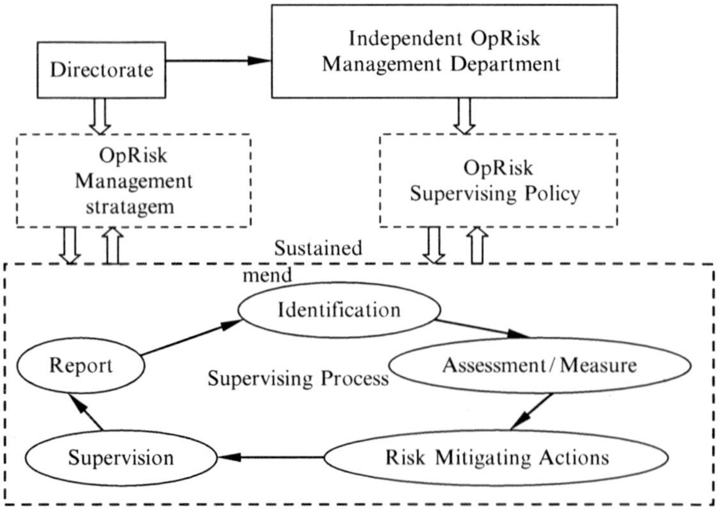

Fig. 13.1 The oprisk supervising frame

Adopting DS Evidential Theory in Oprisk Assessment

Oprisk has no uniform or consensus definition, no general acceptable standards in measuring, no public database and no mature control technique and proper software in China yet. At present, neither the four state-controlled banks nor the joint-stock banks have sufficient historical data of oprisk. These are huge blocks in oprisk management for Chinese financial institutions. Therefore in this paper, we introduce the evidential theory to assess the uncertainty information of oprisk. We can say there are two main advantages in employing the ER approach for MCDM. Firstly, it provides a novel belief framework to model and synthesize subjective information. Secondly the ER approach can make full use of different types of data, including subjective judgments, probabilistic data, and incomplete data under weaker assumptions that may underlie other methods such as the multiple value function theory (MAVT)[12] This paper set up the oprisk measurement according to supervising frame based on DS evidence theory by collecting experts' knowledge and experience in indicators of oprisk source. The uncertain information processing ability of DS theory according with the human being's perceives rules.

Assessment of Oprisk on DS Evidential Theory

The DS theory of evidence originated in the work of Dempster on the theory of probabilities with upper and lower bonds,[13] and improved by Shafer in his 1976 book *A Mathematical Theory of Evidence*.[14] In early 1980s, owing to the study of evidence theory in the expert system framework by Lowrance, Gorden and Shortliffe, it has been popularized in the literature on Artificial Intelligence (AI)[15] and Expert Systems, as a technique for modeling reasoning under uncertainty. The rationale of the ER methodology is demonstrated by many applications, such as business performance assessment,[16] safety and risk analysis and synthesis,[17] product design and selection, environmental impact assessment,[18] etc.

The Evidential Reasoning approach is developed to deal with MCDM problems having both quantitative and qualitative information with uncertainties and subjectivity. The ER approach uses a belief decision matrix, while most conventional MCDM methods use a decision matrix for problem modeling, of which the conventional decision matrix is a special case. In a belief decision matrix, a distribution instead of a single value is used to represent an alternative's performance on an attribute. A modified Dempster's evidence combination algorithm[19] is used for aggregating the information in the belief decision matrix. The aggregation process is nonlinear. The outcome of the aggregation is also a distribution of an alternative's performance on the top attribute. A score can be calculated from the distribution by adding each assessment grade value weighted by the associated belief degree in the distribution.

Evidence, Frame of Discernment and Belief Function

Owing to imperfection and non-exactness of evidences the decision-makers cannot get the optimal scheme directly, although it is feasible to confirm the scope of probability for the optimal scheme. Under this thought, Shafer's evidence theory provided a new construction to interpret probability considering "probability" is that someone constructs his belief degree for a proposition being true under the available evidence.

If we denote the quantity by θ and the set of its possible values by Θ, Θ is called frame of discernment. If Θ is a frame of discernment, then a function m: $2^{\Theta} \rightarrow [0,1]$ is called a basic probability assignment whenever

$$\begin{cases} m(\phi) = 0 \\ \sum_{A \subseteq \Theta} m(A) = 1 \end{cases} \qquad (1)$$

The quantity $m(A)$is called A's basic probability assignment (BPA).
If Θ is a frame of discernment, m: $2^{\Theta} \rightarrow [0,1]$ is a BPA on Θ. Then a function Bel: $2^{\Theta} \rightarrow [0,1]$ is a belief function over Θ if it is given by formula (1) for some BPA m: $2^{\Theta} \rightarrow [0,1]$. $Bel(A) = \sum_{B \subseteq A} m(B), (\forall A \subseteq \Theta$. Subset A of a frame Θ is called a focal element of a belief function Bel over Θ if m(A)>0. There is no requirement that belief committed to a given proposition and allows us to construct and analyze our frame of discernment in a more flexibly way.[20]

Dempster's Rule of Combination

Suppose Bel_1 and Bel_2 are belief functions over the same frame Θ, with BPA m_1 and m_2 and focal elements $A_1,\ldots,A_k$ and $B_1,\ldots,B_l$, respectively. If $Bel_1 \oplus Bel_2$ exists and basic probability assignment is m, then the function m: $2^\Theta \to [0,1]$ defined by

$$m(A) = \begin{cases} K \sum\limits_{A_i \cap B_j = A} m_1(A_i) m_2(B_j) & A \neq \varnothing \\ 0 & A = \varnothing \end{cases} \tag{2}$$

here,

$$K = \left(1 - \sum_{A_i \cap B_j = \varnothing} m_1(A_i) m_2(B_j)\right)^{-1}, \forall A \subseteq \Theta, A_i, B_j \subseteq \Theta. \tag{3}$$

The hypotheses of evidences combining are independency and limited conflict. While relativity and strong conflict between evidence are often exist in banking risk practice, therefore researchers indicated that basic probability assignment of relative focal elements must be amended to avoid over-estimated in combining and to reflect the important and reliability of evidences from different sources; a portion of basic probability number of conflicted evidences was sent to unknown scopes Θ to make results more rational when strong conflict occurred.[21] Thus how to confirm the amending coefficient of basic probability numbers is the key for exact combining. This paper sets the amending coefficient of BPA by measuring distance between evidence bodies.

Weighted Average Combining Model by Evidences' Distances

The weights in combining formula (2) are accordant, while evidence weights in banking oprisk assessment are normally inconsistent; therefore we weight averaged the basic probability assignment by estimating the distance between evidences. According to Bayesian Probability Theory, the lesser the distance between evidences, the more comparability and reliability the evidences have; influence of distance on the evidences reliability has positive correlation with the quantity of evidence sources.

If Θ is a frame of discernment comprising different propositions, and m_1 and m_2 are BPA over Θ, then the distance between m_1 and m_2 can described by

$$dis(m_i, m_j) = \sqrt{\frac{1}{2}\left(\|\vec{m}_i\|^2 + \|\vec{m}_j\|^2 - 2\left\langle \vec{m}_i, \vec{m}_j \right\rangle\right)} \tag{4}$$

$$\left\langle \vec{m}_i, \vec{m}_j \right\rangle = \sum_i \sum_j m_i(A_i) m_j(B_j) \frac{|A_i \cap B_j|}{|A_i \cup B_j|}, A_i, B_j \in P(\Theta) \tag{5}$$

The greater the distance between the evidences, the less their similarity, so we can define the similarity of m_1 and m_2 and the supporting degree of evidence m_i in the system are:[22]

$$Sim(m_i, m_j) = 1 - dis(m_i, m_j), i, j = 1, 2, \wedge \cdots n \tag{6}$$

$$Sup(m_i) = \sum_{j=1, j \neq i}^{n} Sim(m_i, m_j) \tag{7}$$

$$\omega_i = Crd(m_i) = Sup(m_i) \Big/ \sum_{i=1}^{n} Sup(m_i), \sum \omega_i = 1 \tag{8}$$

We get the weight of evidence from same group experts ω_i to combine the evidences using weighted average Dempster's rule of combination.

Indicators of Oprisk's Assessment

To establish a uniform and standardized rating system for commercial banks, CBRC issued *The Internal Guidelines of Supervisory and Rating for Commercial Banking* (IGSRCB) in January 2006. It is based on the CAMEL rating[23] and combined with the actual situation of commercial banks in China. This paper focuses on "management" rating of commercial banks in the IGSRCB and based on the framework of oprisks management (Fig. 13.1), and then used a designed questionnaire to gather the relevant knowledge of operating risk assessment case from experts. We designed the oprisk rating indicators system in following four aspects:

Strategic Plan (f_1)

Strategic plan indicators in oprisk are mainly consisted in careful planning from circumstance analysis, material measures and confirmable inspect ensuring the plan fulfilled. The collocation of resources should be in consistent with strategic plans and integration risk management with planning and decision-making.

Service Quality (f_2)

Service quality indicators involved the extensive communication between bank and clients, efforts by governors to improve clients' relationship, understand potential client needs and reduce credit risk; the competitive power of interest rates; rationality of pricing in banking service.

Internal Control (f_3)

Information System and Technical Safeguard (f_{31})

Assess the bank's risk analysis process, policies, and oversight based on the size and complexity of the credit union, the type and volume of e-Commerce services, technological investment risk. The bank should have a tested contingency plan in place for the possible failure of its computer systems.

Segregation of Duties and Protection of Physical Assets (f_{32})

Banks should have adequate segregation of duties and professional resources in every area of operation, with defined employee responsibility and authority limits, internal and external reporting, and adequacy of the allowance for loan and lease losses account and other valuation reserves are important.

Effectiveness of Audit Program (f_{33})

An effective audit function and process should be independent, reporting to the supervisory committee without conflict or interference by management. Reports should be issued to management for comment and action.

Education of Staff (f_{34})

Staff should be thoroughly trained in specific operations, as well as the bank industry philosophy. A training program should be in place and cross training programs for office staff should be present. Key persona absence and labor force intermitting must be avoided.

Performance of Directorate (f_4)

This was evaluated for compliance with all applicable laws and regulations, reputation, juristic and public obligation, rationality of compensation policies for senior management, avoidance of conflict of interest, responsiveness to audit suggestions, requirements and professional ethics and behavior.

We can get the oprisk indicators system as Table 13.2.

$F = \{f_1, f_2, f_3, f_4\}$ is the set of top indicators of oprisk, q_i is weight of f_i (i = 1,2,3,4), we can conform the weights of indicators q_i = (0.25,0.25,0.3,0.2) according to the analysis of CAMEL system on banking operation management. The top indicator strategic plan (f_1) has four sub-indicators $F_1 = \{f_{11}, f_{12}, f_{13}, f_{14}\}$. Also we can get the sub-indicators F_2, F_3, F_4 of f_2, f_3, f_4.

Table 13.2 Operational risk rating indicators system

Management stratagem f_1	Service quality f_2	Internal control f_3	Assessment on directorate f_4
Operating circumstance f_{11}	Clients relationship/ risk f_{21}	Information system safeguard f_{31}	law-abiding f_{41}
Safeguard measures f_{12}	Exterior exploring f_{22}	Responsibilities and assets safety f_{32}	Prompting measure f_{42}
Communication f_{13}	Loan marking f_{23}	Auditing effectiveness f_{33}	Harmonizing inter conflict f_{43}
Resources collocation f_{14}	Service pricing f_{24}	Personal training program f_{34}	Profession ethics f_{44}
Policy and strategy changing f_{15}	Operation characteristics f_{25}		

Model Structure and Demonstration

Experts Grouping and Weights

We selected the experts who have more than 10-years work experience and more than 5-years management experience in banks as our survey population and grouped them into three types – outside manager, technologist and internal operator by their positions and specialty, denoted experts set as $E = E_1, E_2, E_3$, E_1-outside managers, E_2-technologist, E_3-operator. Therefore we have the grade set $F_{11} = \{E_1(f_{11});E_2(f_{11});E_3(f_{11})\}$ of three groups' experts on f_{11}.

The Weights of Evidences from Same Group Experts

The weights of evidences in same group ω_i were estimated by the distance discussed in formula (8).

The Evidence Weights of Experts from Different Groups

The weights of evidences from different groups were estimated by the experts' specialties and background. We give E_1 higher weights in f_1 and f_4, give E_2 a higher weight in f_3, and E_3 a higher weight in f_2 by experts' meeting. According to the experts' judgments we got the initial weights of different groups on the four top indicators f_1, f_2, f_3, f_4, namely e_{ij} satisfied $\sum_{j=1}^{4} e_{ij} = 1$, e_{ij} means the weight of group i on indicator j. Then get the weights of different groups normalized there are $e^*_{1j} = (0.4,0.267,0.267,0.4)$, $e^*_{2j} = (0.3,0.3,0.433,0.3)$, $e^*_{3j} = (0.3,0.433,0.3,0.3)$.

Data Source and Processing

We designed the survey questionnaire to cover the four top guidelines $F = \{f_1 f_2 f_3 f_4\}$ mentioned in part 3. The experts must estimate the risk exposure, probability and loss of risk events. We adopted three state-controlled banks' oprisk judgments from experts here. The set of evaluation grades is $H = \{1,2,3,4,5\}$ = {excellence, good, neutral, worse, worst}.

Step 1: Distributed assessments (belief degrees) and same group experts' weights

$$E_i = \left\{ \left(H_n, \beta_{n,i} \right), \mathrm{n} = 1 \wedge, 5; i = 1,2,3 \right\}, 0 \le \beta_{\mathrm{n,i}} \le 1$$

Here,

$$\beta_{\mathrm{H,i}} = 1 - \sum\nolimits_{\mathrm{n}=1}^{5} \beta_{\mathrm{n,i}}, (\mathrm{i} = 1,2,3)$$

Following is the BPA of four main indexes from each group of experts using bank A as an example. (The initial BPA matrixes m_1, m_2, m_3, and m_4 as follows.)

$$m_1 = \begin{bmatrix} 0.04 & 0.24 & 0.44 & 0.24 & 0.04 \\ 0.024 & 0.461 & 0.236 & 0.255 & 0.024 \\ 0.026 & 0.683 & 0.239 & 0.026 & 0.026 \end{bmatrix}, m_2 = \begin{bmatrix} 0.04 & 0.36 & 0.52 & 0.04 & 0.04 \\ 0.022 & 0.732 & 0.202 & 0.022 & 0.022 \\ 0.02 & 0.92 & 0.02 & 0.02 & 0.02 \end{bmatrix},$$

$$m_3 = \begin{bmatrix} 0.04 & 0.54 & 0.34 & 0.04 & 0.04 \\ 0.133 & 0.686 & 0.133 & 0.024 & 0.024 \\ 0.028 & 0.673 & 0.243 & 0.028 & 0.028 \end{bmatrix}, m_4 = \begin{bmatrix} 0.04 & 0.64 & 0.04 & 0.24 & 0.04 \\ 0.681 & 0.244 & 0.025 & 0.025 & 0.025 \\ 0.015 & 0.94 & 0.015 & 0.015 & 0.015 \end{bmatrix}$$

Step 2: Confirmed the distance $dis(m_i, m_j)$ of four indicators rating data of bank A, calculated $Crd(m_i)$ as the weight of same groups experts ω_{ij} (i = 1,2,3,4 means four main indicators, j = 1,2,3 means three groups of experts) of basic probability assignment of evidences using formula (6)–(8).

$$Sup_{ij} = \begin{bmatrix} 1.8939 & 1.9336 & 1.9425 \\ 1.8656 & 1.9293 & 1.9222 \\ 1.8839 & 1.9004 & 1.9281 \\ 1.8586 & 1.9116 & 1.8763 \end{bmatrix}, \omega_{ij} = \begin{bmatrix} 0.3283 & 0.3351 & 0.3367 \\ 0.3263 & 0.3375 & 0.3362 \\ 0.3298 & 0.3327 & 0.3375 \\ 0.3292 & 0.3385 & 0.3323 \end{bmatrix}$$

Then amended the BPA according ω_{ij} of bank A, and derived the combining results of oprisk rating by the adjusted combining rule.

$$m_{ij} = \begin{bmatrix} 0.03 & 0.463 & 0.304 & 0.173 & 0.03 \\ 0.027 & 0.674 & 0.245 & 0.027 & 0.027 \\ 0.067 & 0.633 & 0.238 & 0.031 & 0.031 \\ 0.249 & 0.606 & 0.027 & 0.092 & 0.027 \end{bmatrix}$$

Step 3: Normalized weights of experts from different groups and give the basic probability mass (Attribute /expert group *i*):

$$m'_{n,i} = e^{*}_{ij}\beta_{n,i}, (n = 1, \wedge 5), m'_{H,i} = 1 - e^{*}_{ij}\sum_{n=1}^{5}\beta_{n,i}$$

Step 4: Combined probability mass and belief degree:

$$m'_{H} = k(\prod_{i=1}^{3} m_{n,i} + \sum_{t=1}^{3}\prod_{i=1,n\neq t}^{3} m_{H,i}m_{n,t})$$

Combining the probability of each level on four indicators we can get the general score of oprisk management in bank A using integration grade $F = \omega_j \cdot E' \cdot q_i$.

Finally, we can get the general score of operational risk management in bank B and C by same method, and compare the results of the three banks (Table 13.4).

Conclusion

We can find the outcome of the DS evidential approach aggregation is also a distribution on the top attribute (see the shadows in Tables 13.3 and 13.4). A general score can be calculated from the distribution by adding each assessment grade value weighted by the associated belief degree in the distribution. However the score will normally be different from weighted sum method. From Table 13.4 we can detect clearly and easily that where and what caused the oprisk in a bank. We conclude that:

Table 13.3 Probability of each level and score of operational risk management in Bank A

	Probability in each level					Subentry grade	Index weight q_i	Score
	5	4	3	2	1			
f_1	0.03	0.463	0.304	0.173	0.030	3.29	0.25	0.823
f_2	0.027	0.674	0.245	0.027	0.027	3.65	0.25	0.912
f_3	0.067	0.633	0.238	0.031	0.031	3.67	0.30	1.102
f_4	0.249	0.606	0.027	0.092	0.027	3.96	0.20	0.792
Score	1.865	9.504	2.442	0.646	0.115	14.572	1.00	*3.629*

Table 13.4 Comparison of operational risk management results in theree banks

	Bank A				Bank B				Bank C			
E	f_1	f_2	F_3	f_4	f_1	f_2	f_3	f_4	f_1	f_2	f_3	f_4
E_1	3.00	3.32	1.54	3.40	3.50	4.00	3.83	3.80	4.75	4.40	4.50	4.75
E_2	3.21	3.71	1.80	4.53	3.18	3.30	3.55	3.20	4.75	4.20	4.75	4.00
E_3	3.66	3.90	1.09	3.93	3.4	3.53	3.68	3.53	3.63	3.16	3.91	3.00
$\omega_{ij} \cdot Ei$	3.29	3.65	3.67	3.96	3.36	3.66	3.68	3.50	4.19	3.73	4.27	3.69
$\omega_{ij} \cdot Ei \cdot q_i$	3.629				3.561				3.998			

- The results of subentry comparing by main index is: the subentry scores of bank A are in the middle basically for the indicator f_4 (efficiency of directorate) is the best and the f_1 (strategic plan) is the worst among three banks; Bank C has the best score among three banks because of the obvious advantage in its main indicators f_1, f_2 (service quality) and f_3 (internal control); and the f_4 of bank B is the "short leg" for its operational risk management. Before we combined these evidence we also get the assessment of sub-indicators, such as in f_3 (internal control) there are four sub-indicators. Using these sub-indicators' rating, the managers in banks can detect more detailed information on oprisk controlling. So that it is reasonable for managers to change their policy and procedures to control and mitigate the oprisk.
- We can give suggestions on the policies for mitigating oprisk in each bank: managers in bank A need inspect their strategic plans related to operation flew, analyze the circumstance in scrutiny so as to insure the collocation of resources be in consistent with strategic plans; It is important for bank B to improve the performance of directorate. They need inspect the rationality of policies in interest, such as compensation for senior management; although bank C got the best score among three banks, it is necessary for them to make great efforts in performance directorate.
- From the characters of different group's experts we can find that the scores from outside managers and technologist were more steadier and the BPAs were higher, especially the managers' (See the m_{ij} matrixes). The conflicts between the evidences of the three groups' experts were very little.

In this demonstration, DS evidential theory supplied us the tool for mining uncertain information into Scorecard Approach. It was hard to get a rational assessment if we use the methods discussed in Table 1 alone for the insufficient data. Now we can use the uncertain information by DS theory combination rule to improve the Scorecard Approach.

The Function of DS Evidential Theory in Oprisk Assessment

DS evidence theory provides a frame of discernment to deal with ignorant or unaware information. It is accord with gradational perceiving process of human. We can add new evidences constantly into the frame of discernment using the oprisk management circulatory process (Fig. 13.1). This make the risk managers realize the mechanism of belief degree distributing in evidences and support decision-making. Therefore we can build a dynamic rating framework. The key point of DS evidential theory is combining evidences from different information sources so that it has preferable processing ability for uncertainty information. Therefore DS evidence theory is a good quantitatively method for qualitative analysis. This accorded with the information incompleteness and time serial instability in banks' oprisks measurement. DS theory has better application value in inspecting and measuring oprisk. This paper analyzed the availability of the process and results of this methodology by demonstration with three banks, and confirmed the efficiency of DS theory in detecting some problem factors in oprisk control, increased the distinguish ability of assessing to provide better support for decision-making.

We know that measurement of oprisk is only one building block of a sound oprisk management framework and that qualitative models should be associated with more quantitative aspects in order to better integrate the performance of a bank's activities. Using the qualitative and quantitative integrated approaches will be the more rational study manner in banking oprisk assessment.

Acknowledgement This paper has the support from China Natural Science Fund (J0624004) Soft Science Research Program of Anhui (03035005), Literae Humaniores Program of Anhui (2004SK003ZD), and Natural Science Fund of Anhui (050460403). The anonymous referees' comments have made important contributions to the improvement of this paper. We also want to appreciate the help and instructing from Professor J B Yang of the University of Manchester, Prof. Garth Allen of Monfort College of Business of University of Northern Colorado, and the Fulbright Scholar Larry Shotwell in Shanghai University of Finance and Economics.

End Notes

1. Zhengrong, L., and Guojian, L. (2006). Reference and revelation of international advanced experience of oprisk management, *Gansu Finance*, 50–53.
2. Basel Committee on Banking Supervision (2002). Working Paper on the Regulatory Treatment of Operational Risk.
3. Xiaopu, Z., Xun, L., and Ling, L. (2006). The Classification principles of operational risk loss event. *The Banker*, 122–125.
4. Basel Committee on Banking Supervision. (2001). Operational Risk, Consultative Document, Basel, September, URL: http://www.bis.org.
5. Wei, Z., Yuan, W. (2004). Operational risk management framework of new Basel accord. *International Finance Study*, 4, 44–52.
6. Wei, Z., Wenyi, S. (2004). The new basel accord and the principle of operational risk management. *Finance and Trade Economics*.12, 13–20.
7. Shusong, B. (2003). Operational risk measurement and capital restriction under the new basel accord, *Economic Theory and Economic Management*. 2, 25–31.
8. Acerbi, C., and Tasche, D. (2001) Expected Shortfall: A Natural Coherent Alternative to Value at Risk, Working Paper.
9. Mori, T., and Harada, E. (2001). Internal Measurement Approach to Operational Risk Capital Charge, Bank of Japan, Discussion Paper.
10. Federal Deposit Insurance Corporation. (2003). Supervisory Guidance on Operational Risk Advanced Measurement Approaches for Regulatory Capital, July: http://www.fdic.gov/regulations/laws/publiccomments/basel/oprisk.pdf; Kühn, R. (2003). Functional correlation approach to operational risk in banking organizations. *Neul Physica A*, 650–666.
11. Scandizzo, S. (1999). A Fuzzy Clustering Approach for the Measurement of Operational Risk Knowledge-Based Intelligent Information Engineering Systems. Third International Conference 31 Aug. – 1 Sept. 1999, 324–328; Giampiero, Beroggi, E.G., and Wallace, W.A. (2000). Multi-expert operational risk management, *IEEE Transactions on Systems, Man and Cybernetics, Part C*, 30:1, 32–44.
12. Buchanan, B.G., and Shortliffe, E.H. (1984). Rule-Based Expert Systems, Addison-Wesley, Reading, MA.
13. Dempster, A.P. (1967). Upper and lower probabilities induced by a multi-valued mapping, *Annals of Mathematical Statistics*, 38, 325–339.

14. Shafer, G. (1976). A Mathematical Theory of Evidence, Princeton University Press, Princeton, NJ, 35–57.
15. Xinsheng, D. (1993). Evidence Theory and Decision, Artificial Intelligence. Beijing: Renmin University of China Press 3:13–19.
16. Siow, C.H.R., Yang, J.B., and Dale, B.G. (2001). A new modelling framework for organisational self-assessment: Development and application. *Quality Management Journal*, 8:4, 34–47; Yang, J.B., and Xu, D.L. (2005). An intelligent decision system based on evidential reasoning approach and its applications. *Journal of Telecommunications and Information Technology*, 3: 73–80.
17. Wang, J., and Yang, J.B. (2001). A subjective safety based decision making approach for evaluation of safety requirements specifications in software development. *International Journal of Reliability, Quality and Safety Engineering*, 8:1, 35–57; Sii, H.S., Wang, J., Pillay, A., Yang, J.B., Kim, S., and Saajedi, A. (2004). Use of advances in technology in marine risk assessment, *Risk Analysis*, 24:4, 1011–1033.
18. Wang, Y.M., Yang, J.B., and Xu, D.L. (2006). Environmental impact assessment using the evidential reasoning approach. *European Journal of Operational Research*, 174:3, 1885–1913.
19. Yang, J.B., and Xu, D.L. (2002). On the evidential reasoning algorithm for multiple attribute decision analysis under uncertainty, *IEEE Transactions on Systems, Man and Cybernetics. Part A*. 32, 289–304.
20. Shanlin, Y., Weidong, Z., and Minglun, R. (2004). Learning based combination of expert opinions in securities market forecasting. *Journal of Systems Engineering*, 96–100.
21. Ibid.
22. Yong, D., Wenkang, S., and Zhengfu, Z. (2004). An efficient combination method to process conflict evidences, *Journal of Infrared and Millimeter Waves*, 23:1, 27–33
23. Morgan, D.P., and Ashcraft, A.B. (2003). Using loan rates to measure and regulate bank risk. *Journal of Financial Services Research*, 24:2/3, 181–200.

Chapter 14
Case Study of Risks in Cailing Chemical Corporation

X. Kefan, C. Gang, C. Yun, and W. Gui-Xuan

As a Large-scale State-owned Corporation, Cailing Chemical Corporation is located in Hubei province, China, and owes 34.5 million Yuan as working fund and 6,000 staff and workers including 1,210 technicians. its production capacity are mining 2.2 million ton, dressing 2.2 million ton, sulfuric acid 660,000 ton, phosphoric acid 250,000 ton, Ammonia 170,000 ton, Ammonium Phosphate 400,000 ton, Common Superphosphate 340,000 ton, Ammonium Phosphate 140,000 ton, Compound Fertilizer 130,000 ton, sodium fluorosilicate 17,000 ton per year.

Risk management is very important in many aspects of materials processing. There have been studies relative to system components such as purchasing,[1] construction,[2] port construction,[3] and distribution.[4] These represent a diversity of risk types calling for careful management. Cailing Chemical Corporation is currently faced with different kind of risks associated with Chemical corporations. Thus, it is imperative to analysis systemically and dynamically the risks of Cailing Chemical Corporation, which is the basis for risk prevention

Risk Composition of Cailing Chemical Corporation

Risks in process industries have been widely studied in China.[5] According to its business leaders, the risk in Cailing Chemical Corporation can be classified into 14 types as follows:

Quality Risk

Since the establishment of Cailing Chemical Corporation, quality management has been first priority, but there have been some problems, such as:

(a) Low qualified rate of some main raw materials and semi-finished products. High ratio of magnesium and phosphorous has been identified as one of the main causes of the high unqualified rate of phosphate rock. In addition, the quality of some semi-finished product is unstable, which directly affects the quality of products of downstream processes.

D.L. Olson, D. Wu (eds.) *New Frontiers in Enterprise Risk Management*,

(b) Another aspect is that the qualified rates and competitive power of finished product are very low. The most problems of its finished products are low nutrient, which leads to share the profit in low nutrient product market, where low profit margin can only be gained. And their qualified rates are very low, which affects the market share.
(c) Also, Total Quality Management system is not established. Except for product quality is emphasized, the maintenance quality of equipment, decision quality and management quality among other things are not given enough attention. Investigation showed that equipments are often repetitively repaired due to the same act of violation recurs.

Safety Risk

Cailing has done a great deal of work at the aspect of safety production management, but its performance in this area still needs to be strengthened. In 2002, the accident count was 8 but in 2006 the figure elevated to 31. Our study discovered that the safety risk of Cailing Chemical Corporation needs to focus on the accident type, which is concentrated on mechanical injury, injured by vehicles and from heights and others. The distribution of accident is concentrated on Nitrogenous Fertilizer Plants, Sulfuric Acid Plant, Compound Fertilizer Plant and machinery repairing plant. There are several factors responsible for accident in Cailing:

(a) *Equipments and its management*. Three departments and multi-grade management layer are in charge of the equipment management, which is the main cause of their distributive management. So, the efficiency of equipment management is very low. Moreover, quality of equipments have the heavy corrosion aging, which is one of the most potential safety hazards and affect normal production.
(b) *Shortage of competent workers*. The drain of high-class mechanics affects the ability of operation and maintenance of equipments; many operators have indifferent safety awareness; disobedient phenomenon is serious, sometime the same safety accident repeated emergence.
(c) *Safety education*. There is lack of the systemic plan and scheme of safety education, and also implementation of the systemic safety education, which lack the mechanism of routine rescue rehearsals
(d) *Working environment*. There lies some potential safety hazard. For example, narrow workplace potholes pavement etc. some serious potential safety hazards are yet to be improved.

Marketing Risk

Marketing risk is also one of the most important risks of the corporation. There are many factors that lead to marketing risk and such factors are:

(a) *Organization*. Its marketing organization lies in some question, for example, unclear duty and work range, unsmooth information communication, lacks of the flexibility of the system, etc.
(b) *Marketing concept and means*. Nowadays, its means of sales promotion is unitary, lacks of systemic marketing strategy. The function of after-sales service system is imperfect, lacks of given person track after-sales and building the corresponding archives. They do not investigation in the customers in time meanwhile after-sales, so the need of customers can not comprehend in time.
(c) *Competitors*. Since the profit of the Phosphorus Chemical Industry is little, its competition is very fierce, meanwhile some new comers and substitute continuously appears, etc. all of these increase its marketing risk.
(d) *Marketing channel*. There lie in serious Customer losing problems and unitary marketing channel. Meanwhile the development speed of new marketing channel and new customers
(e) *Credibility*. Sometime the need of some customers does not been met in time for inferior quality of some Salesman, as Customer Complaint often appears.

Human Resource Risks

The questions in Human Resource Management are as follows: The quality of Human Resource Management does not match the need of its present development in present. Salary System is not incentive for Technicians, performance assessment can not effectively mobilize the enthusiasm of staff. Serious brain drain and difficult talent recruitment exist at the same time. Staff and workers have no confidence in the prospect of enterprise, poor work force. Some staffs and workers have low morality towards their jobs

Technology Risk

Since phosphorus chemical industry is not high-tech industry, new substitute continuously appears, the need of customers in green product and technology continuously increase, in this background, Cailing chemical Corporation face some technology risks as follows: (a) Technology competitive risk from new substitute, green product and green technology etc.; (b) technology loss risk with brain drain; (c) quality risk for the unabundance of technology capacity; (d) technology advantage loss risk for the development speed cannot meet the need.

Environmental Protection Risk

Cailing chemical Corporation attack importance in the implementation of Environmental Protection Regulation, by strengthening environmental control, improving product technology, Pursue Cleaning Production, the pollutants after treating reached the standard of the national discharge. But there lies still some question in environmental protection management, which can result environmental protection risk, Specific as:

(a) Emission concentration exceeds permissible standard, acidity and alkalinity of pollutants that come in Sewage Treatment Plants is very stable, with maximal uncertainty, which increases the difficulty and complexity of decision in sewage treatment plant.
(b) The ability of environmental protection management is limited, the number of environmental protection accident per year still keep in a relative high level, moreover there is no any improvement tendency.
(c) Old equipment, incorrect operating method and environmentalless technology lead environmental protection accidents repeated emergence and can not been eradicated.

Policy Risk

(a) *Agriculture policy*: to serve agriculture is the main function of the main products of Cailing Chemical Corporation, so any change from agriculture policy can lead risk to Cailing Chemical Corporation
(b) *Environmental protection policy*: phosphorus chemical fertilizer is not Bio-fertilizer and it may bring some pollute to environment, moreover there fill with quantities of potential pollution risk in the product process of phosphorus chemical fertilizer, so, some environmental protection policy can bring unfavorable influence
(c) *Local protective policy*: in order to protect the benefit of local phosphorus chemical enterprises, dealers or peasants, sometime some local government can put forward for new policy, which can bring more uncertainty to Cailing Chemical Corporation

Organization Risk

As Cailing Chemical Corporation has not finished its organization innovation, there lies quantities of question in organization management, these questions have hindered the development of Cailing Chemical Corporation. The main questions are:

(a) Excessive department and overstaffed organization structure lead the function of organization structure to overlap, the possibility of conflicts between departments to increase. Too fuzzy labor division lead to the absence of management, meanwhile system benefit of management displays with difficulty.

(b) Serious in-fighting and lack of effective competition. Organization setting disobeys the principle of authority responsibility profit, and there lack of coordination between organizations.
(c) Complex system and low efficiency of enterprise organization. Updating speed of system is very slow; any system has not explicit valid term; Management system lack of the coherence, systematicness and convenience.

Culture Risks

(a) Cailing chemical Corporation have no established way of confidence building mechanism, staffs and workers distrusts each other, so there is rarely cooperation.
(b) Cailing has the enterprise spirit of working hard, active enterprise, perseverance, but its enterprise spirit lack of innovation, study, organization and cooperation.
(c) Internal Management Communication is inadequate harmonious. Staffs and workers are averse to give themselves advice.

Institutional Risk

(a) Updating speed of Institution is very slow, and therefore unable to meet the changes from the environment.
(b) Excessive and overstaffed institutions, they conflict with each other, and Lack of systematicness and unity, so the Institution System lacks systemic efficiency.
(c) Some institutions have very lower quality. For example, the purpose is unclear, power and duty are not clear, management process far from being smooth.

Planning and Schedule Risk

(a) Inefficiency management objective. Objective itself lack of challenges, object system lack of systematicness, the content of objective lack of guideness and operability, the process of objective implementation lack of supervision, so the efficiency of objective management is very low.
(b) There is lack of comprehensive plan in place, not all of staffs and worker have themselves planning, and are in the range of plan management.
(c) Plan management cannot effective inspire the passion of the staff for lack of corresponding supervision and rewards and punishment.
(d) Plan is not systemic and also lack sense of unity. This often occurs such that the products of upstream and downstream affect each other.

Supply Chain Risk and Procurement Risks

It often occurs that production is stopped and product plan is affect for supply is not enough; (b) the quality of products is affected by the quality of material, equipments and machines; (c) safety and Environmental protection management is also affected by the quality of some machines; (c) Bargaining power of some suppliers can affect financial safety when their repayments occur simultaneously.

Financial Risk

In financial management, Cailing faces some difficulties as follows: High debt ratio, lack of circulating funds, bad credit reputation. Therefore, Cailing face the chance of very serious financial risk.

Investment Risk

Cailing's executive attaches importance to long-term development when in investment decision, but limited information and decision-making ability are the major challenges that brings about some questions in investment management. Some of the challenges in investment decision are: lack of accuracy, equilibrium, harmony and stability in investment. So, (a) the developments of R&D, production and marketing are unharmonious, low input of R&D has resulted in R&D inability to meet the need of marketable; (b) The ratio of investment in person and equipments is mismatch; (c) the production abilities of semi-products are improper, the production ability of mining has affected the development of the whole production system.

In conclusion, there are 14 types of risks in Cailing Chemical Corporation, those jeopardize the development of Cailing at all time. So we must study further these risks and find corresponding countermeasures.

Risk Assessment

Cailing Chemical Corporation currently is facing with 14 types risks, and their intensities are evaluated by subjective assessment technique on the basic of full investigation. In the risk assessment, we took into account the level of harm and frequency of risk. Figure 14.1 shows the 14 types of risks in a Coordinate Graphs.

Figure 14.1 indicates that quality risk, culture risk and human resource risk are the most serious risk in Cailing Chemical Corporation. However, planning and schedule risk, safe production risk, environmental protection risk, supply chain risk and procurement risk, financial risk should not be ignored.

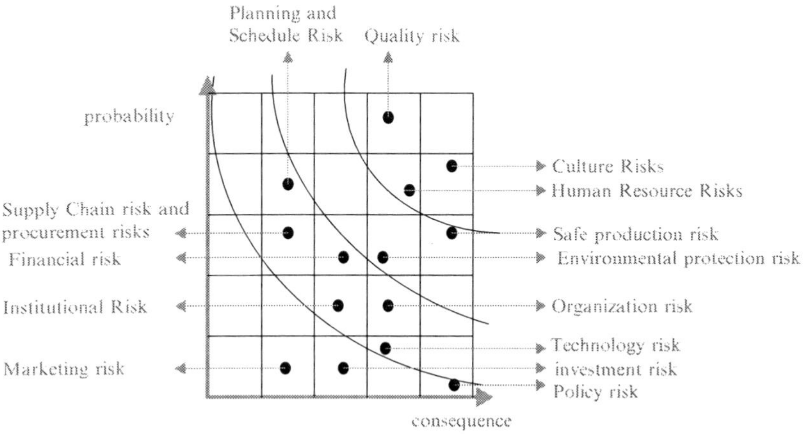

Fig. 14.1 Risk coordinate graphs in Cailing chemical corporation

Risk Analysis

Analysis on Risk Factors

We have identified 14 types of risks facing Cailing Chemical Corporation. Although the influencing factors to every risk are not the same, we can induce some internal and external factors to influence risks. While such internal factors are equipment and machine, chemicals, energy, Three-Waste, technology, Enterprise System, working environment, staff and worker; the external factors are national policy, laws and regulations, Mineral Resources, competitor, consumer, natural condition, social condition, and others. The relationship between these factors and some risks is shown in Table 14.1.

Risk Transfer Relation

The risk transfer relationships among these risks is depicted in Fig. 14.2.

For Cailing Chemical Corporation, since policy risk, investment risk, organization risk, institutional risk, technology risk are not the serious risks (as showed in Fig. 14.1), they could be classified as sources of some risks. For example, unreasonable organization structure can lead unefficient institutional and object management. Thus organization risk is the source of schedule risk and institutional risk. Moreover, institutional risk is the source of human resource risk and culture risk. Investment risk is the source of procurement risk, quality risk and human resource risk. So, in

Table 14.1 The relationship between risks and their factors

Risk type	Quality	Safe production	Marketing risk	Human resource risk	Technology risk	Environmental protection risk	Policy risk	
	Risk factor							
Internal factors	Equipment machine	√	√		√		√	
	Chemicals	√	√		√			
	Energy	√	√					
	Three-waste		√				√	
	Technology	√			√	√		
	Enterprise system	√	√		√			
	Working environment		√					
	Staff and worker	√	√		√		√	
External factors	National policy							√
	laws regulations							
	Mineral Resources	√		√	√			
	Competitors			√				
	Consumers			√	√			
	Natural condition		√					
	Social condition							√

Here, √ indicates risk and the risk factors are related

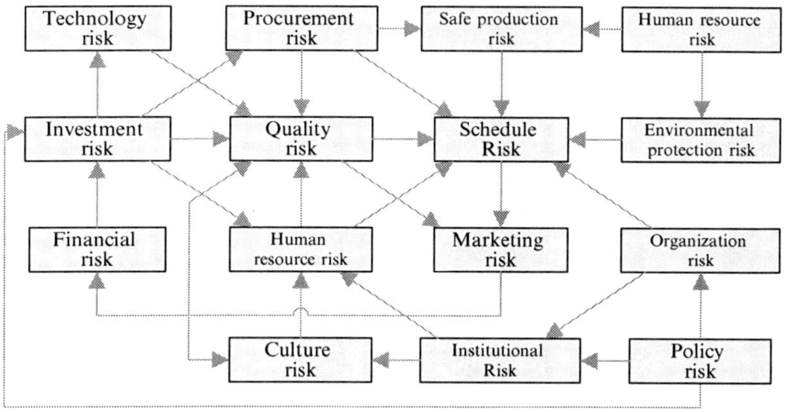

Fig. 14.2 Risk transfer in Cailing chemical corporation

Business Process Reengineering, organization innovation and culture construction, many risks of Cailing Chemical Corporation can be treated efficiently.

Risk Distribution of Cailing Chemical Corporation

The identified 14 types of risks in Cailing Chemical Corporation can not distribute in every organization, every department, or every business process. Moreover, their levels of intensities are incompletely the same in different time and organization. Consequently, it is necessary to study risk distribution from three points of view as stated below:

Risk Distribution Based on Business Process

There are different risks in different business processes. Also, there are different risks in different stage of the same business process. Therefore, it is necessary to study risk distribution based on business process. The identification and analysis of risks in the whole process of the critical business process, which is the basic of the whole process risk management is significant considering the impact of these risks to the modern corporation. Here, we only research the risk distribution of procurement process as depicted in Fig. 14.3.

Figure 14.3 shows some main risk of every stage in procurement process, according to the chart, we can control risk in the whole process of procurement process.

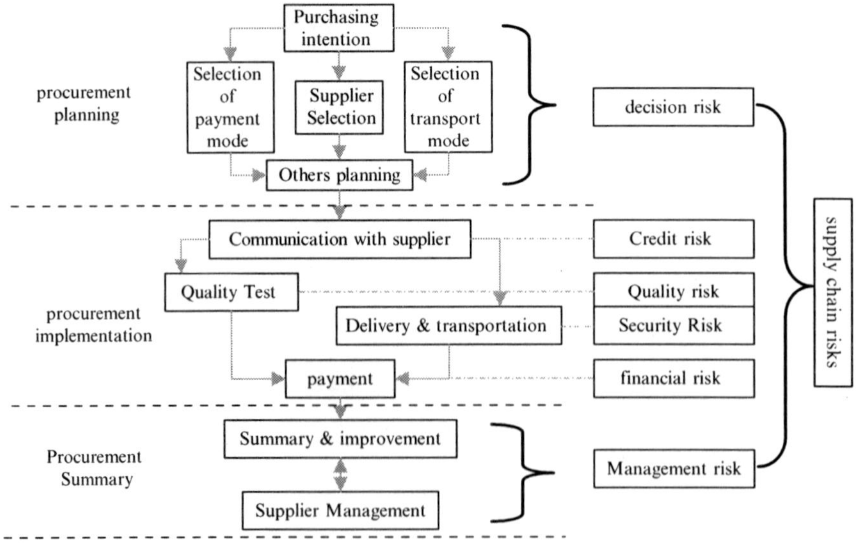

Fig. 14.3 Risk distribution chart of procurement process

Risk Distribution Based on Layout of Factory

It is obvious that the risks in different location of factory district in different ways. Thus, there is the need to research all risks and their position in factory district, which can promote an all-round risk management system. Here we study risk distribution in the sulphuric acid plant.

Quality risk is a major problem in pyrite raw material, in the burning and poison exposure in the roasting plant, and in the oxidation furnace. Environmental protection risks are greatest in fluoride removal and the last absorber. Burning, poison exposure, electrical shock, and corrosion exist at various stages in the production process as well.

Risk Distribution Based on Organization Structure

Every unit has their own business and function, and different business can encounter different risk. Our investigation found that the risks encountered by every production unit as listed in Table 14.2 and the risks encountered by every management unit as shown in Table 14.3 are distinct. Tables 14.2 and 14.3 show risk distribution in organization structure, the two tables make every unit clear of their anti-risk responsibility, so risk distribution in organization structure should be study to strengthen the risk management of all members.

Table 14.2 Risk distribution in production units

Risk type	Quality risk	Safe production risk	Human resource risk	Technology risk	Environment protection risk	Schedule risk
Production units						
Mining team		△	△		△	△
Concentrator	△	△	△	▲	△	
Nitrogenous Fertilizer Plants	▲	▲	△		△	
Sulphuric acid plant	▲	▲	△		△	
Phosphamidon factory	△	▲	△	▲	△	
Compound fertilizer plants	△	v	△	△	△	
Machinery repairing plant		▲	△			
Freight yard		△				▲
Transportation fleet		△				▲
Packaging bag plant		△				

Here, △ represents Production unit has the weak certain risk, ▲ represents Production unit has the strong certain risk

Conclusions

According to our investigation and the characteristics of risks in Cailing Chemical Corporation, we can control risk by implementing some countermeasures such as the implementation of total risk management, establishment of risk management platform and the carrying out of risk early-warning management.

Modern business management theory thinks total risk management emphasize on two basic implications. Firstly, the scope of risk management must include all of risk factors. These factors can come from different risk types, different regions, different departments, or different management levels. Secondly, when we deal with risks, risk factors must be integrated from the integral perspective of Cailing. In order to reduce risk in the business process, Cailing Chemical Corporation needs to implement total risk management, and control risk in systemic and dynamic way.

Cailing Chemical Corporation needs to establish risk management platform, which would include risk management strategy platform, risk management communication platform, risk management monitor platform and risk management organization platform, and their functions are shown in Table 14.4.

Table 14.3 Risk distribution in management units

Risk type	Decision risk	Financial risk	Procurement risk	Human resource risk	Marketing risk	Institutional risk	Organization risk	Culture risk	Investment risk	Technology risk	Schedule risk
Department											
Front office	▲	△			△	▲	▲	△	▲		
Equipment			△			▲			▲		
Instrument			△			▲			▲		
Power			△			▲			▲		
Human resource				▲				△			
Post inspection				▲				△			△
Social charity				▲				△			
Education				▲				△			
Planning and statistics	△										▲
Environment protection						▲		△			
Safety						▲		△			
Mine technology								△		▲	
Chemical technology								△		▲	
Quality	△							△			
Financial		▲									
Marketing					▲						
Supply			▲								

Here, △ represents Production unit has the weak certain risk, ▲ represents Production unit has the strong certain risk

Table 14.4 Risk management platform in Cailing chemical corporation

Platform	Function
Risk management strategy platform	Improve strategy management, promote strategic risk management, implementing risk object management
Risk management communication platform	Promote the realization of risk Management Target Strengthening risk information management, promote the Optimization of Enterprise System
Risk management monitor platform	Establish risk early-warning management mechanism, perform periodic risk identification; Establish risk early warning system, implement all-round risk early-warning; Establishing the review system of the risk management system, promote continual improvement of the risk management system
Risk management organization platform	Promote continual improvement of organization structure, and offer organization and system support for the communication of risk management, risk early-warning management and the realization of strategic objective

Cailing Chemical Corporation should establish risk early-warning management system to ensure risk symptom are found as early as possible and that the main risks are monitored timely with preplans mechanism.

End Notes

1. Wu, C., and Jia-ben, Y. (2000). Risk Management of Material Purchase, *Systems Engineering-Theory and Practice*, 6, 54–59 (In Chinese).
2. Yi, K.-J., and Langford, D. (2006). Scheduling-Based Risk Estimation and Safety Planning for Construction Projects, *Journal of Construction Engineering and Management*, 132, 626.
3. Hogan, J. (2004). Implementing a Construction Safety Program for Seaport Facilities, *Ports*, 136, 134.
4. Lavender, S.A., Oleske, D.M., Andersson, G.B.J., Kwasny, M.J., and Morrissey (2006). Low-back disorder risk in automotive parts distribution, *International Journal of Industrial Ergonomics*, 36:9, 755–760.
5. Jian-jun, Z. (1999). New Preparation Technology of Pure Phosphoric Acid with Variant Phosphorus Ore, *Guangxi Chemical Industry*, 28:4, 13–16 (In Chinese); Jianxing, Y., Cheng, L., and Guangdong, W. (2003). A New Method of Engineering System Risk Analysis Based on Process Analysis, *Ship Engineering*, 05, 53–55 (In Chinese); Xie, K.-F. (2004). Enterprise Risk Management, China, Wuhan: University of Technology Press, P.R. China, (In Chinese); Zheng, L., Shan Ying, H., Ding Jiang, C., XiaoPing, M., and Jin Zhu, S. (2006). Dynamic

Modeling and Scenario Analysis on Phosphor Resources of China, *Computers and Applied Chemistry*, 23:2, 97–102 (In Chinese); Cao, H.-P. (2006). Study on Anhui Liuguo Chemical Industry Corporation Limited's Development Strategy, Guang-xi University, (In Chinese); Feng-Ping, W., and Xu-Xiang, T. (2007). Thermodynamical Analysis of the Normal-Temperance Phosphating Process, *Journal of Liaoning Normal University* (Natural Science Edition), 30:1, 80–83 (In Chinese).

Chapter 15
Information Technology Outsourcing Risk: Trends in China

D. Wu, D.L. Olson, and D. Wu

Introduction

Technology is developing at a rapid pace, outstripping the rate of growth in population (which we hope is slowing down), the economy (which we hope is increasing at a controlled rate), and culture (which we want to speed up). Every year we see at least one significant advance in computer speed and computer system storage capacity. Every year we purchase a new iPod, expecting it to be outdated in a year. Every year we expect last year's cell phone to be an antique, and that Intel will build a faster chip, leading to a new generation of personal computers. This makes long term investment in technology problematic. It is hard to have a rational long-term business plan if the conditions concerning product availability are going to be completely revised. That is one of the factors of life that make the future interesting. We need to learn to keep up with new developments, which lead to new opportunities. It has always been the case that we need to adapt – but now we need to adapt much faster.

The Committee of Sponsoring Organizations of the Treadway Committee (COSO) is an organization formed to improve financial reporting in the U.S. COSO decided enterprise risk management (ERM) was important for accurate financial reporting in 1999 (Levensohn, 2004).[1] COSO emphasized in its ERM framework the importance of IT risk, involving treating IT risk as one of eight key steps.

Outsourcing has evolved into a way for IT to gain cost savings to organizations. Outsourcing is attractive to many types of organizations. Outsourced IT work from corporate America over the past 5 years has grown from \$5.5 billion to over \$17.6 billion. Currently India has 80% of this lucrative market.[2] However, according to the 2005 CIO Insight Outsourcing Survey, China is beginning to offer compelling advantages over India since India's original cost benefits are reaching wage and capacity limits.[3]

Information Systems Risk

Risks in information systems can be viewed from two perspectives. There is a need for information technology security, in the sense that the system function properly when faced by threats from physical (flood, fire, etc.), intrusion (hackers and other malicious

D.L. Olson, D. Wu (eds.) *New Frontiers in Enterprise Risk Management*,

invasions), or function (inaccurate data, reporting systems not providing required information to management and/or operations). Physical security is usually dealt with by one group of people, while IT personnel are usually responsible for risks involving intrusion or function. Anderson called for converging IT and physical security under the direction of a single strategic leader, allowing focus on organizational business objectives.[4] He suggested focus on each organization's unique characteristics considering company size, industry regulations, liability, technical complexity, culture, and risk tolerance. Convergence of physical and IT security are expected to align security efforts with business objectives and allow better risk focus. It also can lead to reduced overhead and administrative duplication. Interaction of system components can lead to better detection of threats, and control of corporate assets. Risk acceptance decisions can be transferred to business units that are most affected.

Systems

Systems are collections of interrelated parts working together to accomplish one or more objectives. In systems, output is not simply the sum of component parts. There are many systems of interacting parts where viewing the whole tells us more than simply looking at the system's components.[5] Components are affected by being in the system, and the sum of the system output is greater than what the sum of individual outputs would have been without being in the system. Systems are purposeful, meant to do something. The distinction of systems thinking is a focus on the whole, viewing the interactions of structure (system components and relationships), function (outcomes), and process (activities and knowledge).[6] Systems thinking enables understanding the interdependency of those system elements working together in some larger environment. Analysis involves taking systems apart, explaining part behaviors, and aggregating parts back into a whole with better understanding.

The complexity of systems has been explored in many fields. Nicolis and Prigogine[7] noted the evolution, diversification, and instability of systems everywhere. Some of these are reversible (like economic policies). Others are irreversible (nuclear reactions). There are important societal issues involved, with popular books by academics[8] and politicians[9] devoted to warning of the dangers of human interactions with nature in the area of pollution generation and control. The complexity of systems across human endeavor was instrumental in the formation of the Santa Fe Institute,[10] which focuses in how adaptation builds complexity in natural and artificial systems.[11] While necessity generates development of solutions in times of crisis (international monetary coordination after the 1930s; nuclear development during World War II; hybrid cars in 2005?) each of the solutions mankind develops can involve unintended consequences. Boston's back bay (the Fenway) was filled in over the period 1850–1880, when it seemed like a very economic idea to use trees for piers, which subsequently led to the need to pay tremendous amounts to repair in the 1980s.[12] The Asian vine kudzu was imported around 1900 to the US to conserve eroded pasture land, but after growing as rapidly as 1 foot per day during peak growing season, it has pulled down telephone poles, damaged electrical distribution systems, and made train tracks more dangerous. Australians imported rabbits to control one problem, and induced another. Environmentally, DDT was considered a miracle cure to insect-borne epidemics in the 1940s. But DDT had negative impacts, leading to its ban in 1972 after many DDT-resistant pest strains had evolved.[13] In medicine, hospitals have become very dangerous places, with up to 6% of patients being infected by microbes after admission.[14] Laparoscopic surgery using fiber optic technology reduced operating costs 25%, which attracted medical insurance companies, and led to double the rate of use, raising costs to insurance companies 11% overall. Pap tests save many lives, but false reassurance can lead to greater risks, and false positives can lead to unnecessary pain and agony. Humans don't seem to do well with complex systems. At least they create the need for adaptation as new complications arise.

Complexities arise in technology as well.[15] The Internet was created to assure communication links under possible nuclear attack, and have done a very good job at distributing data. It has also led to enormous opportunities to share business data, and led to a vast broadening of the global market. That was an unintended benefit. Some unintended negative aspects include broader distribution of pornography, or expedited communication in illegal or subversive organizations. Three Mile Island in the U.S. saw an interaction of multiple failures in a system that was too tightly coupled.[16] Later, Chernobyl was even worse, as system controls acted counter to solving the problem they were designed to prevent. We try to create self-correcting systems, especially when we want high reliability (nuclear power; oil transportation; airline travel – both in the physical context and in the anti-terrorist context). But it is difficult to make systems foolproof. Especially when systems involve complex, nonlinear interactions, conditions that seem inevitable when people are involved.

COSO Application of IS Risk Management

COSO involves a risk management framework including the following steps:

1. Internal Environment
2. Objective Setting
3. Event Identification
4. Risk Assessment
5. Risk Response
6. Control Activities
7. Information and Communication
8. Monitoring.

O'Donnell provided a systems-based taxonomy for information systems risk management.[17] The systems view led him to identify factors influencing business process performance in IS grouped into a taxonomy of procedures (design, support, and externalities) and agents (skill, motivation, and information – constituting personnel-related events in the COSO guidelines).

Procedure design requires complete specification of activities needed to correctly perform the task. It also is necessary to create monitoring capabilities so that management can assure that tasks are being accomplished appropriately. This category in the taxonomy is under procedure support in COSO guidelines.

Procedure support involves the infrastructure of resources and services. This includes appropriate computer technology to communicate with external participants involved, such as vendors or customers. Procedures may require that these external participants be given access through portals, to pass through organizational firewalls. This may seem to lead to a tradeoff between access and security, but industry has generated very effective, secure procedures to allow needed access to systems and information. This category in the taxonomy is under procedure support in COSO guidelines.

Procedure externalities (including external business risks in the COSO guidelines) involve risks from changing economic conditions, competition, disasters (natural and man-made), and changing regulatory controls. Environmental conditions are beyond the control of an organization for the greater part, but risk can be transferred through actions such as insurance, business alliances, and withdrawal from business lines not matching the selected risk appetite of an organization.

Agent skill is the ability to effectively execute procedures. Supervision and training can reduce this class of risk.

Agent motivation is fostered by intrinsic and extrinsic incentives. Risks of insufficient agent motivation for organizational members can be reduced by supervision and incentive programs. Analogous measures for extraorganizational members call for contractual arrangements.

Agent information of sufficient quality and quantity are needed to enable agents to make the best decisions during procedure execution. Procedures involve a series of decisions which can often be automated to gain speed, consistency, and efficiency. Humans are better than computers at making judgments. This judgment can be incorporated into automated systems (in the form of expert systems, for instance), but care must be taken to think of all factors that will be important for future decisions, a daunting task.

Event identification can be accomplished with this taxonomy as a framework as shown in Table 15.1:

IS Risk Identification and Analysis

Information systems involve high levels of risk, in that it is very difficult to predict what problems are going to occur in system development. All risks in information system project management cannot be avoided, but early identification of risk can reduce the damage considerably. Kliem and Ludin (1998) gave A risk management cycle[18] consisting of activities managers can undertake to understand what is happening and where:

Table 15.1 Events threatening agent accomplishment of processes

Component procedure	Functions	Threat events
Engage customers/employees	Identify customer groups to target	Target groups not wanting firm's products Target groups unable to afford firm's products
	Gather and analyze customer data	Target groups unwilling to travel to firm's locations Customer data not available
	Anticipate customer preferences	Inadequate tools for data analysis Inability to identify likely customers
	Develop marketing initiatives	Uncertainty of price customers willing to pay Initiatives not deployed at proper time
	Deliver the message	Inability to effectively communicate with customer base
Provide service employees	Identify services desired	Lack of knowledge of services to provide Service timing
	Services provided in firm outlets	Employee understanding of services Employee understanding of products Services complement marketing
Transact with customers/ employees	Pricing	Prices not competitive
	Inventory management	Products not optimally priced for profit Store layout not optimized
	Deliver checkout services	Ineffective store promotions Product mix not optimal Inventory levels not optimal Sales data not effectively captured Information to effectively sell is not available Information needed to effectively provide service is not available
Engage customers/employee	Customer response to marketing	Customer does not get the message Message does not get customer attention Message does not contain effective information Message does not provide effective incentives
Provide service to customers	Customer appreciates service initiatives	Customers unaware of available services

(continued)

Table 15.1 (continued)

Component procedure	Functions	Threat events
		Customers do not want available services
		Service delivery unsatisfactory
Transact with customers/ employees	Customer value provided	Products hard to locate
		Product information difficult to locate or understand
		Checkout unacceptable
		Products do not meet expectations

Adapted from O'Donnell, 2005

- Risk Identification
- Risk Analysis
- Risk Control
- Risk Reporting

Risk identification focuses on identifying and ranking project elements, project goals, and risks. Risk identification requires a great deal of pre-project planning and research. Risk analysis is the activity of converting data gathered in the risk identification step into understanding of project risks. Analysis can be supported by quantitative techniques, such as simulation, or qualitative approaches based on judgment. Risk control is the activity of measuring and implementing controls to lessen or avoid the impact of risk elements. This can be reactive, after problems arise, or proactive, expending resources to deal with problems before they occur. Risk reporting communicates identified risks to others for discussion and evaluation.

Risk management in information technology is not a step-by-step procedure, done once and then forgotten. The risk management cycle is a continuous process throughout a project. As the project proceeds, risks are more accurately understood.

The primary means of identifying risk amounts to discussing potential problems with those who are most likely to be involved. Successful risk analysis depends on the personal experience of the analyst, as well as access to the project plan and historical data. Interviews with members of the project team can provide the analyst with the official view of the project, but risks are not always readily apparent from this source. More detailed discussion with those familiar with the overall environment within which the project is implemented is more likely to uncover risks. Three commonly used methods to tap human perceptions of risk are brainstorming, the nominal group technique, and the Delphi method.

Brainstorming

Brainstorming involves redefining the problem, generating ideas, and seeking new solutions. The general idea is to create a climate of free association through trading ideas and perceptions of the problem at hand. Better ideas are expected from brainstorming than from individual thought because the minds of more people are tapped. The productive thought process works best in an environment where criticism is avoided, or at least dampened.

Group support systems are especially good at supporting the brainstorming process. The feature of anonymity encourages more reticent members of the group to contribute. Most GSSs allow all participants to enter comments during brainstorming sessions. As other participants read these comments, free association leads to new ideas, built upon the comments from the entire group. Group support systems also provide a valuable feature in their ability to record these comments in a file, which can be edited with conventional word-processing software.

Nominal Group Technique

The Nominal Group Technique[19] supports groups of people (ideally seven to ten) who initially write their ideas about the issue in question on a pad of paper. Each individual then presents their ideas, which are recorded on a flip-chart (or comparable computer screen technology). The group can generate new ideas during this phase, which continues until no new ideas are forthcoming. When all ideas are recorded, discussion opens. Each idea is discussed. At the end of discussion, each individual records their evaluation of the most serious risks associated with the project by either rank-ordering or rating.

The silent generation of ideas, and structured discussion are contended to overcome many of the limitations of brainstorming. Nominal groups have been found to yield more unique ideas, more total ideas, and better quality ideas than brainstorming groups.

Delphi Method

The Delphi method was developed at the RAND Corporation for technological forecasting, but has been applied to many other problem environments. The first phase of the Delphi method is anonymous generation of opinions and ideas related to the issue at hand by participants. These anonymous papers are then circulated to all participants, who revise their thoughts in light of these other ideas. Anonymous ideas are exchanged for either a given number of rounds, or until convergence of ideas.

The Delphi method can be used with any number of participants. Anonymity and isolation allow maximum freedom from any negative aspects of social interaction. On the negative side, the Delphi method is much more time consuming than brainstorming or the nominal group technique. There also is limited opportunity for clarification of ideas. Conflict is usually handled by voting, which may not completely resolve disagreements.

Outsourcing Risks

Viewing enterprise software as a system leads to consideration of the risks involved, and the impact on not only IT costs, but also on hidden costs such as organizational disruption, future upgrades, etc. Managerial decision makers can then consider mitigation strategies, important in initial system selection, as well as in developing plans for dealing with contingencies (what to do if the system fails; what to do if the vendor raises the price of software support; what to do if the vendor discontinues support for this version of software). An alternative approach is to avoid all of this hassle, and rent an enterprise system from an application service provider (ASP). That involves a whole new set of systemic risks. The overall ERP selection decision involves the seven broad categories of alternatives shown in Table 15.2. Each specific organization might generate variants of selected alternatives that suit their particular needs.

Outsourcing has evolved into a way for IT to gain cost savings to organizations. This is true for ERP just as it is for other IT implementations. Competitive pressures as motivation for many organizations to outsource major IT functions.[20] Eliminated jobs make businesses more productive. Often those jobs eliminated are from IT.

Outsourcing is attractive to many types of organizations, but especially to those that have small IT staffs, without expertise in enterprise systems. Some organizations, such as General Motors, outsource entire IT operations. There also are on-demand application providers willing to provide particular services covering the gamut of IT applications. Reasons for use of an ASP included the need to quickly get a system on-line (even to bridge the period when an internal system is installed), or to cope with IT downsizing. ASPs can help both small carriers develop new capabilities quickly, as well as providing faster implementations at multiple locations for large companies, and provide access to automatic updates and new applications. They also provide a more flexible way to deal with the changing ERP vendor market.

Table 15.2 Alternative ERP options[21]

Form	Advantages	Disadvantages
In-house	Fit organization	Most difficult, expensive, slowest
In-house + vendor supp.	Blend proven features with organizational fit	Difficult to develop
		Expensive and slow
Best-of-breed	Theoretically ideal	Hard to link, slow, potentially inefficient
Customize vendor system	Proven features modified to fit organization	Slower, usually more expensive than pure vendor
Select vendor modules	Less risk, fast, inexpensive	If expand, inefficient and higher total cost
Full vendor system	Fast, inexpensive, efficient	Inflexible
ASP	Least risk and cost, fastest	At mercy of ASP

ERP can be outsourced overseas. Overseas outsourcing takes advantage of tremendous cost saving opportunities. As of publication date, India has significant cost advantages over the U.S. and Europe in average programmer salary, while capable of providing equivalent or superior capabilities in many areas. However, relative pay schedules are subject to inflation, and Indian pay rates were expected to increase by double-digit rates over the next few years. ERP skills are one of the areas where higher inflation is expected. However, the expertise available in India still makes them a highly attractive source of IT. Over a period of years, those in other countries such as China are expected to overcome current language barriers and develop sufficiently mature IT skills to draw work from India. As the manufacturing center of the world, China is becoming the winner of most IT outsourcing contracts from developed Asian countries such as Japan and South Korea. It is now poised to compete head-to-head with the traditional outsourcing destination countries, such as India, Ireland and Israel, for the much bigger and more profitable North American and European market.

There is a tradeoff in outsourcing ERP systems, in that costs and some form of risks are reduced by outsourcing, but other companies view ERP as too mission-critical to yield control. The biggest risks of outsourcing are downtime and loss of operational data. Organizations whose systems expand rapidly due to acquisition may find outsourcing attractive for technical aspects of ERP. The tradeoff is between savings in capital investment and technical expertise through ASP, versus control and customization abilities better served through in-house IT.

Government use of ERP has its own set of characteristics. The value of outsourcing financial systems in government can be very beneficial in terms of reduced cost.[22] Benefits of application hosting were stated as lower opportunity costs of software ownership, and avoiding problems of developing and retaining IT staff. Additional difficulties faced by governmental IT directors in the governmental sector include the need to be able to defend proposals in public hearings. Such applications also involved the use of ERP to reduce State jobs, which can lead to difficulties with the state information worker union.

Tradeoffs in ERP Outsourcing

Bryson and Sullivan cited specific reasons that a particular ASP might be attractive as a source for ERP.[23] These included the opportunity to use a well-known company as a reference, opening new lines of business, and opportunities to gain market-share in particular industries. Some organizations may also view ASPs as a way to aid cash flow in periods when they are financially weak and desperate for business. In many cases, cost rise precipitously after the outsourcing firm has become committed to the relationship. One explanation given was the lack of analytical models and tools to evaluate alternatives. These tradeoffs are recapitulated in Table 15.3:

Table 15.3 Factors for and against outsourcing ERP[26]

Reasons to outsource	Reasons against outsourcing
Reduced capital expenditure for ERP software and updates	Security and privacy concerns
Lower costs gained through ASP economies of scale (efficiency)	Concern about vendor dependency and lock-in
More flexible and agile IT capability	Availability, performance and reliability concerns
Increased service levels at reasonable cost	High migration costs
Expertise availability unaffordable in-house (eliminate the need to recruit IT personnel)	ERP expertise is a competency critical to organizational success
Allowing the organization to focus on their core business.	ERP systems are inextricably tied to IT infrastructure
Continuous access to the latest technology	Some key applications may be in-house and critical
Reduced risk of infrastructure failure	Operations are currently as efficient as the ASPs
Manage IT workload variability	Corporate culture does not deal well with working with partners.
Replace obsolete systems	

Qualitative Factors

While cost is clearly an important matter, there are other factors important in selection of ERP that are difficult to fit into a total cost framework. Van Everdingen et al. conducted a survey of European firms in mid-1998 with the intent of measuring ERP penetration by market.[24] The survey included questions about the criteria considered criteria for supplier selection. The criteria reportedly used are given in the first column of Table 15.4, in order of ranking. Product functionality and quality were the criteria most often reported to be important. Column 2 gives related factors reported by Ekanayaka et al. in their framework for evaluating ASPs,[25] while column 3 gives more specifics in that framework.

While these two frameworks do not match entirely, there is a lot of overlap. ASPs would not be expected to have specific impact on the three least important criteria given by Van Everdingen et al. The Ekanayaka et al. framework added two factors important in ASP evaluation: security and service level issues.

Outsourcing Risks in China

China is India's only neighbor in the Far East with a comparable population but far better infrastructure boosted by its fastest expanding economy in the world. China is already the manufacturing center of the world, and the winner of most IT out-

Table 15.4 Selection evaluation factors

ERP Supplier Selection (Van Everdingen et al.)	ASP Evaluation (Ekanayaka et al.)	Ekanayaka et al. subelements
1. Product functionality	Customer service	1. Help desk and training 2. Support for account administration
2. Product quality	Reliability, scalability	
3. Implementation speed	Availability	
4. Interface with other systems	Integration	1. Ability to share data between applications
5. Price	Pricing	1. Effect on total cost structure 2. Hidden costs and charges 3. ROI
6. Market leadership		
7. Corporate image		
8. International orientation		
	Security	Physical security of facilities Security of data and applications Back-up and restore procedures Disaster recovery plan
	Service level monitoring and management	1. Clearly defined performance metrics and measurement 2. Defined procedures for opening and closing accounts 3. Flexibility in service offerings, pricing, contract length

Table 15.5 Relative labor costs[27]

	India	China	Other (Ireland, etc.)
Monthly salary	$700 or more	$500 or less	$600–5,000
Salary increase	10–15% annually	6–8% annually	7–10% annually
Personnel turnover	30%	12.6%	10–15%
IT graduates	150,000 annually	250,000 annually	30,000–50,000 annually
IT worker shortage	250,000 by 2010	None reported	20,000–200,000 by 2010

sourcing contracts from developed Asian countries such as Japan and South Korea. It is now poised to compete head-to-head with the traditional outsourcing destination countries, such as India, Ireland and Israel, for the much bigger and more profitable North American and European market.

According to Gartner Group, the global IT services market is worth $580 billion, of which only 6% is outsourced. India currently has 80% of this market, but other contenders are rising with China now enjoying the biggest cost advantage. On average, an engineer with two to three years post-graduate experience is paid a monthly salary of less than $500, compared with more than $700 in India and upwards of

$5,000 in the United States. India also led other countries in the region with the highest turnover rate at 15.4%, a reflection of the rampant job-hopping in the Indian corporate world, especially the IT sector. Other markets with high attrition rates include Australia (15.1%) and Hong Kong (12.1%). Almost all Indian IT firms projected greater salary increases for 2005, according to a recent survey. Table 15.5 summarizes the labor cost factors.

In light of the increasing labor costs, India's response is also moving to China. In fact, most Indian IT firms that operate globally have begun implementing back-door linkages to cheaper locations. IT giants such as Wipro, Infosys, Satyam and Tata Consulting Services (TCS) have all set up operations in China, given the lower wage cost of software engineers due to the excess supply of trained manpower. TCS set up its shop in China in 2002 that employs more than 180 people; a year after making a foray into the country, Infosys (Shanghai) has a staff strength of 200 to cater to clients in Europe, the US and Japan; Wipro set up its Chinese unit in August 2004.

Business Risks

Two types of risks are perceived in international business operations in China that apply to an ERP IT software company. First, because China is not a full market economy based on a democratic political system, there is some political risk in the government's interfering with free enterprises. Such risks are deemed negligible based on the open and reform policies of the central government in the past two decade, and the economic boom derived from such a more transparent political environment. Second, whereas China's lack of protection of intellectual properties is widely reported, there have been very few cases where business software was pirated. This is due to the requirement of domain knowledge to profit from selling business software.

A crucial factor for China's emergence into the global outsourcing industry is government support. The most important central government policy for the software industry is the June 2000 announcement of State Council Document 18, formally known as the "Policies to Promote the Software and Integrated Circuit Industry Development." The document created preferential policies to promote the development of these two sectors. The documented policies for software companies include:

(1) Value-added Tax (VAT) refund for R&D and expanded production
(2) Tax preferences for newly established companies
(3) Fast-track approval for software companies seeking to raise capital on overseas stock markets
(4) Exemption from tariffs and VAT for software companies' imports of technology and equipment
(5) Direct export rights for all software firms with over USD $1 million in revenues

Conclusions

Information systems are crucial to the success of just about every twenty-first century organization. The IS/IT industry has moved toward enterprise systems as a means to obtain efficiencies in delivering needed computing support. This approach gains through integration of databases, thus eliminating needless duplication and subsequent confusion from conflicting records. It also involves consideration of better business processes, providing substitution of computer technology for more expensive human labor.

But there are many risks associated with enterprise systems (just as there are with implementing any information technology). Whenever major changes in organizational operation are made, this inherently incurs high levels of risk. COSO frameworks apply to information systems just as they do to any aspect of risk assessment. But specific tools for risk assessment have been developed for information systems. This paper has sought to consider risks of evaluating IT proposals (focusing on ERP), as well as consideration of IS/IT project risk in general. Methods for identifying risks in IS/IT projects were reviewed, We also presented the status and trends of outsourcing risks in China.

End Notes

1. Levensohn, A. (2004). How to manage risk – Enterprise-wide, *Strategic Finance* 86:5, 55–56.
2. Asia Times Online: www.atimes.com/atimes/South_Asia/FK16Df06.html.
3. CIO Insight Magazine Predicts China Passes India www.cioinsight.com/article2/0,1397,1776816,00.asp.
4. Anderson, K. (2007). Convergence: A holistic approach to risk management, *Network Security* May, 4–7.
5. von Bertalanffy, L. (1968). General System Theory: Foundations, Development, Applications, New York: George Brazillier, 1968, revised 1969.
6. Gharajedaghi, J. (1999). Systems Thinking: Managing Chaos and Complexity, Woburn, MA: Butturworth-Heinemann.
7. Nicolis, G., and Prigogine, I. (1989). Exploring Complexity: An Introduction, New York: W.H. Freeman.
8. Diamond, J. (2005). Collapse: How Societies Choose to Fail or Succeed, New York: Penguin Books.
9. Gore, A. (2006). An Inconvenient Truth: The Planetary Emergency of Global Warming and What We Can Do About It, New York: Rodale Books.
10. Holland, J.H. (1992). Adaptation in Natural and Artificial Systems, Cambridge, MA: MIT Press, (reprint from 1975); Gell-Mann, M. (1994). The Quark and the Jaguar: Adventures in the Simple and the Complex, New York: W.H. Freeman; Kauffman, S. (2000). Investigations, New York: Oxford University Press.
11. Holland, J.H. (1995). Hidden Order: How Adaptation Builds Complexity, Cambridge, MA: Perseus Books.
12. Tenner, E. (1997). Why Things Bite Back: Technology and the Revenge of Unintended Consequences, New York: Vintage Books (revision from 1996).
13. Carson, R. (1964). Silent Spring, Greenwich, CT: Fawcett.

14. Tenner. (1997). op cit.
15. Feenberg, A. (1999). Questioning Technology, London: Routledge.
16. Perrow, C. (1999). Normal Accidents: Living with High-Risk Technologies, Princeton, NJ: Princeton University Press, reprinted from 1984.
17. O'Donnell, E. (2005). Enterprise risk management: A systems-thinking framework for the event identification phase, *International Journal of Accounting Information Systems* 6, 177–195.
18. From Kliem, R.L., and Ludin, I.S. (1998). Reducing Project Risk. Aldershot, England: Gower.
19. Moore, C.M. (1994). Group Techniques for Idea Building 2nd ed. Thousand Oaks, CA: Sage.
20. Bryson, K.M., and Sullivan, W.E. (2003). Designing effective incentive-oriented contracts for application service provider hosting of ERP systems. *Business Process Management Journal* 9:6, 705–721.
21. Derived from Olson, D.L. (2004). Managerial Issues of Enterprise Resource Planning Systems. Boston: McGraw-Hill/Irwin.
22. Joplin, B., and Terry, C. (2000). Financial system outsourcing: The ERP application hosting option. *Government Finance Review* 16:1, 31–33 (Feb).
23. Bryson and Sullivan (2003), op. cit.
24. Van Everdingen, Y., van Hellegersberg, J., and Waarts, E. (2000). ERP adoption by European midsize companies, *Communications of the ACM* 43:4, 27–31.
25. Ekanayaka, Y., Currie, W.L., and Seltsikas, P. (2003). Evaluating application service providers. *Benchmarking: An International Journal* 10:4, 343–354.
26. Derived from Olson, D.L. (2004). Managerial Issues of Enterprise Resource Planning Systems. Boston: McGraw-Hill/Irwin.
27. MetaGroupConsultancy: http://insight.zdnet.co.uk/specials/outsourcing/0,39026381,39150917,00.htm;ComputerWorld, March 19, 2001.

Printed in the United Kingdom
by Lightning Source UK Ltd.
131073UK00008B/246/P

9 783540 786412